Praise for *Toy Fights*

"*Toy Fights* is a portrait of the poet as . . . well, that's what's articulated so perfectly by this book: as a potential anything, in the sense of terminal mess-up, unrepentant head case, autodidact, exceptional and typical product of his place and times. It's wonderful, aggressively wise, and always—especially at its most serious—devastatingly funny."   —Geoff Dyer

"A tremendously engaging memoir, seasoned with Don Paterson's customary wit, total recall, and love of language. A classic of its kind."   —William Boyd

"One of the greatest poets now writing anywhere."

—Colm Tóibín

"Already compared to *Shuggie Bain*, *Toy Fights* is a story of family, the working class, money, and all the things in between that we do to avoid boredom."   —*GQ*

"Anyone wanting a quiet book should read elsewhere—it will make you laugh aloud."   —Kate Kellaway, *Observer*

"The language crackles. . . . This is a poet's memoir. . . . Some of the best writing on mental health I have ever read."

—*The Times*

"Paterson is arguably Scotland's finest writer at work today; his sense of the absurd is acutely honed, his wisdom hard-won." —John Quin, *Sunday National*

"You'll be lucky if you find a more thought-provoking, hilarious, sardonic and scarily brilliant self-portrait this year." —David Robinson, *Scotsman*

"These 360 pages scorch and crackle with the joy of revenge and revelation. *Toy Fights* is a memoir in a million, yelping with real-life experience, aghast at the ways human beings manipulate each other and screamingly funny about the absurdity of our pretensions. If a finer memoir is published this year, I'll eat my own sporran." —*Sunday Times*

"Part treatise, part guidebook, part intimate confessional, this is a book that swan-dives into the filthy waters of growing up and resurfaces clear-eyed, bearing pearls." —*Financial Times*

"The book is beautifully crafted. The language is precise, balanced and every other sentence has me wondering 'How did he do that?'" —*Irish Times*

"Uproarious joy and unbearable pain—*Toy Fights* is a potent mix, and a memorable read." —*Tablet*

"It is rare to read an autobiography which balances acerbic, almost visceral, anger with moments of genuine tenderness and affection. What makes this stratospherically better than most childhood memoirs is the searing anger about injustice that burns through the book." —*Scotland on Sunday*

"It's a searing, raw read, alternatively laugh-out-loud funny, and heartbreakingly painful." —*Herald on Sunday*

"A coruscating portrait of his first two decades that simultaneously celebrates, undermines and ruthlessly takes the mick out of the memoir form." —*Mail on Sunday*

"*Toy Fights* is a work of dazzling craft."
—*Times Literary Supplement*

"Should you find a better memoir all year than this wonderful book, you'll be very lucky. . . . The funniest, most truthful, moving and honest account of a boyhood I have read: witty and dry, profane and brutally hilarious in a laugh-out-loud way, it is full of wincing moments of recognition. . . . [I]nstant classic." —Roger Alton, *Daily Mail*

"Memoirs by poets—the Top Ten? . . . [S]traight to the top spot this week, *Toy Fights*, by Don Paterson. . . . Frank and fearless, *Toy Fights* therefore charts not only as a great poet's memoir but also, unexpectedly . . . a selflessly helpful book of self-help." —Ian Sansom, *Spectator*

Don Paterson

Toy Fights

A Boyhood

LIVERIGHT PUBLISHING CORPORATION

A Division of W. W. Norton & Company

INDEPENDENT PUBLISHERS SINCE 1923

Copyright © 2023 by Don Paterson

First published in the UK in 2023 by Faber & Faber Ltd.

For information about permission to reproduce selections from this book, write to Permissions, Liveright Publishing Corporation, a division of W. W. Norton & Company, Inc., 500 Fifth Avenue, New York, NY 10110

For information about special discounts for bulk purchases, please contact W. W. Norton Special Sales at specialsales@wwnorton.com or 800-233-4830

Manufacturing by Lakeside Book Company

Library of Congress Control Number: 2024936534

ISBN 978-1-324-09519-4 pbk.

Liveright Publishing Corporation
500 Fifth Avenue, New York, N.Y. 10110
www.wwnorton.com

W. W. Norton & Company Ltd.
15 Carlisle Street, London W1D 3BS

1 2 3 4 5 6 7 8 9 0

for my mother and in memory of my father

I am not me. I am the one
who walks unseen beside me.
The one I sense, from time to time,
but often forget; the one
who is silent and still while I'm speaking;
who forgives me when I'm spiteful;
who is where I am not;
who stays standing when I finally lie down.

— after Juan Ramón Jiménez

Contents

1 Pre Face

I recall nothing of my being born in Dundee Royal Infirmary in 1963. Which, of course, doesn't mean it didn't happen, but the possibility must remain that I may not have been. If I hadn't known someone who claimed to have been present, I'd be within my rights to think I simply manifested, piecemeal, flickering off and on like a broken torch, until the age of three or so, when the light I shone on the world seems more steady. At that point, whatever calls itself me seems to have gained a more secure fix on what one must grudgingly call reality, reality being defined as 'that to which there appears to be no alternative'.

Thereafter the memories are more vivid, but they still can't be trusted. I am wont to confuse memory and photographs, other folks' memories with my own, and things I saw on television with things that happened to me. I am pretty sure that was me standing up to take a bow at a Francie and Josie concert on my fourth birthday, but only because I also remember exclaiming to my mother something like 'I can't *believe* these global superstars bothered to give an insignificant wretch like *me* the time of day!', which sounds way too much like me to be anyone else. I remember playing my dad's mandolin in my grandfather's back garden, but only because I have a photo of me doing so. And while I am 87 per cent certain no Scottish schoolboy participated in the Apollo 11 moon landings, I am not at all sure I wasn't an extra in a clown routine at Billy Smart's Circus. I can smell the sawdust and the tigers.

It doesn't help that all our memories are of someone else. After a day or so, the hippocampus hits some point-of-view toggle and the camera flips from first to third person, and into our little archive of home movies, horror shorts, blooper reels, sketch show pilots, public information films and amateur porn it goes. We are not wired to identify with ourselves. I mean: it would be unbearable if all that stuff had actually happened to us.

Anyway, I definitely occurred. Some gratuitously complicated lump of meat spat out from the evolutionary process cooked up an ego, rather circularly declared itself to be me, and started to suffer. As to the form of that suffering: Aristotle tells us that what we do is who we are; neuroscience tells us that who we are is what we do. While Frank Sinatra did not sing *are do are do are do are do are do*, Abba kind of did, and we propel ourselves into the future via just such a rapid switching, like an electromagnetic wave, only made of karma. But that just tells us the means of transport. Our desires, or lack of them, will commit us to a destination, and thereafter all is the vagaries of route, terrain, weather, car maintenance, local hazard, the folk we pick up along the way, the new maps they bring with them and the stronger appeal of the strange and distant cities for which they were bound.

I think I'm *some* kind of determinist. I suspect all environment and parenting can really do is keep the neuroses down to a working minimum; they add little in the way of positive trait that wasn't already there. And I don't see any evidence of free will, which is mostly a happy retrospective illusion; we've learned the trick of taking immediate credit for decisions already unconsciously made. But if I believe in fate, it's only as a godawful, unreadable mess. Someone may have the vantage to take it all in, but it'll never be us. (I think the strong odds are on all this being a simulation in which the gamers have either long lost interest or are waiting to see how it plays out from initial conditions. 'See! They *do* rise up from the algae and then set themselves on fire.') The life-map may be in our genes alright, but between blueprint and phenotype there will have been many a mumbled instruction and drunken transcription error, and once we're here, the fates of others constantly intervene in and supervene on our own. Our lives suffer the tidal pulls of far too many moons to accurately predict this evening's TV, never mind the hour of our deaths.

All we have to go on is the past, and the current state of the 'am' and the 'do'. One senses it most keenly in that moment when, just after waking, one witnesses that airy creature of infinite potential rapidly contract to the aching weirdo desperate for his coffee. And having painfully recalled oneself, one might then reflect that it didn't take very long; the little book of one's life is a light read these days. So we can dispatch this quickly: at the time of writing, I 'am' in my mid-to-late fifties, the age when qualifications like 'mid-to-late' seem especially important again, as they were when I was six and three-quarters. My name is Donald, which is a stupid name. I am a man. I am obsessed with – that is, my mind naturally and immediately turns to, and is filled with thoughts of – painkillers, sex, music, US billiards, guitars, avoiding the attention of my employers, television, food, ailments real and imaginary, poetry, family, politics. In any order. What else. I am a Scot; I do not think of myself as British; I love England above all other nations, excepting my own. I believe social media has been a disaster for the species and has driven us suicidally out of step with reality. My politics, which increasingly dominate my casual conversation, are radically centrist, which is to say hostile to that which involves any systematic belief in anything. I can't stand the right, I can't stand the left, and I *really* can't stand the appeasing, quietist, weedy, non-radical, status-quo 'liberal' centre. (The rad cent approach is pretty much just 'go in fear of all ideology and be of no tribe', 'pay your damn taxes', 'capitalism for the rich, socialism for the poor' and 'reality always bites your ass'. Mostly, one is animated by the staggering indifference of both right and left elites towards the poor I grew up among, the former through venality and open contempt, the latter through fashionable idiocy and hidden contempt.) My state in repose is bored, slightly afraid, agitated, and for some reason really dehydrated. That's pretty much the 'am'.

To swiftly do the 'do': I sometimes 'do' poetry (I suspect anyone who *really* imagines 'I am a poet' to be a coherent declaration has little genuine acquaintance with the stuff). I know a lot about it, and have been previously encouraged to behave as though I am quite good at it, although fashions change and my talents feel increasingly redundant. (Poetry these days is mostly short-form experimental prose, which is to say it's now open to anyone clever – this is important, as we have a lot of expensive MFA places to fill and qualified poets to turn out – and has, increasingly, little use for the quaint and dinky skills of old-school versifiers like me.) In exchange for money, I lecture, and for years also worked in publishing; I am pretty good at teaching and editing but a bitterly incompetent administrator. I play the guitar and write music, mostly jazz, though I've programmed a lot of electronic music (and along the way played a lot of folk and country, and written a lot of 'straight' music). The guitar was once my living, and for no reason but pride I try to keep my playing at a vaguely professional level, which involves a lot of daily practice. I shoot US billiards (okay, 'pool'); from the length of my warm-up drill you would correctly infer that I am very short of talent. I am almost certainly better than you, but still way worse than him, to whom I regularly lose money. I watch a lot of TV and movies while I play guitar. I play the flugelhorn in the kitchen, and by God no one will ever hear it in any other venue. I eat and drink, and cook regularly if indifferently; I exercise resentfully and painfully. I play the odd video game, and in my time have reviewed them for newspapers; I recently wept, screamed and sat open-mouthed in wonder through *The Last of Us Part II*. I somatise my distress and I nurture my symptoms; I worry about money; I drink to forget about money; on those occasions I appreciate quality alcohol ('cheap booze is a false economy'); I indulge my terror of authority. Pre-pandemic I spent enough time on the east coast Edinburgh–London line to get mail on it. I try to look after my partner, my kids, my family and those friends I've co-opted into it. I could do a lot better. I walk and hug my dogs, who change every decade or so and are currently a broken toy poodle called Yentl (some other time, but I'm a sort of honorary self-hating Jew), who knows exactly four things, two of which are wrong, and a standard poodle called Furny, which is short for Furnival, which is short for Sir Martin Furnival Jones CBE, which he gets called only when I'm angry with him. Since 'everybody has to be somewhere', I live in Kirriemuir, where my kids grew up, because the Angus glens and the Cairngorms are almost as pretty as the west coast, only deserted.

And that's it. I know that was boring, and I know you didn't really ask, but that's *all*. Literally the whole show. The end. The life we end up with should ideally be far less interesting than the one that got us there: we contribute most when we specialise, and this generally means we have to simplify ourselves. The prospect of having a rich and eventful life right *now* seems exhausting. But now also seems the moment to figure out how it came to this, and the first two decades seem like the obvious place to start. And possibly end. I may go on, but I'll see if anyone reads this part first; if they do, I'll wait for a few folk to die, and if one of them isn't me, we'll see. But eventually one's writing would merely converge asymptotically upon the subject of one's writing, and things like my current wrangle with Janice at Angus Council over the speed limit signage on the Brechin Road. One has to know when to stop, and it's usually far sooner than one's inclined to. Besides, it's already a monstrous presumption to think anyone might want to read about this bit, which at least has the merit of being fairly eventful.

So. Why did we end up *this* guy? is the question I ask, drunk, in the mirror these days, although it's increasingly likely to take the form 'The hell are *you*?' as the ageing white-bearded stranger grows more and more distant from the boy within. The explanation seems to lie in the years one spent in rehearsal for real life, but those rehearsals often turned out to be more real than the thing we were rehearsing for, to the point that I sometimes wonder if we get it all the wrong way round. 'Toy fights' was how we referred to a horrible childhood game in Dundee, the announcement of which would see the blood instantly drain from my head into my socks. 'Toy' was supposed to indicate 'not serious', but it really meant 'senseless'. It was basically twenty minutes of extreme violence without pretext. Childhood lacks all pretext by definition, of course, but as a kid you constantly had the urge to anticipate real conflict before life strictly required you to. I could have deferred my fights with God, drugs and insanity, but at some level must've known it would save time; and much like the 'toy' variety, they were the worst fights I've had in my life. I had other reasons to seek conflict. If your mum and dad refuse to fuck you up, or display no talent for it, or leave the job half done – you have to fuck yourself up, if getting completely fucked up is the only way you're ever going to become yourself. This means to some extent it's a recreational pursuit, which is an odd category in which to place something that might kill you. Toy fights, indeed.

This book is about a lot of things but is notably music-obsessed. I'm the kind of writer who writes because they do what they are, not because they love what they do. But I am also the kind who writes about what they love, helplessly, for which I apologise when it gets too geeky – as all real love does, being partly just a condition of emotional hypervigilance. (Here, this occasionally takes the form of extended sleeve notes on some records that rewired my brain.) And since I make little mention of poetry in this tale, which ends before I started writing the stuff, let me mention it now and then park it. Poetry isn't a calling, and even less a living. I'm not even convinced it's a real art form. I have painter, novelist and composer friends who hit the studio or desk or piano at nine and knock off at five.* I know of no poet who does this. Our art seems more like a helpless disposition. To call yourself 'poet' strikes me as either a mistake, a tasteless vaunt or the confession of a mental illness. To be called one is either a mistake, a compliment or a diagnosis. Okay, perhaps 'mental illness' is a bit strong, but poets don't have the same relationship to language as other folk; yours is sensible. Poets' brains have a wiring error that makes them think words are real things. They keep trying to use words to magically influence reality, and to drag bits of it into words that just

---

* Okay, the successful novelists usually manage twelve noon, often declaring this the limit of human concentration. They will be livid to read this, since they are all, to a man and woman, convinced they work like dogs. Poets all have *jobs*.

8

don't go. These moves don't strike them as magical at all, but perfectly logical. Since magic doesn't work, it can often lead to a life of disappointment, pain and confusion. (Among all the various professions, mental illness is statistically most prevalent among artists; among the artists, writers; among the writers, poets.) They often instinctively seek out or bring about extreme situations that 'inspire' them – O how we laugh when you use that word! – and will often wreck their lives and the lives of those close to them in their pursuit of the extremities of feeling. So your *actual* poet generally doesn't think being a poet is that cool. Of course one can, and definitely should, be other things besides. Anyway, I'm not claiming poetry came out of the blue: it ran like the third rail through the track of my childhood, but only on emerging into my twenties did I see what was not only causing the buzzing, the fear and the sparks, but propelling the whole damn train.

I started this book a good while ago – I think it was originally commissioned by T. S. Eliot – but stopped almost immediately, having spent the advance on a guitar. I also lost interest in myself. While this may have performed a temporary service to the reader, it didn't help me much. Then my dad died, and I got very angry, mostly over his having spent his life working far too hard because he was usually broke. My getting angry was some accomplishment, since propranolol has made the emotion alien to me for years. I then wrote the book with the swearing in, took it all out, and put about half of it back in again. I think it adds fucking nuance, personally, but I agree it can sometimes make the prose sound boorish; however, it leaves it a little closer to the way I often speak at home, i.e. like a ned off the scheme, and that particular verisimilitude is sometimes important here. One often hears the swearing of the working classes dismissed by their betters as a 'form of punctuation'. *Au contraire*, my new friends. We swear for just the reason you do: fury. The difference is that it tends to run through our every conversation like a crimson thread. But my anger is really only about one thing: the unfair treatment of the poor, and the fact that they are the only social class who are forced to believe that money is real. (It isn't. Not even slightly. The middle classes suspect as much. The rich know it.) Once in a while it will spill over into what I have learned to call intersectional issues, particularly the younger left's current habit of dismissing my generation's entire engagement with the subjects of gender and race as irrelevant, as if they were the first in history ever to consider these matters, and the way in which they will happily divorce these injustices from the poverty and class prejudice which exacerbate them.

Because this book is often quite music-fixated, it was going to be for my father, who was a musician. He died before I completed it, though, so it's dedicated to my mum too, which makes sense, as much of it has turned out to be an attempt to understand myself through understanding my parents. The timelines of its chapters sometimes overlap a little, as the same childhood and adolescence is regarded through a succession of different windows, but they're train windows, and the thrust is forward. This book stops when I get to twenty, at a natural and literal watershed. Nonetheless, I hope the end seems a little abrupt; I'd hate to leave you with the sense that anything had come to a conclusion.

Besides my family, very few folk I mention here are still in my life. The most notable exception is my friend of forty-odd years, the Scottish music journalist, agent, promoter, reluctant bassist and anecdotalist supreme Rob Adams, aka 'Big Rab' on account of his preposterous height. Several cautionary tales drawn from Rab's infinite reservoir appear here, with due acknowledgement; a few others may appear here without, since they were so oft and well told that I may have believed they happened to me. (Indeed, they sometimes did: our early experiences not only overlapped but were sometimes repeated identically, a few years apart.) Big Rab is easily abashed, so I will write little more, but his older-brother steerings and nudges at various stages of my life – they continue as we speak – were the sort of small kindnesses and major interventions that were so thoughtful and well timed as to be life-shaping, and occasionally -saving. I know I have been a disappointment to him as a musician (Rab has always taken my duff gigs personally, as if he'd played them himself), but I'm glad that he persists in his misplaced faith in me, and I am determined to make him averagely proud before either he or I have wound up the leads.

As a jazz musician I was never good enough to keep the company of the best; but I managed to share band members who did, mainly because I'm a better composer than I am an instrumentalist, and write the sort of tunes other musicians enjoy playing. I made my living at it through the eighties and nineties, but I kept some terrifying company that required me to work three times as hard just to keep up. Because I'm lazy, I didn't. I plumped for the path of least resistance, which in my case was poetry, and my minor curse is that I seem to be a bit better at the thing I love a bit less. (Emil Cioran talks of 'the shame of not being a musician'; he should've tried being a merely average one.) I then pretty much quit playing around 2002 and took an idiotic twelve years off, had an unnecessary operation on my left hand and practically had to relearn the rudiments of my instrument. I'm sort of back to where I was now, and to this day I don't know what I was thinking. So I originally thought this book would be a way of reminding me how crucial music is to any coherent sense I have of myself. In a way it has been; but not in the way I anticipated. I discovered that the line music paid out into the past was unbroken, and it allowed me to remember everything else; and then remember why I'd forgotten it. The result is a book that's about schizophrenia, hell, money, narcissists, debt and the working class, anger, swearing, drugs, books, football, love, origami, the peculiar insanity of Dundee, sugar, religious mania, the sexual excesses of the Scottish club band scene, and, more generally, the lengths we go to not to be bored. Since you don't know me, I won't assume that you are starting from the position of the slightest curiosity, so I'll deploy the usual sympathetic magic, and try not to bore me in the telling, in the hope that I won't bore you.

– Kirriemuir, 2022

2 The Man with the Blue Guitar

My father was born in 1937, in St Cyrus, on the stark and beautiful north-east coast between Stonehaven and Montrose. Lewis Grassic Gibbon had already written *Sunset Song*, his stream-of-consciousness paean to the rich red earth of the Mearns and the considerable and generally non-voluntary sacrifices of its working women. The Mearns fetishised the Protestant work ethic to the point of death cult. Gibbon's own tombstone celebrates 'the warmth of toil, the peace of rest', as if the latter couldn't come quickly enough; he rattled off twenty books, then sparked out at thirty-four. But as Mearns families went, the Patersons were relatively easy-going. Dad spent his days playing on the endless, empty beaches below the high cliffs that stood lookout over the North Sea. Eventually my Granny would appear on the clifftop, clanging a brass bell (I keep it on my mantelpiece) when it was time for him to start on the long, looping tack back up for his supper. Dad didn't really notice there was a war on. There were few hardships bar the little hell of the outside toilet, and the Germans could find nothing in the area worth bombing. My Granny baked, kept a kitchen garden, bred hens and ducks. My grandfather, 'Pappy', was a builder and worked on airfields during the war, and later in municipal construction in Montrose; he always claimed the old bridge over the South Esk – a lovely cantilever design built in brown reinforced concrete, like a wedding dress made out of sandpaper – was his personal handiwork. It looked it: Pappy was a sensitive, and spent his life trying to make sure no word of it ever escaped. Prior to Dad's arrival, there had been an incomprehensible move to Moose Jaw, Saskatchewan, but like most moves to Moose Jaw, Saskatchewan, it hadn't worked out, which is why you're reading this sentence. My dad's grandparents lived nearby at Mill of Morphie, where his grandfather had a joinery. All his machinery was turned by a great web of leather pulleys and belts driven by the waterwheel in the millstream outside. Its perpetual motion was a thing of hypnotic wonder to my dad, and he'd sit below its whirring lattice for hours.

Pappy was a double for Picasso, which was pretty misleading. He was a gruff, rough man of few words and often less, and he regarded my mild, artistic and dreamy father as a bit effete and feminised. Dreamy, in those days, had too many downsides for a family economy. The irony was that Dad inherited all this from his father; Granny was the real hard-head, and oversaw the family budget. Pappy loved his children dearly, but his time, place and class denied him the means to express it. He was given to unfunny, misjudged pranks, like promising my dad dogs and ponies which never turned up. My dad loved him in return, but was early resolved to be a different kind of father.

Pappy took a new job, and moved the family to Tayport, in Fife, a working-class harbour town that lies facing Dundee and Carnoustie across the Tay estuary. He hated anything touching his arms, which impeded movement, therefore work. When my Granny bought him a new white dress shirt for my parents' wedding, he cut off the sleeves with garden shears. When they got to the church, my Granny handed him a carnation for his buttonhole; failing to find anywhere to stick it, he took out his knife and stabbed a hole in his lapel. Pappy had four fingers on his right hand, having lost one, he would relate with an unaffected indifference, on the way to work one morning. On the *way*. (When I was small, I'd count them over and over, mystified that I couldn't get them to add up. In my tinfoil-hat episode in my teens, I decided that there was a whole number between four and five that had somehow concealed itself from the human mind; I'm entirely certain Pappy's missing digit was its origin.) His machismo killed him. One day in midwinter, a valve in a drainage pipe burst in a downpour, and he jumped into the hole to fix it. After three hours working in freezing, chest-high water, he dried himself off at a brazier and then squelched home to die of pneumonia, in his early sixties.

Dad's memories of St Cyrus Primary School were blissfully thin: the screak of the writing slate, the sting of the tawse, and the worst soup in Scotland. He ended up dux, or head boy, but would be the first to volunteer that the competition wasn't steep. He spent the summers berry-picking and tattie-howking to pay for his school clothes. (Having had some miserable, if resolutely minimal, experience of both jobs – a week at the berries and one fuck-this morning at the tatties – that sentence hurt my fingers to type.) However, his labour meant that he was the only first-year at Montrose Academy who had long trousers. School clothes then consisted of a corduroy suit and 'tackety' boots, meaning the soles were studded with metal 'segs' – small, flat, trapezoidal studs hammered into the heels and toes to save on wear. They sounded like the approach of the Polish cavalry, and showered a welder's arc of sparks on the pavement if you slid on them. Segging persisted in the council schemes well into the late seventies, although it legislated heavily against some essential schemie activities, mainly silent escape, and it soon fell to the homeopathic levels of fashion statement. (A few years ago, my friend, the artist Eddie Summerton, was working on a conceptual piece called *Northern Sole*; the Northern Soul dance movement was known for its seg-studded leather shoes and their ruinous effects on the dance floors of north-east England and Scotland. His idea was to cover a stuffed North Sea grey seal, liberated from a mothballed natural history museum, completely with segs. Many segs had therefore to be bought. There is a cobbler's up our way in Kirriemuir, staffed by a short, terse Hephaestus of the ancient guild, who stocks traditional supplies for the local farming community; after five thousand years, surprise is a stranger to him. Eddie approached the counter. The conversation went as follows:

– I need some segs.

– How many are ye after.

– Enough to cover an adult seal.

– Male or female.

– Male.

– You'll need about four pound.)

Dad's first regular job was organ pumper, the boy hired to work the bellows for the church organ on a Sunday morning. This job neatly foreshadowed his two principal callings: music and sleeping. Three or four times each service the organist would find himself getting quieter and quieter, until he was miming 'Death May Approach I Shall Not Flee' as if he was trying to escape its attention. A swift kick to the backboard would be met with a grunt, and a suddenly restored airflow.

It was a literate household, though. Pappy might have been practically aphasic but had hours of Robert Service and Burns by heart. Dad read constantly. It was rarely high literature, but never total rubbish; the purpose of the book, for most of the labouring classes, was to swiftly remove you somewhere else. Jack London's *White Fang*, written in the voice of a dog, was the first book in which he lost himself completely. But he detested secondary school and couldn't wait to get out of Montrose Academy. He then worked as a film projectionist, which offered him, if anything, too much in the way of first-rate kipping opportunities. Seeing his life about to slip by like a dog's, he apprenticed as a painter and decorator.

Meanwhile, the skiffle craze was reaching its berserker climax. Skiffle resembled a kind of St Vitus's Wank, a clearly unsustainable blizzard of strumming, garbled patter, madly thumbed tea-chest basses, washboards attacked like untreatable eczema. My dad was desperate to get a guitar and join in before it was all over. One day, Pappy found one floating in the dock of Tayport Harbour, or at least that's the way he told it. I'm certain this was a cover story for a kindness he didn't dare admit to. Dad restrung the suspiciously dry guitar, painted it blue and taught himself to play. (Thereafter my dad measured time, quite literally, by whatever box he was playing. Even when his memory had been blasted to rags by dementia, you could go: '1967?' And he'd answer: 'Epiphone.')

Dad did his national service in Cyprus, in the catering corps. Though he emerged as a competent cook who'd often take a shift in the galley at the weekends, he was famous for a friendly-fire incident in which he incapacitated his entire unit with a fish pie. His comrades survived their tour mooning and moaning over the picture in their wallet; in my father's case, this was a photo of his Antoria Cello acoustic. When he made it back to Scotland, after what I assume was an explosive reunion with the Antoria, he met my mother at a Valentine's dance at Tayport. It was love at first sight, at least for my mother, who particularly liked the look of his backside.

3 The Ball of Clava

As a daughter of the manse, my mum had had it considerably harder. For all the appearance of middle-class gentility, the kids who grew up inside the vicarage often lived in poverty. The dissonance can be the source of considerable shame. It's far harder maintaining the appearance of what you aren't than just being what you are, even if what you are is skint. The family were just that, but my grandfather's ministry in the United Free Church of Scotland placed them under the obligation to appear middle class, despite his pittance of a wage. Appearing comfortably off at all costs became Mum's leitmotif, and the costs were considerable, both for her and for my father. (Sixty years later, she still blanches at the thought of the terrible old curtains she put up upon her arrival in McLean Street, and what on earth the long-dead Alice McFarlane next door must've thought of them.)

Unlike my father in his rural Mearns cocoon, Mum had a bad war, and spent it in terror. She was born in Carnoustie, but the family soon upped sticks to Glasgow, where my grandfather, Francis Cougan – later 'Papa' to all his grandkids – had been posted. Her own mother's diabetes and heart condition left her far too large and unwell to make it down the garden to the air-raid shelter when the sirens went off. Papa was in the Home Guard, and therefore ironically not home to guard anyone. Mum would be pushed under the bed, more symbolically than protectively, in a gas mask kitted out with Mickey Mouse ears just to make it all maximally horrible. The rising wail of the sirens terrified her; she knew she wasn't safe. For years afterwards she avoided the Tayport sawmill, whose whiny bandsaws sent her running for cover.*

Mum was only six when her mother died of heart disease. There was talk, for a while, of having her adopted by my Aunt Maggie, Papa's sister and the matriarch of a mining family in Lochgelly. Mum and Young Frank, her wild and beloved older brother, strongly resisted this, and Papa muddled through with help from her schoolteachers, who'd snatch her off the street to clean her up before she went into class; she'd often be covered in black molasses, the only readily available source of sugar, and acquired the nickname 'Treacle Jeannie'. Food in the Cougan household was plain and not in rich supply. The manse in Dysart had eleven rooms, but it was impossible to heat more than a couple of them. To make matters even more complicated, my Great-Aunt Kate was working as a housekeeper for Robert A. Taft in his huge pile on First Avenue; she would send back care parcels several times a year, and my mum would receive barely worn hand-me-downs from the wider Taft family. In other words, Mum often ate like

---

* Yes, triggering is a thing: but it involves your involuntary shaking, terror and need to be somewhere else immediately. Best not to use the word to describe your mild discomfort, or some offence you're hosting on behalf of some notional third party.

a pauper and struggled to keep warm, but lived in a mansion and dressed like a senator's daughter. The disjunction between appearance and reality added another shame to her mother's abandonment. The struggle to keep that shame hidden and maintain the appearance of wealth later led to a hire purchase habit, and my father working two jobs to cover it.

My mum recalls her Aunt Mary forever getting lost in the Dysart manse, and calling out for her younger brother, 'Mr Coug-ing, where are you?' In this there will have been much pride – that one's family boasted a member who must be so formally addressed! – but the improvement of the family surname to a gerund is perhaps the ultimate 'properism'. I suspect the phenomenon is universal, but probably most common in cringe-cultures like Scotland, where a word is erroneously understood as having been pronounced in a slovenly fashion, and is then corrected by your socially aspirant auntie, who will restore the imaginary dropped consonants. Thus one often heard things like: 'If you're really going out in this cold to play badmingting after *Jack and Nory* is finished, then at least put on your Ball of Clava' (a piece of headgear presumably commemorating the famous shindig held by the Duke of Clava). My Papa was also given to the exaggerated pronunciation of anything of French origin. 'Your Uncle Iain went to an Indian *rest-you-wrong* last night'; 'Your Aunt Margaret is having an *ong-guh swate* bathroom put in'; and 'I put your bike in the *gah-rarzh*.' My mother still follows his pronunciation of 'pouffe' as *pouffée*. (My all-time-favourite properism was allegedly overheard in a Dundee cake shop, where a well-dressed woman had requested the West Country millefeuille cream-and-jam confection she identified as a 'Diving Slice'. 'Diving' would be pronounced 'dehvin' in street-Dundee, which is, I suppose, quite close to 'Devon'.)

But as good a single parent as my grandfather was, his calling came first; this meant Mum being dragged to wherever a flock found itself short of a denominationally appropriate shepherd. The move to Tayport frustrated her desire to go to catering college, and she instead left school at fourteen to work in a print office. She was always her daddy's girl, though, and initially found the upgrading of my Nana from housekeeper to wife – and the subsequent arrival of her two half-siblings – very hard to accept. (This change of status may have been a while in preparation. There's an old family photo with my mum's vast birth-mum foregrounded, the only position she was capable of occupying, the poor woman, and looking like she wouldn't make it through the camera spool; my Papa and Nana are standing in the back row, staring at each other with what looks like considerably more than a platonic regard.) Nana, while she warmed up delightfully in her later years, arrived on a war footing. The kids did not go hungry again, but often wished they had. She was a fine woman but a splendidly awful cook who worked from ration-book recipes thirty years after the war was over and could not be coaxed out of the jungle. Powdered eggs, waterlogged veg, tripe and onions; junket (a milk pudding, set by demonic means); custard with skin like a trampoline; grey second-day mince thinned with water that was soon third-day water thickened with mince.

Mum dreamed of little but her own sweet-laden pantry, her own warm, weather- and bomb-proof home with its own safe, sealed-in, indestructible family.

Following the Valentine's Day dance, Mum immediately twanged Charlie (Charlie went on to amass a fortune, and in broke years was wistfully recalled as 'the man who was almost your father', as if Dad had intercepted him at the point of insemination). She then declared her intention to marry my dad, and had all her teeth removed and replaced in anticipation of the big day. (Folk didn't mess around back then. Mum had lost her tonsils merely by having casually accompanied her brother Frank to the hospital when he was having his own whipped out.) Dad found a little flat to rent in Main Street, off the Hilltown in Dundee; he and Mum then married at Papa's church in King Street, Tayport. All his ancient colleagues and relatives were dutifully invited, leaving few seats for Mum's own friends. On the day, she got stage fright and hid upstairs in the glory hole on an old packing trunk; she didn't know any of these people. My lovely mad Aunt Bett was one of the bridesmaids but had declined the uniform in favour of her own red-rose-themed creation, and had done herself up like Carmen Miranda. She found my mum weeping on the trunk and helped her get dressed. My mother had desperately wanted to come down the aisle to 'Here Comes the Bride', but Papa selfishly vetoed it for 'The King of Love My Shepherd Is'. Billy Gibson, the father of the local undertaker, was inexpensively hired to play piano at the reception. The couple left at 5 p.m. for their honeymoon: two nights at the Bay Hotel in Stonehaven. It was pelting with sleet by the time they got there. They managed one night, and then headed to where they really wanted to be: home.

4 All I Can Remember Before 1967

The rough-to-the-touch, black-and-white paisley pattern of the settee we had in Main Street. On my hands and knees in the lobby, too terror-stricken to cry because my mum's disappeared. Sitting in a pram in School Road, parked outside the blue tin shack that stinks of peroxide where Mum gets her hair done. Watching fireworks being set off in the front garden from the living room window, and feeling I'm getting too old for this nappy. Granny's incomprehensibly complex underthings. Chewing Granny's teeth after I'd fished them from the glass of water on her nightstand. The weird taste of the vitamin-infused orange juice at the Young Mothers' Club down the bottom of Macalpine Road where the fire brigade is now, opposite the crematorium. Turning the gold lid of a jelly jar shut on the honeybee I'd caught in the back green, the prize of its tiny gold pelt.

Because they're all I have, I want these things to mean something. But they won't. They're nothing, just memories of memories.

———

I am three years old, in bed in the dark. There's a ribbon of yellow light at the foot of the closed door. On the far wall is, I know, the picture of the bug-eyed kid in striped pyjamas holding a golliwog. Drifting off, I hear that little song again, the one the balloon man sings – O! that filthy satyr, that Transylvanian louche, that prince of removals – and I know I will have precisely until it ends to start screaming and raise my parents from across the hall. As ever, though, the song is so dreadfully beguiling that I get lost in it, like a sprite inside a demon-trap inside a medieval prayer inside a psalter. I forget to shout out, and the last notes fade away, and it's now too late. The hunched shape of the balloon man hirples off, pushing his squeaky wooden cart, his whistling lost in the rising tide of radio static; and before I can open my mouth to shout, I'm fixed by a flat vision of a huge satanic golliwog, staring at me. I'm wide awake but I can't move or scream, and now have to ride it out. Because the golliwog doesn't move, its perfect fixity means I've no idea how long the vision lasts. Time doesn't seem to pass. I know at some point it will fade, and I'll be able to yell out – but I'm not yelling yet, and even when I start, it seems to take long minutes for the scream to rise through my paralysis into my real lungs. At the age of six or so, I heard the song for the last time. I've forgotten it, every word and note. But then nothing is truly lost, only mislaid, or hiding.

—

O this dream: I love this one. I'm in a walled garden, very very high above the world. A river of mist is winding through the grey mountain peaks below. It's a bright, blue morning. The garden is very pretty, with trees and silver streams and glassy ponds. Strange, tall, organic rock-forms make a natural encircling wall. I am waiting, I think, to be born, to be called down; but so painless, so free from anxiety or boredom is the waiting, I'm happy to sit here forever. Take your time.

———

Again and again, I dream of a substance. It's a small ball of something grey and fuzzy and caustic and prickly, not made of anything I can recognise. Someone, a grown-up, insists that I touch it, hold it. As soon as I do I feel I am being internally dismantled. The only way I can describe it is as the intensification of known, mildly unpleasant sensations – boredom, discomfort, the ticklish feel of Granny's blue Wedgwood bowl – to the point that they undergo a change of phase state and become a horror. It's as though half the million little magnets that had been making me up had flipped their poles and were repelling the other half, trying to rip me apart from the inside. In an effort to contain it I seem to be contracting, so the sensation is of simultaneous implosion and explosion, the two working to produce a single unbearable force that is both balanced and at virulent odds with itself. The substance hums and prickles and it's toxic and radioactive and has been plucked from the dead centre of a failed star. I fear this dream more than any other, and this stuff more than anything.

———

Tonight as I lie down to sleep I pray to god my soul to keep god bless mummy and daddy and stephen and granny and pappy and nana and papa amen. I can't sleep facing that side, the side of the bed that's pushed to the wall, because that's the devil's side, so I have to sleep on my left, but my heartbeat is so loud in my ear that I can't. One night I tried sleeping the other way, but as I was falling asleep I could feel the bedclothes being pulled down by unseen hands at the foot of the bed.

———

Again and again, laid like a weightless dimension on the heavy world, the spaces. A space will open unannounced, with a feeling of huge melancholy, passing, aftermath, intolerable beauty, yearning, an articulated mystery that speaks in late shadow and in gold light, grass and hill and sky and passing cloud. In the future, a landscape or a face or a change in the light will raise their ghosts again, and their silent soundtrack will resume. Each space is a kind of definitive qualifier of being, and each has the quality (and I want to write *I cannot stress this enough*) of being both utterly distinct from all the other eternities and so far 'beyond verbal description' that my inability to articulate them is almost their only common feature. One enters any one of these states and never wishes to return, no matter how heavily are some tinted with sadness or regret. They are that deeper realm of feeling and living within which only the dead or the unborn can reside. Don't worry, I won't have to write like this often. Because they pass, or rather they occur less and less frequently as the soul dies into life, and after thirty years only music can summon them again, weakly, through its strange empty signs, and its way of combining them to conjure up sensations one has never known before.

—

I keep getting really upset by the emptiness of my parents' faces, which seem underfurnished to the point of near-blankness. What is it with the two-eyes-and-one-mouth thing? I feel bereft, and I often weep over it. It's accompanied by an awful hollow and abandoned feeling, centred in my stomach. Drinking water helps a bit. A hug both helps and makes it much worse. Also I hear voices as intensely rhythmic. I can hear an underlying beat to which they're synchronised. To be honest, sometimes I think I may have come here from somewhere else.

5 Happy Birthday to Me

Nonetheless, one pieces things together. For the first couple of years I was too continuous with the world to tell you much about it. Then, like a flaming shit-tipped spear flung into the timeless Eden of which I recall nothing, will have come the news that I was to be a father. I mean a brother. My mum and I would have been fatally confused at this point; Winnicott wisely prefers 'nursing couple' to 'mother and baby', as there's little point in trying to consider the child a separate entity; the mere fact of one person not being stuffed inside another isn't necessarily a sign of their independence. I will have been happy for this arrangement to have obtained indefinitely, so this threat to my mother's immaculate devotion won't have been welcome.

However, my parents had a stroke of luck. Lord knows what it is about the stimulating power of the Burns Supper, but houghmagandie was clearly the side order, and my sibling was due to arrive close to my own birthday, on the 30th of October. This meant that, with a bit of clever reframing, they could turn subtraction into addition. My imminent sibling was offered to me not as the dread usurper and thief of my mother's love, but as a *birthday present*. Genius! I may still prefer the little bastard not to exist, but at least I would *own* them, which is the next best thing to killing them. I couldn't speak much yet, but as my birthday approached I was taught a little catechism.

– Whose birthday is it soon?

– Mine!

– How old are ye going to be?

– Two!

– What are you getting for your birthday?

– A baby brother!

– *Or?*

– A baby sister!

Scott was born on the 28th of October and died two days later, on my birthday. His lungs hadn't properly formed. He was tiny and dark-haired; Mum fed him twice before he was taken away, and her arm ached for weeks where she'd cradled him. Papa visited Mum in the hospital, and was shocked to find her in the same bed on the same ward where his first wife had lost a child, my mother's namesake, Jean; the baby had died of the same condition. Mum couldn't face the funeral. Dad and Papa saw him out in a tiny white coffin at the crematorium.

Mum made as much of a fuss as she could of me when she got home; I've no idea what they told me. But I'll have been aware of two things: her dead-faced grief, and the fact that my present hadn't turned up. I will have quickly done the maths. It had already been made clear to me that presents are for good boys. Certainly my mother looked disappointed in me, to the point of tears; what on earth had I done? Oh yeah . . . I'd *wanted* it to go down this way. Indeed, I'd *willed* it so, and was now paying for it. (In my more manic phases in my thirties I occasionally experienced, and unwisely expressed, a sense of my Kali-like, all-powerful destructive talent, and suspect its origins lie here.) As for my mum: yet again she will have seen someone she loved die far too soon, and she may have started to take it personally.

I then embarked on a lifetime of elaborate apology. My mum used to say 'Sorry' would be on my gravestone; it really is the sound I make on exhalation. In my mind the apology has long been antecedent to the sin, and probably creates the necessity for it. One can't be forever apologising for nothing; you need something to feel guilty about, so let's do that, then. The sensation of guilt feels *right* to me. I also feel good being physically burdened, and barely notice the effort. While not particularly fit in any other way, I've ended up a packhorse who'll carry your luggage half a mile, even if I already have my own on my back. Pile it on. I literally can't feel it. My back and shoulders are misshapen through decades of carrying absurdly heavy gear and heavy bags, many of them yours. It also accounts for the nickname of 'Women's Rescue' one girlfriend gave me, and my initially attractive habit of doing my utmost to alleviate the pain of women (though there's a point in every relationship when one finally gets exhausted and resentful doing so, usually at the point the woman has come to rely on it), and my less attractive habit of unthinkingly siding with the woman in any argument. I didn't really register how deep this reflex ran until, during a conversation on *The Wizard of Oz*, a girl who knew me better than most stopped me halfway through some thoughtful remarks I was making in defence of the Wicked Witch of the West. (But I mean – see it from her point of view. This little shit drops a house on her sister, then turns up wearing her slippers. *I'd* want to kill her.)

It has also, as will soon become clear, made me an ideal narcissist's 'supply', and to say that they see me coming would imply that I wasn't looking for *them*. O who will forgive little Donald? Will you? There's a class of narc (maybe best learn that abbreviation now, if it's new to you) who always come on like they have the power to redeem you. Their beauty will take away your repulsiveness, their eternal youth your physical corruption, their love-bombing your self-loathing, their certainty your doubt, their moral infallibility or godliness your sin, their demand of sacrifice your blood-debt. For your redemption to occur, though, you need to believe in them; their virtues have to be *real*, even if they aren't. My instinct to enable any good quality someone credits themselves with can border on the lunatic. (In the nineties I had a brief relationship with a saintly, beautiful, profoundly wise and intelligent individual – I know, because she told me – who then declared herself also in possession of a wonderful singing voice. At least then I discovered where my credulity drew the line.)

Through no fault of my parents, I came to dread my birthday, and even now I still prefer to spend it alone. I used to pass this off as a deep distaste for self-celebration; that anyone would ever throw a party for themselves strikes me as practically disgusting. In my childhood, my birthday always seemed slung like a rope bridge between my mother's grieving and Halloween, where the souls of the dead rise up and walk the earth. My favourite birthday ever occurred in Borneo: I'd been booked for a jazz gig up a tree in the rainforest – long story – and was uncontactable for days. I got to the 1st of November, realised I'd missed it completely, and felt a whole year younger.

By way of a postscript: I've resolved to do as little skipping ahead as possible, but in this case a note on karma seems appropriate. My twin boys were due to be born on the 28th of October – again, what's in the haggis? The night before, my mother was in barely contained hysterics as Scott's own death-day swung into alignment. Because I can't deal with the pain of women, I want to do anything I can to relieve it; my solipsistic instinct is still that it's all on me. Annie was doing fine, though – and in no pain, following what I remain convinced was an epidural I encouraged her to take when it was offered. She'd already brought three girls into the world on nothing at all, and had felt every contraction; but why experience more pain than was necessary? One lad was already out, home and dry. Unfortunately, when the effects of the epidural started to ebb away, her body had forgotten how to push, and Jamie got stuck. Ideally constructive panic would've set in immediately, but our useless obstetrician was nowhere to be found; the midwives were frantic, for all that they tried to disguise it. Finally he was located, and even then I recall his approach as oddly louche, given the condition of Jamie's heartbeat. After first trying calipers, ventouse and everything short of a rope and a donkey, he belatedly directed an emergency Caesarean.

By now the epidural had worn off, and there was no time to administer an anaesthetic. So much for me being the human analgesic. Everything suddenly went authentically medieval: there is a world of difference between a doctor saying 'This may make you feel a little uncomfortable', which one may hear a few times over the course of a lifetime, and a furious surgeon saying 'I'm so sorry; this will hurt you', which ideally you never will. She was too drugged and out of it over the next two days to do much. I held both our kids before she did. In contrast to the Satan's slapstick of his delivery (the hospital moved immediately into don't-sue-us PR mode, following an official complaint from the midwife), Jamie then spent an age in the miracle of human competence that is the NICU, though for about a week or so it was fifty–fifty. They drew fluids from Jamie to confirm how far the oxygen levels had dropped, something accomplished by spinal tap, to which – I later saw in his notes – 'he responded appropriately', one of the grimmest turns of phrase I have read in my life.* Had this gone down differently, what it would have done to not only his mother, but his brother and grandmother, Lord alone knows. Likely this way of telling the story is deluded, and

---

* These readings were alarming but somehow he got away with it unscathed. Indeed, the experience seemed to accidentally overwire his mirror neurons, so he's an empath; if there's a way of doing this painlessly as standard, we probably should. I mean, I don't want to cramp his style if he wants to be an asshole or a mass murderer in later life, but he's never been able to help being the sweetest kid, like his granddad, who was the sweetest kid. Russ: so are you.

6 I'm Out with The Inn Folk

One day, while my dad was waking up in Draffens, the department store where he now worked in soft furnishings, he saw an ad for 'fine brush work' at DC Thomson (the venerable Dundee publisher of not just the *Sunday Post*, but about half of the UK's major comics and magazines), and figured his City & Guilds in painting and decorating might get him through the door. It did, and he settled down to forty years of colouring in Dennis the Menace and Desperate Dan, which is to say that for decades there was barely a child in the UK unacquainted with my father's anonymous handiwork. Willie Whyte, a DCT co-worker, got wind of the fact he played the guitar. The era was now thankfully post-skiffle and the folk revival was in full swing, but Dundee still had no regular venue. Willie had a big voice, prodigious ear hair, and – having no kids to waste his cash on – a big Gibson J45 (of which my dad remained perennially covetous for decades: 'It just sits under his bloody bed!' he'd exclaim, about once a year, before consoling and tormenting himself with the thought that Willie's neglect had left the neck warped, and the action unplayably high).

Dad upgraded to a half-decent Levin, and together he and Willie founded the Dundee Folksong Club, which initially gathered in the function room of what was then the old Royal British Hotel in Castle Street. They also formed its house band,

The Inn Folk, a complex pun which at the time was something of a brilliancy. They soon gained some popularity on the circuit, touring the country and making several radio appearances on BBC Scotland, though one spot went south when Willie got dry mouth during a whistled chorus of 'Mama Don't Allow', adding at least one success to the list of Mama's prohibitions. They also recorded one record. Literally, one: there was a slot-machine recording booth in the train station which would cut you a disc, and the two of them crammed in on their dinner break to lay down a version of 'Stewball Was a Racehorse'. ('. . . and I wish he were mine. / He never drank water, / he always drank wine.' Tenner on Stewball! Yeah okay, maybe each way.) The session went well until the arrival of the 12.45 to Aberdeen on Platform 2, which despite its late running still beat both Stewball and the needle to the end of the tune.

My folks had supernatural faith in the ability of a good pram to keep one safe, and mine was a Sherman tank, gifted from their parents. My mother spent the day lowering it down then shoving it back up the Hilltown, as if Sisyphus had been hit with a second ticket. The Hilltown, that Alpine thoroughfare any other city would have declared only traversable by funicular, has the contour of a ski jump, and if my mum had ever forgotten the brake when she stopped to get fags I'd have been catapulted over the Tay into Fife. Since my parents didn't yet know anyone who could babysit, they could only both attend the folk club and its numerous afterparties if they brought me along. Dr Denovan was the club's convener and party-animal-in-chief; my parents had no car, so this pram was often ferried in the back of Dr Denovan's jeep, as my mother calls it. (I was minorly perplexed, as I am sure are you, as to how one crammed a pram the size of a cow into a jeep, but through the miracle of the internet we need fret no longer: conveniently, Dr Denovan's only net presence is an anecdote in the *Courier* detailing his preservation of 'The Balaena', an old Dundee whaling song, and his Dundee vehicle registration for 1956, where I can confirm his ownership of a grey Thames van with rear double doors. What a time to be dead.)

At the club, I would be parked at the back of the room in my giant pram, so my exposure to live music began at a few months old. Not all of it was of the highest calibre. The evening would invariably kick off, as Willie later recalled, with some hippy dressed as a returning trawlerman in a sou'wester, who stood with one hand on his ear and the other resting on his waders while he sang forty verses about the 1894 Whelk Pickers' Strike in Buckie, while atmospheric sea-sounds were supplied by an accomplice who'd prop open the door of the gents with his foot while he repeatedly flushed the cistern. But then they'd have the main act, drawn from the zodiac of talent then wheeling round the club circuit. This might be Bert Jansch, Shirley Collins, Jeannie Robertson, Ewan MacColl and Peggy Seeger, John Renbourn, The Incredible String Band or The Watersons. A regular was the man-mountain folk-roarer Hamish Imlach, who one night brought along his sixteen-year-old protégé, a Glaswegian psychopath and monstrous talent by the name of Iain McGeachy, yet to change his name to John Martyn, and then in possession of only one of his nine accents.

(Older Martyn aficionados tend to resent his later popularity, and play the 'I was into him first' card. I can usually beat them: my father recorded the date as 25/11/64.)

Parties would begin sedately enough, with the shanty dude in netting and plastic lobsters giving it fifty verses on the Auchmithie Sperm Whale Explosion, and end six hours later with everyone stuck to the ceiling on cough-syrup punch and Drinamyl (the little blue pills then known, oddly, as 'purple hearts', for their emboldening powers) that Dr Denovan supplied by mass prescription, and which anyone under thirty with a job used back then as a way of wringing sixty hours out of the weekend. I was then driven home at 3 a.m. in the grey Thames van my mother claims was a jeep by a plastered GP on an ass-ton of speed. I am alive because there were very few cars on the road in the sixties.

The Inn Folk kept working into the early seventies, but Willie then lost his young wife to cancer. (I remember Sheila, probably inaccurately, as a Tolkien elf-queen, tall, beautiful, with impossibly straight silver-white hair so long she could sit on it.) He had a wise and compassionate aspect to his nature that this event seemed to focus, and he began studying for his social work exams in the DCT toilets (he later rose far up the ranks within the city), and left the band. By then the bassist had long since been replaced by the well-known Scottish fiddler, multi-instrumentalist, debauchee and conductor of chaos Allan Barty. Barty was my first musical inspiration. If my dad ever dragged me along to a gig of his in the seventies, my first question was always: 'Is Barty playing?' Barty looked disconcertingly like a reflection of Rolf Harris's actual soul, essentially the god Pan with square glasses; nor was this false advertising. He regarded my father's sobriety and sexual continence as a miracle of practically Benedictine restraint. Like many great natural talents, Barty didn't really put the work in, and indeed confined himself to musical situations where he didn't really have to; that way there were fewer interruptions to his drinking. He should have been the Scottish Dave Swarbrick, but fell short of Swarbrick's almost Jean-Luc Ponty-esque virtuosity. (Nor, it turns out, did he quite have Swarb's constitution, for all that the two of them put their bodies through a regime most lab rats might have regarded as taking the piss. Swarb was king of the premature obituary, once or twice literally so; Barty managed just the one.)

Barty had taught Swarb his own signature tune, the classic Scottish set 'The Hens March Through the Midden / The Four-Poster Bed'. The set features two violin techniques yet to enter the classical vocabulary: the first tune contains a plausible chicken impersonation, achieved by a violent, scraped bounce of the bow-end that makes a decent cluck; the second, a less plausible four-poster bed impersonation, where the bow is raised upright and its screw thumped rhythmically four times round the corners of the fiddle. Swarbrick always nailed the chicken but chickened out on the bed, preferring his instrument to keep the original number of holes, but Barty's fiddle was completely fucked from years of committed performance, with a worn and splintered patch in each corner. Audiences loved a random dash of panto, I noted, and after

Barty's four-poster turn they would turn to each other in disbelief as to its incomprehensible wizardry. He was permanently off-colour, a master of the pre-curtain fart, and was once ejected from the Statue of Liberty by the tour guide for yelling that he'd 'never been this far up a woman'. For a while Barty opened a Home Brew store in the worst mall in Dundee, The Keiller Centre, and next to one of the city's oldest pubs, The Arctic, an old whaler drinking hole whose coffin-shaped windows commemorate six whalers lost at sea in the mid-nineteenth century, and in whose honour the clientele continued to drown themselves. He manned the shop between tours with The Clancy Brothers, and this played out exactly as you'd expect. If ever a guy was certain to die from being Allan Barty it was Allan Barty, and he did, in middle age, to heartfelt if by then proportionate lamenting. He had a laugh as deep as a well and he swung like a bastard, and I thought he was wonderful.

My dad's now complete, so permit me to complete him here, so you know the kind of living man you're meeting throughout this book, where he's woven in everywhere. It took a while for me to appreciate my dad's musicianship, since what we hear every day we soon take for granted. As his sole expertise, it should really have shone out. At home on the St Mary's council scheme, Dad would occasionally attempt the odd bit of DIY, but to say he lacked patience would be to grossly understate his talent for closing the gap between commencement and conclusion; he really could've built

Rome in a day, but it would've looked like our patio. This was finished in the local vernacular known as 'hashy-bashy': he built its wall without a string line, and passed off the chaotic results as a 'rustic effect', to which cinderblocks are ill suited. I came to dread his guitar repairs. His astonishing, call-Norris-McWhirter fifteen-minute re-fret of my crap Chinese Strat led to an expensive trip to the pawn shop to buy me another guitar, after the results cut my left hand to ribbons. (The incident led me to quit making excuses on the grounds of my artistic temperament and learn how to use the damn toolbox; I am, for a normal citizen, no better than barely competent, but, for a poet, outrageously handy.) His craftsmanship was all in car maintenance, in which he was necessarily expert, and his music. He was a bluegrass flatpicker in the style of Doc Watson, unflashy but utterly rock-solid. I once imitated his playing during a gig, and took a jokey solo in his style, using all his stock licks and boom-ching rhythms. I fluffed it. He was magnanimous: 'Son, don't take the piss until you can do it at least as well.' It was a decent life lesson. By the time I could, I had way too much respect for it, and eventually bought myself a Nashville Telecaster to do his music some justice. But he was one of the best accompanists I've ever heard, and had an ear like Jodrell Bank. There was no wedding drunk, no obscure Barry Manilow B-side, no unannounced key change that my dad didn't seem instantly to have covered, and he could make anyone sound great. It was a wholly thankless craftsmanship, always unappreciated by those he accompanied; they noticed his existence only if their sudden lurch into 7/4, M-sharp,

F-minus or another song entirely had not been followed with his usual presentiment, when they'd turn to give him a hard glare. Mostly, they'd return to their seats heroes, to the loud applause and back-slapping of their loved ones, and my father's selfless and invisible expertise meant that they would all go to their graves not knowing how, that night, he'd stitched a golden cape of harmony around their Brownian leaps of pitch. But he was a family man, loved and with love to spare, and the sight of these last-round Sinatras being cheered to the rafters by their own loved ones lit him up.

In his last twenty years of playing, my father worked solo, and this could be solidly lonely work. He was a nervous and socially awkward man, and far preferred the company of other musicians. It took me many years to appreciate the bravery, the steeled nerves and the pre-gig vomiting it took for someone like him to shoulder the whole show alone, but he did, because solo work paid far better and we needed the cash. He did his best to make himself plural; he sang, he played, and he developed a strong style where he could alternate rhythm guitar, bass lines and somehow solo at the same time; he played the harmonica with a neck brace while he accompanied himself, and as a gadget nut he was an early adopter of the electronic drum machine, and he'd spend the evenings programming songs into his Roland Dr Rhythm. He often took me along as a sideman. On one occasion I brought a bassist pal with me; my dad enjoyed the gig, and we both received a healthy bung. But we were sixteen, and my friend was an avowed socialist, appalled to discover that the gig fee wasn't to be split three ways. I was rather cowed by him, and I'm mortally ashamed to recall I took his side. Dave needed the money for weed; my dad to feed his family, me included, and pay off the guitar he was playing. He didn't hire the two of us together again.

He'd often have to travel very far afield, and he would cover any distance to avoid an overnight stay. I often think of him now, driving back at 2 a.m. through Glencoe in winter from a gig in Fort William, with no radio signal and not another human heartbeat for ten miles in any direction, and nothing for company but the silence of the mountains and the cold moon, just for the sake of three hours in his own bed, in his own home.

Statistically, dementia tends to kill the carer more efficiently than the sufferer. Nonetheless, my mum was resolute: my father would not end his days in care, since it would have added a horror to a horror for him. He was permitted to die at home, in her arms. His last coherent sentence was: 'Alexa, play Lyle Lovett.'

7 Nickety Nackety Noo

Between the ages of nothing and twelve, at least one weekend in two we'd head to Tayport to visit my grandparents in the manse. I'm just old enough to remember making the crossing on the *Scotscraig*, better known as 'the Fifie', the ferry that plied the vast Tay estuary before the road bridge was built, when Tayport was still known as Ferryport-on-Craig; I can see the wake unfurl between my bare knees as I sat on the pine benches towards the stern. (It enjoyed an odd, late career revival as Popeye's barge in Robin Williams's unfairly trashed movie.) I can even summon the train that ran over the two-mile rail bridge directly from Dundee to Tayport, pre-Beeching. Taking the guard's assurances at face value, my mother would sling the giant blue pram in the guard's van with me still in it. He promised to come and fetch her if I woke up, then sent her off with a cheery smile, which in my mind grows more smirk-like as the camera tightens on it, and his eyes narrow and his nostrils flare a little; then again, the age has made us paranoid. But then my brother Stevie was born, and the skyway of the Tay Road Bridge was opened, and the boat and the train were cancelled, and my dad bought a Ford Anglia that looked like a duck, and we all drove to the manse in it.

My grandfather was a short, stocky, charismatic man, a fine sermonist, a dedicated shepherd of his flock and inveterate pipe smoker who smelled of Condor and occasionally, and wonderfully, of Clan. Papa was mad for bowls, golf, cards and Scrabble, and he cheated at them all, often through the late introduction of a new rule no one had heard of but which mysteriously and retrospectively accommodated his last play. This was in some ways down to his too-competitive nature, but also his reflexive need to find some weakness in the system: the Church gave you a big house, but paid you a subsistence wage. He made jokes about his own parsimony to cover for the fact that, for years, it had been a life skill. His years of single-parenthood had taught him how to get the ends close enough to wave to each other, if not quite meet: soup was thinned, socks were darned, dog collars fashioned from Fairy Liquid bottles, and he prided himself on being able to carve a joint so you could watch the sunset through the slices. In the early days, my mother inherited aspects of his thrift; when I first heard the phrase 'sandwich filling' it sounded like an oxymoron. Whatever went on bread was strictly in two dimensions.

My brother Stevie and I spent most summers hanging round the manse and playing daft, topologically specific games in its sheds and cellars and wall-gaps, often with our cousins Catherine and Claire, who'd come over from Belfast for the school holidays. Whenever Stevie and I got too rowdy my mum would whisper-scream, 'Sit at peace! This is a residential area!' This led to two misunderstandings. The first phrase made no sense, but I heard it as 'syrup piece', the name of a reward-sandwich involving Tate & Lyle's golden syrup, and assumed this was some kind of minced oath of the sort Papa the year to recover from one summer she spent in hot pants, those especially short short-shorts briefly legal in the mid-seventies. (Sorry, cous: I suspect you knew.) Catherine further added to her mystery by occasionally refusing to talk to me in anything but Spanish; this, she recently confessed, was total gibberish. The manse would have merely passed as a decent-sized semi elsewhere, but coming from the scheme it was Balmoral. To the rear of the house was a wide gravel path bounded by a low wall; behind it a great frothy breaker of pansies and hydrangeas and red-hot pokers fell away into the walled garden below. At one side of this raised bed there were steps down to a lawn where one could gaily sport and cavort, and play with the ancient, cracked, white-marble 'bools' Papa kept in the green shed in an old brass coal scuttle; then a row of apple and plum trees which separated the lawn from the kitchen garden that had fed the family for years. On the right, there were drills of potatoes, carrots and cauliflower; on the left, rows of raspberry canes with wild strawberries growing between them, and then a very jaggy row of gooseberry bushes, whose bristly fruit we resentfully stole in August. At the eastern extremity of the garden was another very old, gnarly, green-lichened apple tree we climbed up to see out over the Tay estuary. (Google Maps now reveals what looks like thirty yards of Astroturf.)

Downstairs, besides the yellow kitchen and dining-cum-living room, the house had a book-lined study where Papa wrote his sermons, and a drawing room where he met his parishioners. If you stood in the back garden, though, you could see a small window between the living room and study. It seemed to be boarded up on the inside. This made no sense at all: you couldn't have fitted a cupboard, let alone another room, in there. I suspect now that it was evidence of a maid's room that had been knocked through to enlarge the living room, but as kids we were greatly troubled by this window. It was a space we just couldn't account for, but not for want of trying.*

I became obsessed with Papa's library and dreamed of inheriting it. It regularly features in my one recurring dream, of which more shortly. I have the capstan chair in which he wrote his sermons; I used to think of it as a magnificent, throne-like object. It's a flimsy thing, and the kids have broken it several times just by failing to sit perfectly still. His books were all theology. Papa had grown up dirt poor in central Fife; he was a coal miner who'd done his seminary study part-time, and had learned his New Testament Greek by the light of a Davy lamp. He was a kind, reflective and articulate man, and venerated to the point that it will be difficult for my family to read that he was also a self-important one; but it was hard for a man like him not to believe the world revolved around him when it actually did. He was also generous with what little he had, even if his generosity could be a little performative. A favourite story involved a tramp who turned up at the door, who was sent away – after a good meal – with some decent shoes and an old jacket, the punchline being the 'five pounds

* Don't read *House of Leaves*. I'm serious.

in an envelope' (I put it in quotes, as he said it with such reverent emphasis) posted through the door by a mysterious benefactor a few days later. Papa would relate this tale, a lot, as an instructive miracle on God's own generosity to those who give. But he was discreet and wise in a genuine crisis, and wonderful with kids, with a daft song constantly on his lips, the dafter the better.* He was also a quite brilliant storyteller, and his tales of Paddy and Pansy the Irish fairies and the scuzzy John-the-Baptist figure of Caravan Johnny kept us rapt, because we starred in them, each of us playing to our stereotypes: Catherine the epitome of calm and bold leadership, Stevie generally covered in shit, Claire custard-obsessed, me terrified to the point of immobility. They all began *in medias res* with, notoriously, 'Well: to cut a long story short . . .', and then ran like the *Mahabharata*.

My Nana was generally silent and invisible. When you caught sight of her, she was a handsome, white-haired woman with what I almost described as a rosy complexion, but now I think of it, her face was just red from labour: she worked like a dog, from dawn till dusk. Her official duties as a minister's wife were often almost as onerous as her husband's, but these were added to her housekeeping and childcare. She was, of

---

* His favourite was: 'There was a wee cooper who lived in Fife, / Nickety, nackety, noo, noo, noo, / And he had gotten a gentle wife, / Hey Willie Wallacky, hey John Dougall, / Alane quo rushety, roo, roo, roo. / She wouldnae bake, she wouldnae brew . . .', etc. Thereafter follows a familiar tale of a lazy, haughty and vain bitch, finally battered into servile obedience by our bold hero.

course, of those endless generations of Scottish women for whom a husband was the one route to financial security; she not only deferred to him in everything, but did so on strongly held principle, and proudly signed her name as his. At least Old Frank, while he expected to be waited on hand, if not foot, treated Mrs Francis E. Cougan with love and, as far as we could tell, with honour. (My family will just have to forgive the mild qualification. Charismatic men in positions of power can never be merely trusted to behave well.) It was decades before I learned her name was Margaret Weir.

Old Frank was a devotee of his exact contemporary, the Caithness-born theologian William Barclay, and aligned with his views: pacifist, scientistic, generally (despite the tramp story) sceptical of miracles, non-literalist in regard to the Bible, and with a view of universal salvation that was really more bodhisattva vow than Pauline. For all that the extramarital was abhorred, he had healthy views on sex – occasionally a bit too healthy – and was explicit in his praise of his wife's attractiveness. (When he decreed that my father should court my mother for at least a year before they wed, he knew exactly what Mum meant by her firm 'That's going to be too long' without her going into detail, and convened the wedding post-haste.) He also lusted openly after Doris Day; he would frequently claim to have spent the afternoon attending to his parishioners, but the smell of the disinfectant they dropped from the ceiling of the Tayport fleapit would give him away, and he'd have to confess to a second or fourth solo viewing of *Calamity Jane*. On skint weeks he'd drive to Dundee, where the Green's Playhouse was owned by a Catholic family. He'd slap on his dog collar and be ushered in with a whispered 'On you go, Father', with only the gentlest protestation and the most cursory of two-fingers cross-blessings on his part.

He was also actively anti-racist when no one else was, and admired Dr King and the heroes of the US civil rights movement, Paul Robeson in particular. (His oft-stated heart's desire was to 'stand next to Paul Robeson in heaven', though I could never work out why there wouldn't be any chairs.) He once bollocked out Uncle Jimmer the psycho-Nazi when he'd started to expound, in his appalling Bumfuck Dumfriesshire half-gargle, half-yodel, some half-witted eugenic theory he'd just been reading on 'the crghanial capacity of yourgh averghage n—rghh' at a family dinner. It was a tone I didn't know he had outside of the pulpit. He rapped the wood with his knuckles. 'There. Will be. No. Talk. Of that kind. At this table.'

Barclay's evangelical bent led Papa to admire Billy Graham and attend at least one of his rallies. Britain had developed few antibodies to Graham's evangelism: Graham, like all stadium preachers, was a huckster and a charlatan, but his charisma blinded even the most conservative Christians back then. Had my grandfather known he was an anti-Semite who had denied his daughters an education and encouraged Nixon to bomb the dikes and kill a million innocent Vietnamese, he would likely have been less enamoured. (Graham was an early master of 'I do not recognise myself here' defences, which became popular with the advent of recording equipment.) Graham merely deepened Papa's faith. The United Free Church had mostly re-dis-un-united with the Church of Scotland in 1929, after Scottish Protestantism had emerged from eighty years of bewildering schisms, creaky alliances, flounces and petted lips ('Tonight in the Toon Ha': the Auld Lichters and the Seceders Try to Agree on Precisely Whit They Are Fechtin' Aboot'), but the small UFCoS that remained stayed true to its beliefs of independence from the state and interdenominational harmony. Papa's Saturday sessions at the bools with young Father Aldo did not go down well with that Knoxite faction in the Kirk who still maintained that Catholics were not Christians of any kind, but he could not have given less of a toss.

He died in a side room in Ninewells Hospital in Dundee, understandably knackered from almost sixty years of ministry, and pleading to go home. The day before he died, my cousin Claire and I were regaled with the final episode of *Paddy and Pansy* as we sat on his hospital bed. He was too lost in his daft storytelling to see the mess we were in. Among his last words were a typically operatic but wholly sincere 'I loved my fellow man.' He did, and was loved in return. His final instruction to me was the same as my Nana's a few years later: 'Be good.' (I was not good.)

The manse, though, has never left my dreams, and appears in the handwritten notes of my therapists as 'the house behind the house'. In the dream I have just bought a house (ex-schemie kids are often obsessed with home ownership). This new pile is accessed by a wide driveway through its laid lawns and manicured beds; it's a huge, transparent, polished affair, modern and spacious, all glass and steel and sunlight. But then the seller mentions, casually, that the house comes with another house. Oh yes, sorry, forgot to mention it in the schedule. This house lies at the bottom of the long, overgrown back garden. It stands alone, and its ground floor is entered by strikingly grand ornamental steps, which arc across a sunken basement level. It is a fabulously decrepit nineteenth-century pile in the Scots baronial style. I sense most folk would condemn it on sight, but I *know* it can be renovated; it'd be a tragedy if I don't. It seems recently and hastily vacated – lamps have been left on, and books lie open on the tatty Victorian couches. I explore upstairs. There are holes in the ceiling and in the roof, and a light rain is misting through the bedrooms, soaking the rumpled linen on the wonky four-posters. There's green mould on the walls. The lamps are still on in the bedroom too, and are buzzing and sparking in the rain. I'm frightened, but rarely to the point of waking, as it's far too interesting. It needs three phone calls made there and then: one to the roofer, one to the sparky and one to the priest, as a couple of the previous occupants clearly need to be persuaded to leave.

Slowly, I become aware of the house's deranged complexity. I make a mental note that I'll need to set aside several days to map it out: it starts to hint at warrens of connected chambers, crawl-spaces, secret panic rooms, priest holes and lofts; I daren't even think about the basement, though I have already seen its grimy, cobwebbed windows cluttered with books and gardening equipment. Back on the ground floor, though, I find

8 From Secret Admire

After Scott died, I needed a way of keeping Mum's focus, and she needed an excuse to shower me with all the attention she'd set aside for two kids. She'd already made the critical mistake of going away for a three-night trip down south. Nana looked after me, but not, I must report, with any of the warmth that would later exist between us. I recall that weekend as many weeks of cold scrubbing, early nights and harsh words. I suspect her own teenage children were then making plenty of maternal claims on her without the addition of a whining grandchild not even related by blood. I think Mum was attending a funeral; either way, I was determined that she was coming back to another one. I wept and howled; I fell head first into the fire and burned my face; I developed a hideous impetigo. On my mother's return, it was clear some compromise had to be worked out. So between the two of us, we struck upon asthma, which could be summoned whenever the occasion demanded. I became, with Mum's encouragement, a hypochondriac, for which I was immediately and handsomely rewarded. Days off school, weeks in bed and, most importantly, notes for PE. *I am afraid Donald cannot attend gym today as he is a wee bit chesty.* Asthma was the reason I was the only kid in the entire class – bar the lassie in calipers – to fail Grade 1 gymnastics ('The Forward Roll'), and why I still can't swim. Swimming took place in the Dickensian sewer of Lochee Baths, and was taught by a prune-faced old sadist who saw her job as teaching us to overcome our resistance, not our fear. Her last act was to administer one thirty-second ducking, only ended through the humanitarian intervention of my teacher. I then argued successfully for a lifetime exemption. This was signed off, under some pressure from Mum, by Dr Carswell.

Dr Carswell was the godlike figure who had tended me from birth. He was a tall, bald man of negligible senescence – he might have been anywhere between forty and ninety-five – and a patrician, rather doctrinaire figure, though he had a ready smile and a gasping, narrow-eyed laugh that lasted ten seconds longer than was comfortable. He was also wise to my mother, and once threw her out of my bedroom during a particularly hysterical attack, as it was obvious she was playing The Globe to my choking Hamlet.

Something else for apparently mortal concern was my flat feet. I am yet to experience the terrible musculoskeletal problems in later life that were then promised to flat-feet sufferers; I was also told I would be prevented from joining the marines, but the asthma and the cowardice had surely ticked that box twice already. Nonetheless, once a week I was dragged off to a gloomy, draughty, high-ceilinged clinic in red-bricked Kemback Street to do semi-mystical stretching and waddling exercises. These had names like 'the swan', and 'the mermaid', and 'the tightrope walker'. I'm not sure they made a blind bit of difference; maybe they cured it. Who knows. I am not knock-kneed but still not a marine. I also had to wear shoes with built-up insoles, which could be made only of real leather – much to my mother's dismay, as she loved the sheen and cheapness of the new synthetic fabrics. I was otherwise a prince in polyester, a viscount in viscose, and slept in red nylon pyjamas between nylon sheets. If I turned over suddenly in the night, I got tased, so I slept standing horizontally to attention. In the morning my hair was like Eraserhead's, and I had learned to automatically put a foot on the floor to earth myself before I turned the lamp on. If there'd been a fire, I'd have died by a kind of instant plastic en croute.

Because it was then the law in child-hating Scotland, I was obliged to go to school at four years old. I was barely out of nappies. I was also still a regular bedwetter. While hardly convenient for my mother, it was marvellously so for me. Dad tried to incentivise my continence by putting a star on the door when I had a dry night, with the promise of reward once the door was full. This isn't a great system, but it works much better than battering the child into compliance, or humiliating them before their peers. That, I could manage myself. I recall sitting outside on the close steps in front of the tenement with the bigger kids, who were discussing what guns and outfits they were saving up for. I don't know what possessed me to breezily chip in with 'Yeah, if I don't wet the bed for another six nights I'm getting an Action Man', but the remark didn't quite win the nods of chin-stroking approval I'd hoped for.

Yet I was already quite independent, and ran, or at least

waddled, errands to the shop at the bottom of McLean Street.*
The idea that this *wasn't* safe didn't arise; there were very few
cars, and while I assume folk fiddled with kids in the sixties,
no one seemed to regard it as a crime worth heading off at
the pass. In a total inversion of current practice, strangers, let
alone neighbours, were to be trusted on principle; it was plain
bad form to ascribe wicked intent to someone you didn't know.
(There's a net gain here for any community, but like *those*
days will return.) Mostly these trips only involved me getting
milk or bread, though those two three-pound bags of potatoes
were a bit much, Jean. I once lucked out and came back with a
ten-bob note from Mr Depta, the drunk Polish tailor. Despite
my sobs that it had been legitimately secured, Mum handed it
straight back to Mrs Depta, whom he notoriously kept short.
One day Mum put sanitary towels on the shopping list. In
those days sanitary towels had loops. I know this because I
returned wearing one as a kind of chin-sling with a loop round
each ear, and will have thought it made me look quite striking.
Mum stopped putting sanitary towels on the shopping list.

My independence must have reassured my parents that
I would handle school well, even though I was still just a
foetus in a blazer. Though I'm not convinced anyone properly
explained to me what school actually was. I thought it was

---

* The Scots phrase we used for 'shopping' is 'getting your messages',
'message' here being transferred from one's 'mission', which is
actually closer to the Old English sense of 'errand' (*ærende*: message,
mission, news, tidings, etc.).

something we were trying out, like a new kind of cereal. I went willingly enough and tried to keep an open mind, but did not enjoy my first morning, a demanding programme of sand, water, coloured blocks, farting and wailing. Playtime came at 10.30 a.m. I made an executive, and strode out the front gate with a whistle: I'd just explain to Mum that this wasn't for me, and was certain she'd see it my way, as she did most things. I walked the half-mile home – it really was half a mile, I've just checked – and gave Mum a cheery wave when I saw her at the window, though I clocked that she didn't wave back. The school was called. I took the rest of the morning off, but Dad took me back in at lunchtime. I had to be carried bodily into the classroom, flailing and flexing like a landed conger eel and roaring my head off, my distraught father holding my neck and the atrocious Miss Fabb, the assistant headmistress, grabbing my ankles. Miss Fabb, a bitter old hag of maybe thirty-eight who'd joined the profession to batter children, was disappointed that she wasn't allowed to belt anyone under eight, and had to make do with slapping my legs as hard as she could get away with.

After a few months of extraordinary rendition, things got a little easier. I went quietly, if not willingly. Luckily, I had Miss Houston as my first teacher, of whom I recall nothing but her kindness, and the fact that she was so young even *I* knew she was young. I also recall nothing because I learned nothing. I made cool friends, though, and now walked home with Alex Tosh, who had permanent shiny green plugs of hardened snot up either nostril, which lent his speech a sing-song quality;

and Jimmy Neeley, who could take out his cock and pee while walking without breaking the flow of the conversation, which I thought was a pretty suave move. More crucially, there were girls. Girls with *pants*. I was genitally obsessed from the age of three or four, possibly earlier, and in any game of doctors and nurses always played a consultant proctologist. My various shrinks sometimes have remarked that this premature sexualisation may point to some early abuse, possibly by the guardsman on the Dundee–Tayport line. I mean, if that *was* the reason, it was definitely worth taking the hit. I was enjoying myself too much. Obviously things had to be more discreet in the classroom, and the obsession was metonymically transferred to Debbie O'Hanlon's knickers, a glimpse of which would send me into a venereal delirium. It was then that I became aware of the vast gulf between love and sex, which my brain has, miserably, always regarded less as kissing cousins than as a principled separation of church and state. What on earth had they to do with each other? Conditions that obtain from the very beginning are never interrogated, or at least not until it's too late. My deep instinct to investigate any item of clothing that contained a bum or a fanny was irrelevant and unrelated to my burgeoning love-junkie career. (In other words, everything that made me an arsehole at forty was pretty much solidly in place at five.)

I started to fall in love, serially, and endlessly. At seven I wrote my first and last valentine, for Mandy Martin, a small, fast-legged, red-haired, freckle-faced alpha girl. I thought I was in with a shout because we were already comrades-in-arms: we'd marched side by side on my first political demo, protesting the BBC's decision to cancel *Scooby-Doo*. (The BBC had announced they were to ditch it after two seasons, and we responded with a Scotland-wide campaign. Thirty thousand signatures were gathered, and the Glasgow contingent proposed burning down the BBC Scotland HQ. Glasgow weans weren't big on empty threats, and the BBC backed down. Pesky kids!) On the sheet of folded white card I drew a heart, and I inscribed it with the words 'Love, Likeness and Beauty'. I thought 'likeness' was the quality of liking someone a lot, or rather their ability to provoke that in oneself. I think the word I was reaching for was 'likeynessitude'. Mum suggested I also add 'from secret admire', though I may have written that down wrong. I posted it through Mandy's front door in far and away the bravest act of my young life, and I'd had nine teeth out at once. Admittedly, I had been vague on the effect I'd hoped for; but whatever it was, I'd definitely hoped for something else. In class the next morning, there was a lot of behind-hand snarfing, pointing and loud whispering. I will have given myself away by my blush, which gave off an audible hum; it then entered the infrared to turn my head a shade of black, and had every kid within three yards loosening their tie. Mandy and her entire family then moved to Carlisle to get away from me.

We'll get round to the sugar that rotted them in their sockets later, but a word on those nine teeth. My fear of dentists is like my fear of flying: rational. My first dentist was Mr McMadden on Strathmartine Road, who had started his career in a travelling fair, and would also put your dog down for a fiver. I appreciate the no-nonsense school of extraction, but he regarded anaesthesia as the sort of absurd rigmarole one only performs for the aristocracy. Besides, for the young light- or non-brusher, the application of extreme pain was a not-to-be-wasted teachable moment. It certainly taught me not to go near Mr McMadden, and Mum was then obliged to switch me to Dundee Dental Hospital. This was literally the only place on earth where things could have gone worse. This is a training hospital: yes, 'training', like hairdressers. 'Dental practice' here meant something else. Since baby teeth were destined for the bin anyway, they were regarded as perfect for getting your eye in, and their being in the mouths of babies seemed to trouble no one. One memorable two-hour session began with three twenty-year-olds making space for a small filling in a molar; they seemed to be only lightly supervised. Euphoric from having successfully located the mouth, they then fell victim to overconfidence: drilling turned to grinding, grinding to routing, my mere pain into agony. Eventually, the consultant came over to check on the screaming, then removed the older kids to a side room for what I could tell was a furious whispered word. By this stage I had long given up on the brave-wee-soldier shtick, and was howling. About twelve jabs were swiftly administered to my soft palate, like an attack squadron of hornets, which at least shut me up; then what had very recently been a perfectly viable part of my head was ripped out of it. I rode home in silence and hid in a cupboard. Mum then insisted all serious dental work be conducted under general anaesthetic. My team of dentists reckoned a mass cull was the only way to properly clear space and prevent my heart giving out to caries. The day came, the way the day always does; suddenly we were here, in the orange waiting room. I was terrified, and told Mum. 'So am I,' she said, in honest solidarity, but it wasn't quite what I needed to hear. I was led alone into the operating theatre. The blunted yellow lights, the huge chair, the leather ankle- and wrist-straps, the trays of rusty pliers (I have a selective imagination but a lively memory). A nurse said something distressingly poetic about 'breathing in the sweet smell of sleep'. Then the mask, the hiss, the horrible smell of sleep, the rising buzz and blur. I started thrashing around and had to be restrained. 'Hold him still! Hold him still!' were the last words I heard on this earth, as I was sucked into the void like a dying bee up a hoover. I woke to my own loud moans, covered in blood and vomit. When my next appointment came round, I went into full-scale denial, and didn't tell my teacher. On the day, when Mum came to pick me up, I hid in the bike shed in the playground. I could hear her asking the other kids where I was; I was dragged out of hiding and marched off to the car, in a half nelson. I was then reported as having been violently kidnapped by a strange woman, and the police were called. All was swiftly resolved, but the next day I had to face Mr Dryden, a towering old dominie with a black cloak and the huge bushy eyebrows that were standard issue for headmasters in those days. I assumed I was down for six of the tawse. I sat in his office staring at, of all things, a print of Dalí's *Port Lligat at Sunset*. But Mr Dryden actually liked children, and immediately saw what had happened. Next

(In my case: the exile, the loneliness, the madness, the girl, the loss, the books and the example.) I didn't give poetry another thought, beyond a very short and predictable white-charger rescue-fantasy obsession with Sylvia Plath at fifteen, and some terrible lyrics for the sub-John Martyn stuff I was writing a year later. Though I'm struck now far less by my six-year-old prescience than by my fatalism. Not I *want* to be. I am *going* to be. One has had little choice, and I know this because I would have chosen differently. I have a tattoo of a line from Antonio Porchia which reads 'BEFORE I TRAVELLED MY ROAD I WAS MY ROAD', more in tribute to my genetic determinism than to any great belief in destiny, though most folk read the latter. It functions variously as a poor excuse, an explanation and occasionally a source of consolation.

(By the way, if you don't yet have a tattoo and are considering it, they're *really* sore. I had mine done blind drunk and it was still awful. As soon as the needle touches your skin you know two things: this is going to be hell, and it's already too late. But it's only hell to begin with. The tattooist kept asking me, 'Are you getting it yet?' All I was getting was tortured by a man with a big ink gun, and I had an hour and a half of it to go. But on his third time of asking, I noticed myself following the tip of his descending needle with some sense of anticipation. By the fourth, I was *definitely* getting it – 'it' being the surge of endorphins your brain makes to offset the pain, to which it soon adds the dopamine spike of anticipation. When I left the parlour I was high as a weather balloon, and wanted to book myself back in at the weekend for a full-length koi carp

9 Bungopolis

When I was four or five, one game I played with Mum a lot was hiding in the hall cupboard. It was an odd game, and it could be randomly initiated by the other team, and only when Dad was at work. The object of the game seemed to be that the other team wasn't allowed to hear you. They started the game by ringing the doorbell. At the hollow, falling-third bing-bong of the NuTone, Mum and I would race to the cupboard and stay as quiet as we could and only speak in whispers. They'd ring maybe three more times, and if you stayed quiet until the end you got a biscuit. I liked it. We played it a lot and we always won.

Later, there was a bloke who came round to collect for the catalogue; he was kindly and forgiving and open to extensions. Mum was as sweetly attentive to him as she was to the minister. One later heard of other arrangements being come to with the catalogue men elsewhere on the estate, with some folk putting out more than their traybakes. When I was about twelve, I caught Mum crying in the kitchen, and she confessed to the huge debt she'd racked up. It was wrong of her to burden me with this, but she found it far easier to share bad news with me than with my dad, who had a tendency to worry himself sick about everything. (It gave me a lifelong fear of debt. I've never owned a credit card, nor ever will.) But eventually my father got wind of it, and was plunged into a black, catatonic funk that saw him signed off and staring out the window for weeks. It just wasn't possible for him to work any harder than he did. Dad would occasionally just collapse from exhaustion, but his body had to find a physical excuse to justify his sick pay, so his back would go and he'd be laid up for a fortnight. Dad was so much the axletree of the household that any suggestion of frailty on his part sent great shudders through the whole caravan, and these occasions scared us mightily.

But to air a familiar ex-schemie observation: mostly we didn't feel broke, being no better or worse off than our neighbours. If every bairn in the street is also being sent out to collect the lumps scattered across the road by the coal lorry, there's little stigma attached to it. (I did think about hamming this stuff up in that poor-mouth Kailyard 2.0 way that still defines the Scottish literature written for the export market, because I'm not a total idiot, but it was bad enough.) Though my dad did once attempt an economy too far. One day Mum and I got off the bus back from town to encounter a freakish meteorological phenomenon: while it was blue and bright elsewhere, our corner of the scheme had been plunged into a sunless, Cimmerian fog. We soon traced its origin to our chimney. Inside, we found Dad attempting to burn some wet peat he'd bought off a country cousin at the weekend. This was not the most discreet plan in a smokeless zone, for all that it did a fine job of completely concealing the house.

However, I owe something else to my coal-scavenging. At some point in my ninth year, I spent half an hour helping

Mrs Grant down the road pick up a couple of bags'-worth the lorry had shed in front of her house by taking the corner a bit fast. Mrs Grant was a primary school teacher, and by way of payment she gave me a copy of *The Greek Gods*, in the Scholastic Press edition. I was initially sceptical; 'reading' then meant Enid Blyton, who was regarded as a self-contained genre, indeed an inexhaustible branch of world literature within which one might forge one's own distinctive tastes. I favoured the Brer Rabbit books and *The Book of Brownies*, especially any story involving comeuppance and small underground trains. But one day, tired – for all its intertextual layers – of rereading 'The Saucepan Man', I opened *The Greek Gods*. It was illustrated with fake-Cocteau line drawings, and was written mostly by Bernard Evslin, who had added a number of lurid details I was subsequently unable to find in either Ovid or Graves. It was a book of unbelievable drama, mad love, crazy transformation and spectacular vengeance, and I read it till it fell apart. In this telling, here is how the ugly little smith-god Hephaestus gained the hand of Aphrodite in marriage: Aphrodite: 'But what could you possibly offer a girl like me?' Hephaestus: 'I work late.' It took me five reads to understand it. Oh. Even though it was for kids, it opened a window onto the world of non-Blytonian adult emotions for the first time. I then tried to branch out in the Blytonverse, and had a crack at the Famous Fives. While they didn't quite trigger class war, they were obviously set in a foreign country. (Though one friend tells me her political awakening began one day on reading something roughly along the lines of 'One day,

Mary turned into a street where all the houses had *numbers*, not names.') But moreover they were *childish*. No: it was time to tackle the classics. Molesworth, Tom Sharpe, Para Handy, James Herriot, and my father's precious hardback library of Dennis Wheatleys.

In the size of our household debt we were very far from untypical. There had been a shift in thinking: it was the beginning of the era when not only were the material aspirations of the poor starting to be monetised, but the poor were seen as a commodity in themselves: they could now be taxed for the privilege of their own existence. As well as all the traditional lower-order scourges, one could also now die of hire purchase. Mum's cuboid pal Anne McShane was a sweary, funny and popular woman who slowly fell out with the entire cul-de-sac, my mum included, over unreturned loans. It was always a fatal mistake to ask to borrow even a small amount of money from outside the family, if you either could not or had no intention of paying it back. The creditor might have had the generosity, but they won't have had the capital to stop thinking about it every time they saw you; they had their own HP debt to service. Anne just started to avoid folk. The borrowing habit had been partly forced on her through her husband, a slightly saft-in-the-heid, gentle-natured and nervous door-to-door salesman, dying suddenly, and young. (The whisper on the street was: 'So they took Stuart into the DRI wi' that pain in his belly, and they opened him up, and they took one look, and it was aa black everywhere, so they sewed him right back up again, and that was him awa' by the weekend.') Anne's main crime in the eyes of estate seemed to be an unforgivable *nerve*: she did not cut her cloth according to her freshly reduced circumstances, and continued to live the high life, i.e. she occasionally replaced her couch and still went to the bingo. Slowly, her circle dwindled as debt made her a liar, then a recluse, and she died drunk and alone.

Fortunately my family had my mum's elder brother, Frank. Uncle Frank was a businessman of some means (Mum was sketchy on the matter: 'He owns a factory that sells shirts to Iceland') who not only conformed to the mortifying-uncle trope in all the usual regards, but showed the kind of commitment that smacked of true calling. One could not take Frank anywhere. His golf club bacchanalias were the stuff of you'll-never-darken-these-lounge-doors legend; he'd spontaneously buy champagne for the queue at the chip shop, and walk down the line doling it out in plastic glasses; he'd come down to breakfast dressed as Rod Stewart, having gone to bed as Tina Turner. A certain what-happens-in-Troon *omertà* surrounds his activities, and frankly we do not know everything Frank Got Up To, nor are we much inclined to enquire further. His natural gift for the totally inappropriate was pretty versatile. Frank once pitched me 'a great idea for a novel' he strongly felt I should write. It was, as he put it, 'about a tribe in Africa' who'd been discovered deep in the jungle, but who had primitive machinery – cars, windmills, typewriters, etc. – only built from twigs and creepers and fur and whatnot. They were unusually advanced because generations before 'they had bred with the white man'. Mainly, Frank had a strong vision of its bestselling cover. 'Picture this. Lad's face. Black as the ace of spades. Black black *black*. But get this – bright blue, blue eyes staring out. *Sky*-blue. Get this title.' Drum roll. '. . . *Ebony Blue.*' He said it again. '*Ebony. Blue.* There ye go.' I was fixed in an attitude of such winded disbelief it was likely taken for gobsmacked wonder. But while Nineveh had been more thoroughly reconstructed, Frank was the opposite of Uncle Jimmer the psycho-Nazi (of whom more shortly). He was his father's son. No one knew the extent of Frank's family interventions. All we did know is that if you called Frank weeping, he'd be round in half an hour to dry your tears, restructure your debt and repurpose your assets. If that wasn't possible, he'd just bail you out. He would hear no word of gratitude, let alone of any repayment plan that might leave you in the same position. He was also beyond discreet. His handouts would be stuffed into my pocket with such sleight of hand I'd only discover them days later. He had known the shame of poverty himself, and he wasn't going to let you, if he could avoid it.

We spent a lot of time taking the 20 bus into town to Goldbergs department store, where Mum would queue to pay off another bit of the store credit she was beginning to rack up. (Mum still sweetly claims, 'I just wanted you to have the best,' but Jeannie, I've been onto you for years. Wipe that treacle off your face.) Afterwards, Mum would take me for toasted cheese and hot chocolate in Forte's Italian cafe, and then we'd go to the tenebrose, spooky labyrinth of the amusement arcade under the Caird Hall, or the one in the old Wellgate, where they had dodgems. The Wellgate was then a drunken grid of eighteenth- and nineteenth-century streets clinging to the talus of the Hilltown. I loved it for its picturesque grime and its haggle culture. On Saturdays, we'd head for the huge indoor flea market of Dens Road, where one could also find the cheap butchers and grocers that could stretch out the family food budget. Dens Road was the last place to sell the Dundee delicacy of the 'buster' – a poke of chips with hot peas drenched in vinegar – and I'd be sent off to scald my mouth and stroll round the stalls alone. Every rented pitch was screened off from the next by a swathe of jute, that most wonderfully Dundonian of smells, whose sweetness filled the entire hall. Each booth had its mad specialism – jewellery, comics, ceramics, Victorian dolls, books, musical instruments – though I loved the bric-a-brac stalls that looked like upturned attics. Now that eBay has taught us the price of everything, what one wouldn't give for an hour amongst their filthy treasures.

Then one day we stopped going to Forte's, and instead headed for the Lite Bite, a trendy diner that The Inn Folk had officially opened one lunchtime, in the new, freezing, brutalist wind-tunnel of the Overgate. The arcade under the Caird Hall closed down. Then they bulldozed the streets of the Wellgate and threw up a huge brown mall the size of a football pitch that took a mere twenty years to turn into four levels of empty lets, remainder shops and jakie benches, which in bad weather would alternate prettily with junkie benches. (The two constituencies did not mix, and shared very different tastes in communal singalongs.)

If we'd kept these wonderful precincts intact, Dundee would

have been preserved as a kind of boreal Naples, with the most breathtaking natural situation of any city in Scotland. (Let's not get into the specifics, that's to say the bulldozing of Dundee West train station, or the Royal Arch, or a hundred other lost glories; I couldn't bear it.) What first-time rail traveller to Dundee has not crossed the 'mighty long bridge'* at sunset to gaze upriver at the broad, mountain-flanked Tay, shimmering like the rainbow-crossing of Bifröst itself – then turned to see the glittering, twinkling city rise up on its twin green hills, and not dreamed herself bound for some inexplicably unsung Shangri-La? And then pulled into Dundee station and gone: 'Oh.' My childhood consisted of watching almost every building of any architectural worth razed in a systematic programme of municipal vandalism – one not even driven by a misguided modernising instinct, but by the realisation that dodgy contracting was an end in itself. The possibilities for legitimate self-enrichment in Dundee were so limited that to use one's elevation to the council chambers as an opportunity for public service alone would have been perverse. Slowly, all became ugly-ass concrete malls and office blocks, multistorey parking, pissy underpasses and a ring-road system designed expressly to twang you out the way you came in, without ever revealing how it had spun you around. There is no way on God's earth this work could have been undertaken in the name of good-faith 'improvement'. Visitors to the town looking for

* Ulysses S. Grant's one recorded remark on the town; he was very tired.

its putative centre would often be guided onto the ramp to the Tay Bridge for a scenic four-mile detour into Fife and back, via the tollbooths. (On the Dundee exit, though, next to the booth, was a magic tree that the toll guys would point out to the kids in the back seats: it was full of shiny, bright lemons which grew all year round. God knows how many plastic Jif lemons they'd bought up and squeezed out over the years to keep this tree in permanent flourish, but our parents were in on it, and the authentic miracle of the Tay Bridge Lemon Tree was as stoutly defended as the existence of Santa. As a child, this sweetened one's re-entry into the city considerably.)

Quite deliberately, the town was never finished. The council regarded it as a bent dentist regards an open mouth, an empty canvas for unnecessary fillings, veneers, root canals, crowns and bridges, implants and extractions. I never knew it not to be in a state of upheaval, of perfect uproar, a vast circus of temporary traffic lights, cones, cranes, puddles, dug-up roads, closed lanes, whole quarters fenced off and under redevelopment. Social immobility meant that most folk just didn't *know* Edinburgh and Aberdeen didn't look like that too. Weren't all towns permanent works-in-progress? Had Dundee appeared in Calvino's *Invisible Cities*, one would turn a corner in Bungopolis and head for the bus home; but, realising one had left one's wallet in a cafe, turn back, only to find everything already altered beyond recognition: the street name changed, the flow of traffic reversed, the cafe now a betting shop and the Victorian pub next door a smoking, blackened shell.

The absence of any town planning whatsoever left Dundee

as a town one could only know as an insider, though, and learn by walking it. Aberdeen makes an instructive contrast; it looks as if it was cut out with a grinder five minutes ago. Dundee, on the other hand, is a palimpsest of every Dundee there ever was. Turn a corner into a side street and you'll find medieval wall, Victorian slum, thirties deco, eighties postmodern and illegally jerry-built. And what one memorises one inevitably comes to love. It is a city that's difficult to be bored by. (Students, in particular, love Dundee: it's cheap, full of pubs, dementedly hospitable in the way poor towns are, and it's hard to get them to leave.) But Dundee was not only poor; it was determined to look it, and show its population it should not dare aspire to better. We believed we had the city we deserved.

This carefully inculcated apathy worked as a fine cover for a council strongly inclined to a mid-period Ornette Coleman approach to its accounts. Corruption was simply how the city ran, and in turn it encouraged the population to behave in a similar way. In Dundee, 'Closed for Refurbishment' was just a way of giving the fire brigade three days' notice. Am I allowed to even whisper the name of former lord provost Alexander Ogilvie yet? Yes, I think so; though for years his exploits were a matter of record only in the dark murmurs of late-night taxi drivers, with the reflexively nervous addition '. . . but onywiy you didnae hear that from me'. I see Eck's obit in the *Courier* describes him as a 'rough diamond', much in the way *Pravda* finally conceded Lavrentiy Beria had been a bit of a cheeky monkey. Although they were forced into reform, Scottish Labour never expressed any contrition, conducted no public renunciation of the old carrot-and-stick way of doing business (my first run at that phrase contained some apparently litigable metonyms for both the stick and the carrot), never explained any number of miraculously well-compensated McHoffas within the unions, and yet still have the nerve to airily wonder why almost no one wants to vote for them anymore.

By way of a coda one must add that, to the town and the council's considerable credit, Dundee is now attempting to finish itself; colourful plans are posted round the city centre showing the wonderful parks, public spaces and marinas that are scheduled to be completed after I am dead. I didn't say we were Germany. Dundee's starring role in HBO's *Succession*, while the beneficiary of some selective camerawork – some of it selected other cities entirely – nonetheless showed a town one could be architecturally as well as tribally proud of. A climactic scene sees *Succession*'s Rupert Murdoch figure, Logan Roy, receive a civic honour at a fancy bash in his home town; the masterly Brian Cox's persistent Dundee twang was easier to build into Roy's backstory than it was to train out of him, this late in the day. When the hotshot NYC crew rolled up to shoot the civic reception scene in Dundee's superb new Victoria and Albert Museum, they needed extras, and I gather a call was put out on Facebook for '200 Dundonians with black-tie evening wear'. You guys.

10 The Lore and Anguish of Schoolchildren

When I lived on the St Mary's council estate, this was all fields, son, stretching up to Baldragon Wood and Clatto Reservoir and away north towards the village of Bridgefoot and up to the Sidlaws, the 'fairy hills' that separated us from the great Vale of Strathmore slung between the Sidlaws and the Cairngorms, and running from Perth in the west to Stonehaven in the east. Behind the last row of tenements on the schemie was exactly nothing. McLean Street, where we lived until I was ten, is a short, steep ramp running downhill off the Macalpine Road circle (roundabouts are known in Dundee, and in Dundee only, as 'circles') into a square of three-storey tenements, as safe as a ring of wagons, where we lived. In the north-west corner between the tenements was a tiny patch of undeveloped wasteland known as 'The Dump'. This was a 15 × 15-yard scale model of the Highlands, rugged, wild, crawling with life, throbbing with sex, mud and holes, and off-limits to adults. In The Dump we devised elaborate tag and forfeit games for higher and higher stakes, games which left me so breathless and ecstatic I needed to go inside to lie down every half-hour. The McLean cul-de-sac (we naturalised the word, 'culdysack') was almost a closed community. Two exits led off it: McLean Street proper, which ended in a grocery-cum-butcher's and Strathmartine Church, and a leafy, shady back lane that ran past the orphanage with which we were often threatened, which was sealed off behind a high-wire fence. All this, from the three-foot perspective, provided as much topological variety as you could conceive of. TV was crap, so we lived in the street.

Very few of our most popular games are to be found in Opie. Granny was the game for connoisseurs: by way of equipment it required only a ball and the high side of a tenement, but its rule book was dafter than royal tennis. You threw the ball against the wall and caught it; but *where* you threw it, the height you threw it, the manner in which you threw it, caught it or missed it, and the points granted or deducted, and the various benefits or forfeits involved, were perfectly deranged. Like most games adapted to very specific bits of local architecture, it ceased to exist as soon as you turned the corner. McLean Street Granny was effectively one of those species of orchid that only grows in one crack in one rock in one tiny bit of County Clare, in its own freakish microclimate. Another skilful game was Cribby, known more sensibly as Kerby everywhere on the planet except McLean Street. You stood on opposite pavements and tried to bounce a football or a tennis ball off the corner of the kerb so that it bounced back in such a way that you could catch it again; for this you got one point, two if you could catch it without leaving the pavement, and much other stuff. Now that I think of it, it was exactly the same as Granny, only horizontal. I was quite accomplished, and dreamed, vaguely, of getting into a decent Ivy League on a Cribby scholarship.

Then there were the usual dressy-up role-playing games, but you came in what you had. This led to some odd *mises en scène*, and many fires had to be put out at hospitals on the moon, or pirates read the Miranda following their stabbing of Snow White. For some reason Stevie was obsessed with being a Red Indian. One December my Papa's brother, Uncle Johnny from Canada – 'the bigamist', my mother would always add, without explanation – brought him a full outfit, complete with bow and arrow, which he claimed he'd purchased from the gift shop on a Canadian First Nation reserve but had 'airport' written all over it. Stevie begged Santa for a wigwam to go with it. There's a photo of him standing, on Christmas morning, arms folded and very proud, before his yellow wigwam in full feather headdress and buckskin, holding a plastic tomahawk. This picture was taken about five minutes before he discovered Santa had got every other kid in the street a cowboy outfit. History then took a familiar course, with Stevie featuring as a one-man genocide, and his three sucker-tipped arrows no match for the massed firepower of forty potato guns. He was back in his shorts by teatime.

Truth Dare Double-Dare Promise or Command was a just-before-supper game played in variants everywhere, but in Dundee with the added idiotic and non-metrical addition of 'Love Kiss Opinion'. 'Double-dare' was variously interpreted – the correct meaning is 'If you do that, I'll do it too' – but we took it as just a suicidally extreme version of 'dare', so it came up a lot. There was a question-master, and perched on the steps into the tenement close we stuck to an urbane, relaxed, late-night *Parkinson*-style interview format as the shadows yawned around us.

– Do you *double-dare* to fill this Tudor Crisps bag with dogshite, set fire to it outside Snouter's door, ring his bell, then watch him stamp it out?

– I do, Brian. I accept your challenge. Snouter is not only loathsome but old and frail, and will be unable to pursue me.

– What is your *opinion* of wee James here?

– I feel – as I know we all do – that Jamesy was weaned too early, and we now see the consequences of this in his very short stature and general insecurity. In the long run I think this will play out badly for him, especially in the workplace, assuming he ever secures employment; most of us here feel circus work may be his only available option. Sorry, Jamesy.

– Nae worries.

– Do you *love* Sally McGinty from McLean Place?

– Honestly? Yes; yes, I'd call it love. I suppose you're going to tell her now! God, that'll be a little embarrassing.

– What is the *truth* of the rumour that you pished in the bucket at the berries?

– Not only was it true, it was worse than you describe, Brian. From observing your own actions, I discovered an even more effective way to weigh down the scales.

– Will you *kiss* Big Sandra – right here, right now?

– No, Brian, I'd prefer not to. No offence to Sandra, who is horny and well developed for ten, but Sally McGinty has my heart.

– Do you *promise* to give Big Sandra a kiss?

– No, I do not; I refer you to my earlier answer.

– What if I were to *command* you?

– Ha! Well, you could try, Brian, but I will instead opt for the standard forfeit, and stand on top of Snouter's Cortina and shout: 'I'm My Mammy's Big Bubbly Bairn.'*

The one variable in our unchanging little gang was Terri, Jackie Caithness's US cousin. We met her only once a year, in the summer holidays. Terri looked like the alien she was: pale verging on albino, with hair the colour of bleached straw, her face beautiful, but her expression blankly unreadable, as if she hadn't been issued the right number of facial muscles – though what came out of her mouth was hyper-nuanced, and far sharper than anything we ever heard round our way. She seemed to have a finely developed sense of herself, and I hadn't yet met anyone who did. Dundee got self-aware irony round about the same time it got yoghurt, well into the 1980s, which was still some way off. Terri's appeal was of course enhanced by her cultural exoticism and her September-through-July unavailability. Love in those days was so strange: one fell in love *only* at first sight, when a face seemed immediately to take the shape of some perfectly distinct and elemental yearning that had somehow always been there, waiting. Sometimes I think these innocent early loves make such a deep and almost literal impression, they form the shadowboard for all the others that follow, which is why we greet them with such an immediate and inexplicable sense of recognition upon later encounter.

* To 'bubble' is to produce bubbles with snot, i.e. to blubber and cry.

Certainly I know exactly who Terri materialised as, thirty-five years later; but also who that dark and curly-haired, already-maternal little girl on the bus turned out to be, and indeed the tall and aloof lass at Sunday School who looked like Dudley D. Watkins's very occasional cartoons where Ma Broon featured as a young woman: towering, proud, her eyes on a future no one would deny her, and to which others were only a means. I should have averted my eyes the first time round.

Sally Arthur was notable for being the first girl I fell for so hard I had to actually talk to my mother about it, as it was giving me sleepless nights and a crippling stomach ache. (My other in-love symptom has always been a stigmata-like ache in the palms of my hands. That's just me, right.) Sally ran with our gang, to which I was far more peripheral than I admitted to myself. Indeed, my gang often ran without me, and sometimes ran right past me. I'd pretend not to see them and turn away quickly, hoping they wouldn't see me. Well, look at me now, suckers. What are you up to these days, Ryan, of the withering put-down and the slick quiff? Fat-baldy driving a cab, I hear? Way to go. And yourself, Calum, of the sudden, unannounced jab to the guts that had them all in stitches, where I had to laugh along, winded as I was, pretending it didn't hurt? How's the (googles) being-dead thing working out for ya? Graeme Esson also ran with the gang, quite literally non-stop, as running was Graeme's primary USP. Graeme could outrun a horse. He had a helium-assisted falsetto voice, which one usually heard in Doppler. I was tolerated in the gang occasionally, as a reliable source of free sugar: Mum had a job in the wee shop at the foot of McLean Street by then, and swiped the half of the penny tray left at the end of the day, which was heavy on unsold liquorice and the tuppence-costing 'lucky tatties'. (These looked like a kind of flattened potato, and were made from a sweet chewy mush covered in cinnamon. Lucky tatties came with a free choking hazard, a tiny plastic charm embedded in them – a cowboy, a soldier, a tiger – and if you were lucky, your teeth would find it before your throat did.) Sally Arthur was a slight, quick, ash-blonde girl with olive skin, and would have been a low mezzo if she'd sung. She went out with squeaky Graeme, presumably purely because of his rate of acceleration, since he was otherwise a man without qualities. 'Going out' with someone was then little more than a formal declaration, and only involved sitting a bit closer when you'd stopped running, but it still killed me fairly.

My sexual development continued, albeit glacially. The slow pace was largely down to misinformation. Having read a line in my dad's *Melody Maker* about 'mutual masturbation' in some exegesis of a Rolling Stones song, I asked Dad to explain. I think he barely understood the phrase himself. I had heard the second word used once before, when Sharon McLaverty's granny had talked about allowing the teapot to masturbate, but I think she'd meant 'mast', which folk sometimes said in Dundee for 'mask', i.e. 'steep'. Dad was useless and suddenly only able to speak in koans.

– It's . . . one of those things that you only know about when you know about it.

– Eh?

– Before the . . . thing that happens, you can't know what. It's like. Erm . . . Do you remember before you could walk?

– No.

– Erm there you go. So before, you could walk, you didn't know. What it was like. To walk.

– But I'd have *seen* folk walk. Can you watch folk ma—

– But you wouldn't know what it was *like*. From the *inside*.

– I don't want to know what it's like. I just want to know what it means.

– Aye but I have to put the tea on.

Although we were all tuned faithfully into Sex FM, our reception was terrible. All we got was static, garbled broadcasts, or what seemed to be straightforward bad intelligence from the enemy. Sharon McLaverty said her mum had taken her aside and told her that at some point, she couldn't say when, blood would come out of her bum instead of jobbies. End of newsflash. We were terrified by this, and had no idea if it applied to everyone, or just to girls, or even just to Sharon McLaverty. There were occasional jokes I laughed along with but didn't understand: 'I hear Tam's after your blood.' 'Tam who?' 'Tam Pax.' Ha ha ha ha ha. No idea. Derek Taylor of the dark and mysterious tenement in the corner was a year or so ahead of us, and had received some basic instruction at school, but the confidence of his delivery was balanced by the shakiness of his recall. 'Okay – so there's this stuff that comes out of your wullie, and it's called . . . spunkolania, and you rub it on the lassie's tits, so they get full of milk. Then you pee inside her, and then she has a bairn and the bairn sucks the lassie's tits.' That's me up to speed. My *Ladybird Book of Your Body* also contained the necessary information, but imparted it in a way that rendered it deliberately incomprehensible. Reproduction was buried between the function of the liver and the structure of the eyeball, and there was no pronunciation guide. I assumed 'penis' rhymed with 'Dennis', and 'vagina' with God knows. 'Mag in a'? As in jazz mag, in a bush. Porn was retrieved in the traditional fashion from rural hedges, where it grew naturally, and railway sidings, where the wheel-tappers and shunters of the rail network formed an unusually concupiscent guild. Pages were stuck with rain and the extra glue that all porn publications seemed to require.

Our little posse was peripherally attached to another, more dangerous group that revolved around Lena Murray. Lena was trouble incarnate. Looking back, there was likely abuse. There was certainly neglect. Her popularity stemmed partly from her always being left in the house alone while her parents hit the town. She had what definitely counted round our way as a middle-class family, meaning they owned their house, a 1920s bungalow on Dare Street. Her older sister was a dedicated clubber, and never home either. We'd lurk round the corner and wait for her folks to drive off; then we'd all roll up at her front door and throw what ten-year-olds imagined an adult party to be, which was way more fun than the reality. There was drinking, there was fighting, there was nudity, and there were swetchies. (I'll explain.) To Lena's infinite licence was added the terrifying catalyst of Arthur McClumsky. Arthur was having sex at ten, and we gathered Lena was one of the many with whom he had coupled (Arthur's phrase was 'I've shagged more lassies than you've had Mivvis, Donald', a turn of phrase both hurtful and impressive); there was, inevitably, an invited audience, though I always declined. Lena, for some reason, fancied me, though I was careful not to be left alone in her company. I expect I made her feel safe.

A typical evening at Lena's would begin with sharing round the Cointreau and the Advocaat from the drinks cabinet, and a skipping game called Cat's Cradle, where if the rhyme stopped and your legs were crossed, an item of clothing had to be removed. Sharon McLaverty was playing against Lena, and had started with her coat, balaclava and scarf on, and would be divesting herself of the Kleenex in her pocket. Lena was faking her oh-no-not-again eyerolls, but was desperate to get down to her vest and knickers. Arthur would be getting stuck into Lena's dad's porno mag stash, and helped us to interpret what the hell was going on, though it was very hard to work out what was going on, because everyone had pubes like Afros and it all looked like fish being sold through a hedge. Lena had also trained her dog to simulate humping her, but part of me worried she actually let the dog do it. So much of this seems less hilarious in retrospect.

One terrible night Lena's parents returned early, and we had around twenty seconds to vacate the house. We poured out the back door and climbed the side fence into the next-door garden, and then into the side lane. I made a mental note to never do this again. (A note I misplaced, though located, belatedly, at some point in my mid-thirties; specifically at the point I was making an escape over a fence, having been caught in flagrante and locked in the back garden, presumably while the other dude looked for a hammer.) Arthur was naked when the car pulled up and had only managed to get half dressed, and ran out minus his coat and shoes. He was forced to make a weeping return to the front door later to ask for them back. I'd never seen Arthur afraid; his fear, he confessed, was not the wrath of Lena's dad but that of his own, for returning without his coat.

Arthur was one of those feral terrors you no longer see; or maybe you do. How the hell would I know? Short, spiky-haired, wiry as a boxer, a creature of pure appetite and pure reaction, too much animal to be called wicked, he was lightning-quick of tongue and fist, and terrifying to be around. Not for any violence he was likely to do to you – I mean he probably would, but it wouldn't be personal – but for the fact that an invisible dome of pure anarchy and chaos extended outward for about twenty feet in any direction, and if you found yourself within it, you might fall into the blast radius, or be swept up in the mass arrest. (Arthur was probably trying to cram a life of adult experience into what he knew would be a short span; ten years later, on its regular appearances in the *Courier*, the name McClumsky was rarely attached to a feel-good news story. He was dead in his twenties: he'd murdered someone, and was killed in prison.) We took a group decision to avoid him. As for Lena, she made one more attempt to seduce me, but seemed viscerally disgusted by my suggestion that perhaps we should 'just kiss'. Lena and her entire family then moved to Carlisle to get away from me. What was it with Carlisle.

McLean Street is now a flu dream of McLean Street, and a tribute to the ideological insanity of the Thatcher years. The mini-Cairngorms of The Dump has been flattened and fenced in by steel spikes, keeping out the kids from nothing at all. Cars are everywhere, sloppily half-parked on the pavement like silent drunks propped at a bar; good luck finding three clear feet of opposing kerb for your Cribby league, kids. All the pretty gardens, once such an expressive way of distinguishing yourself from your neighbour, are gone; the perversity of Thatcher's supposed liberation of the housing market in the name of individual freedom led to not only the collapse of social housing stock but complete homogenisation, for all our glued-on porches, cartwheels and coach lamps: as soon as council houses became purchasable, gardens were requisitioned for off-road parking, and are now identically horrible, badly paved, muddy carports. The neat bin recesses behind the tenements seem to have been replaced with on-road stinking rubbish silos, chained in place with concrete slabs, presumably for ease of uplift for council workers. The population seems broke as hell. The great larch we surrounded as kids to stop the council taking an axe to it is still there, but looks brown and dried out and dead. You can cut it down now.

11 Got Any Swetchies

For every family on the street, debt was a constant low drone. If you could hear it, it turned the harmony of daily life above it from major to minor. One did one's best to drown it out. The estate defaulted to the usual analgesic escapes: bingo, gambling, alcohol and sugar, the latter being the most effective way to make yourself feel instantly better. Mum addicted me to sugar as a way of sharing the feeling it gave her – love, embrace, and anaesthesia. It seemed to dovetail seamlessly into her encouragement of my illnesses. Sweets would lighten my terrible suffering on my days off school; my medication would be washed down with buckets of sugary Lucozade, and the taste of it removed by small balls of butter rolled in sugar. Mum put the munch into Munchausen's by proxy. Contrary to received wisdom, we are often turned into addicts by those who love us best. Sometimes they want relief from the guilt of the pain they cause us, and offer the drug as a way of killing it; sometimes they just use the drug as a proxy for love they don't have the capacity, or the language, or the energy, to show; and sometimes, like my mum, they just want to share the nice feeling it also gave them.

Her sugar addiction had its roots in the loss of her own mother to heart disease. This unthinkable void in her six-year-old life coincided with sugar rationing during the war, meaning that most days there wasn't even the comfort of a jujube or a liquorice stick to numb the pain. Mum once ran home from school, howling like she'd slammed her hand in the door, upon discovering that one of her classmates was allowed a spoonful of jam in his custard, a luxury my skint grandfather could do little to match. Once rationing was lifted and you could have all the sugar you wanted, she wanted all the damn sugar. My mother's kitchen cupboard is still a shrine to the white stuff, with biscuits, cakes and sweets stacked in Tupperware boxes marking various hierarchies of occasion (everyday; special; ministers) and strength ('plain', i.e. anything between a Rich Tea and a Bourbon; chocolate; illegal). I get an insulin spike when I drift within five miles of her postcode. I can't stop over, because if I do I'll find myself howling into a box of Celebrations at three in the morning. I can't keep sugar in my own house any more than I could OxyContin. My mum mostly kept her weight down through a forty-a-day Consulate habit and then, when she kicked it, Slimming Club, which in Scotland tends to be a lifelong commitment, i.e. Slimming Club does not work.

Mum was nonetheless svelte compared to some of her vast friends. Anne McShane of the unreturned debt was almost perfectly orthogonal. Jess, a childhood friend of Mum's from Dysart, was the size of a triple-door wardrobe, wore marquee-like blue pinafores and was as benign a soul as you could meet. Her husband was a wiry and perjink wee nyaff of a physics teacher called Jackie.* Celtic drinkers often choose between

---

* 'A fussily presented little person of no worth', sort of, but if I'd meant that I'd have said it.

whisky and beer in a straight fuck-the-head or fuck-the-gut trade-off, and Jackie had opted for the former, the better to keep his shape and to emphasise his wife's. He had a raw, red face and steel-wire hair, and sported fisheye glasses and bristly Harris tweed jackets; his voice was throaty like a frog, and always drenched in bitter sarcasm and contempt. I can still hear it clear as a cracked bell, and it makes my blood run cold. One evening, out for a meal with my mum and dad, he spoke to Jess in a way that was so demeaning, my father bollocked him out at the bar – another non-anecdote of Dad's, only memorable because Dad *never* bollocked anyone out. (Whenever I recalled this story, I'd wonder how much of a threat my dad could ever present; but I forget that, for all his meek bearing, he was a country lad and had forearms like seams of oak. I saw them tensed just once: I was thirteen, hormonally unhinged and bullying my wee brother atrociously, and he pinned me up against the wall, balled his fist and called me a little shit; I decided I wasn't going to see them tensed again.) Jackie had a line in unfunny and really painful tickling, that perennial cover for child-hating sadists, as well as a local move known as the 'craw dab', where you ground your knuckle hilariously into the child's scalp.

Jess's three boys were fond of the non-game of Toy Fights, which was the last item called in the game roster, after Reely-Fo and Feechs. Reely-Fo was – unknown to us – a corruption of the well-documented game of Relief-O. Its Dundee incarnation was a kind of dry run of Zimbardo's prison experiment, whose now-disputed conclusions I can nonetheless confirm as broadly correct. Feechs was what the English called Tag, with added infection. 'The Feechs' was sometimes invoked as a likely fatal – at least socially – contagion of indeterminate nature, possibly involving tiny invisible shit-eating fleas or something. One did not want them.* The announcement of Toy Fights was met with a resigned dread. At least it meant an end to the afternoon, albeit possibly in the morgue. Toy Fights was the same as Fights, only with the need for even a nominal justification removed. There were no sides; it was a kind of Atherstone Ball Game without the ball. You choked or kicked or walloped whoever was nearest. The end was declared when more than half the kids were crying. Jess's lads were brutal and efficient boxers, and each rabbit punch they landed on a kid was, I assume, one emptied from the sack they had likely received from their father. Jackie was a horrible little cunt and no one lamented his early death from liver cirrhosis, which Jess nursed him through with a dedication and sacrifice he was not owed.† He died early enough for his boys to all

---

* 'Feech' has a relative in 'flech', an unidentifiable but visible fleck in your tea or soup which has to be removed immediately. The '-ech/ -eech' phonaestheme in Scots connotes misery, filth, infection and disgust, as in the children's nonsense rhyme 'Eech, Meech, Hen's Keech'; this could be concluded 'Toly, Bum, Fart', but the first four words were routinely used as a 4/4 count-in by Dundee club bands. A 'keech' is a shit, and will be traceable to the PIE root *kakka–*.

† We need to talk about cunts, don't we. Especially as they're liable to come up again. Words have no intrinsic meaning and are merely how you use them, so one really shouldn't judge others just because

turn out well, once they'd been removed from his brutalising sway. Jess found love soon after with Archie, who – being poor, and not the sharpest tool – had been considered a little below her station the first time round, but who treated her with the kindness and honour she deserved.

The Scottish diet draws heavily from the Tan Food Group, and is not famed for its nutritional balance. It also contains so much sugar, it's amazing that the Scottish pancreas hasn't done a kidney and cloned itself to split the workload. In my

---

they use them differently to the way you might. No one is denying the c-word's misogynist history, although the genitals of both sexes have long supplied us with versatile terms of abuse. But a word can eventually become distant enough from its original meaning for its relationship to it to be sensibly described in terms of etymology, not ugly metaphor; this point is reached when folk use the word without the original sense consciously in mind. Then, you're effectively talking about two different words that are now only homonyms. In Dundee, the word is used in three ways. None of them refer to the female part. I've never heard anyone except the middle classes indicate it by that name, and then, honourably; in Dundee, 'fanny' or 'fud' are your gentler alternatives here. 'Cunt' is sometimes deployed as a non-gendered synecdoche for the whole person, much like the US 'ass': 'I have spent all week knocking my cunt in and I am exhausted.' And as is now well known, it is also used across Scotland by both sexes to mean, neutrally, 'person': 'I went into the pub last night and aa' cunt [i.e. 'everyone'] was there/I did a poetry reading last night but there was nae cunt there,' etc. A female taxi driver recently described her father to me as 'basically a decent cunt'. Finally, there is the sense in which I deploy the word here, by which I intend 'cunt'.

childhood, sugar was initially delivered at breakfast, in the form of Coco Pops, Frosties or Weetabix, which we heaped with more sugar, like heavy snowfall on a Cortina. Throughout the day, one could top up with boiled sweets, sold by the quarter-pound (this was a near-daily habit, and sometimes at the weekend you'd have a *half*), or with chocolate bars. I mean, let's not do that *À la Recherche des Bonbons Perdus* thing no memoir seems complete without or we'll be here all year; but suffice to say that from Aztec bars to Zoom lollies, I have a little song for each of them. Several favourite items were banned, as what made them delicious or fun turned out to be carcinogenic, or self-combusting, or not really food. Take the weird adhesive rice-paper of the flying saucer, which I'm still not sure you were meant to swallow; once wet, it would stick to the back of your upper palate and choke you, unless you overcame your gag reflex and scraped it off with a fingernail. Then there was the first iteration of Cresta, a suspiciously opaque and pastel-coloured drink which put your mouth to sleep and was promptly removed from sale; Space Dust did the opposite and was ordnance for your face, and actually crushed and snorted by the brave. Space Dust was later banned following the entirely false story that a kid had exploded in gym class when she combined several bags in her stomach with a can of Fanta. This experiment was, of course, aggressively pursued while the stuff still remained on sale. (The theme of extracting more danger than necessary from an already edgy practice is a Dundee cultural meme. My brother would occasionally execute 'The Lochee Slammer', where you snort the salt, squeeze the lime juice into your eye, drink the tequila, and go to the hospital.) Worst of all were the bags of 'kelly', luridly coloured and flavoured crystallised sugar you bought by the quarter and dipped your wet finger in, leaving it stained blue or pink for days afterwards. (This replaced, in what we thought was a space-age way, tubes of old-school white kelly, a powdered sherbet conducted into your face with wet liquorice.)

As for the hard sweets or 'boilings' which filled our quarter-pound pokes, I can direct you to several nostalgia websites that will help you tell your soor plooms from your granny sookers. (The hard, green, bitter 'soor ploom' commemorates a border skirmish in the fourteenth century, when English raiders were repelled by being pelted with unripe plums. Scottish victories over the numerically superior English are few and far between, and each one is immortalised, even if it was just a square go in a car park in Coldstream.) Sweeties had the tough urban vernacular name 'swetchies', delivered with much the same swagger as one might say 'jellies' or 'blow'. 'You there, ya wee prick. Got any swetchies.' One very hard-man, street-cool way of eating them was in the form of a bag of 'mushies', sold by an unscrupulous vendor from deep in the Kirkton estate. These were mixed bags of the shattered boilings left at the bottom of the jars after all the quarters had been sold, and looked like a lump of crushed stained-glass window.

Dinner, which in Scotland and the north of England is the midday meal, was usually the portmanteau of soup'n'puddin: the soup eaten with a ziggurat of white bread and margarine, and dessert being some tin of delicious gloop with a shiny puddle of sweet stuff in it. Tea concluded with yet more pudding, generally with more structure to it (rice pudding, sponge pudding, jelly and piss-tinted vegetable-fat ice cream). Dessert of some sort has been an ineradicable and, despite the efforts of many, non-negotiable feature of the evening meal all my life, and even if I now have it down to one symbolic square of 85 per cent cocoa Lindt, it's still, in my mind at least, my goddamn pudding, and from my cold dead hand.

But these were merely the *staple* forms of sugar, the ones you'd obviously die without. Treats were a whole different classification. One had to up the ante at Christmas and New Year, obviously; nothing that wasn't pure sugar could be consumed before teatime at all, and one was expected to have destroyed one's first twelve-item Cadbury's Selection Box before sunrise. New Year would begin with a hair-of-the-dog toast at Aggie and Mary's, our kindly mother-and-daughter babysitters. (Mary had a brain injury from a childhood skating accident, and the ancient Aggie had stayed aboard well past her station for fear of leaving Mary to fend for herself.) While Mum and Dad took a whisky or a sherry, we too were encouraged to have a little of the hard stuff, in the form of a glass of 'cordial'; a word you may think you know, but here it designated only *undiluted* cordial, a fluorescent syrup concentrate like an alien's drool which would gnaw through your tooth enamel on contact.

Otherwise, treats came in the form of the historical Scottish delivery system of the traybake. The chocolate crispie, made of cornflakes, melted chocolate and horse glue, was a jagged confection as painful to eat as a pinecone. Millionaire short-bread: in our imagined gilded futures, what Caribbean cruise, what Learjet trip, what cocktail at The Ivy would be complete without a slab of shortbread covered in toffee and cooking chocolate? I stuffed my face with it and felt like 007. ('The nameff Bomff. Jameff Bomff.') There was something lumpy called tiffin, which appeared to be made of reconstituted traybakes, and the rare peppermint slice, which was regarded as a health food because it tasted like toothpaste.

But the doyen, the dauphin, the *deus pater* of traybakes was of course Scottish tablet, which essentially dispensed with all the other ingredients and got straight down to business. The feeling of tablet is as hard to describe as masturbation; can you remember how it felt to walk before you could walk? No. You can't. So stop asking me. Nor can you watch me eat it, for I am going to eat it like a fat Labrador in the corner, angrily and alone. Tablet is a sort of crystalline fudge made from sugar, condensed milk, more milk, butter, more sugar and – that might be all, actually. It is an alchemical procedure, not a recipe. All is stirring, adding, pausing, timing, condensing, cooling and waiting. The result is a semi-hard square of fawn heaven that tastes like what it is, forty pints of milk squashed into a block of gold. It is milky and buttery and crumbly and both hard and soft; it is sweeter than anything you've tasted in your life, and electricity rushes up the sides of your face as your dopamine surges in anticipation of the next bite, and your inhibitory neurons throw down their rifles, tear off their uniforms and join the lack of resistance. Tablet puts all thoughts to rest, bar those of tablet. To say that you cannot stop eating it would imply that you'd contemplated trying.

My Manhattanite ex pointed out that the way my mother sold and packaged tablet – in a cut square, taped up and wrapped in parcel paper, and placed individually in a ziplock sandwich bag – was identical to the way you bought a quarter of brown in the South Bronx. My mum basically owned the corner where they sold the good shit. One day she had made an excess batch for the church sale of work. (Another phrase that made no sense for years, and which I heard as *c'est-la-ouierg*, along with the working arrangement known as *de-la-rees*, i.e. 'day release'.) Word got out to the kids in the estate. They started to turn up at the door, 10p in hand, and the discreet exchange would be made. Within an hour a queue had formed, and snaked back down the garden path to the bus stop, the kids getting taller as you went down the line, which ended in several shifty adults on a dinner break, keeping their eyes firmly on their shoes. I once had my 'play piece' confiscated at school. ('Piece' was a contraction of 'piece of bread', a working lunch; as a metonym it also covered 'sandwich', and from there, anything put in your face between breakfast and teatime.) Mum, for fear that I'd expire on the ten-minute walk home, had crammed around ten thousand calories two-storey Bento-style into a large piece of Tupperware, including a bar of tablet the size of my head, and even the teachers could tell it was killing me.

All this made me a fat kid. The West had only just left the era of 'Doctors Smoke Camels', and no one had by then made the slightest connection between sugar and obesity – but, as with tobacco, only because no one wanted to find it: who wouldn't invest in a product that sells itself? (Early-seventies cigarette advertising basically went 'Smoke Fags: They're Great'.) Brian Hughes christened me 'Fatty Patty the Tudor Tatty', after the popular brand of crisps I was rarely seen without. Slick-haired, dark and tall, Brian was really more an alpha than a bully, only averagely violent, and picked only on hard kids. I quite liked him. Brian fancied he was in possession of a fine singing voice – a matter over which you were expected to promptly concur – and kept practising his crooner's vibrato on what he took to be the first line of a Dean Martin-esque swing ballad, which he sang over and over, for weeks on end: 'Leanin' on the oboe . . .' (I have found it impossible to locate this subsequently. He or I must have misheard. I mean, how could one *lean* on an oboe? Was it propped against a wall, perhaps, for stability? Since when was a fucking *oboe* a cool thing to lean on? And where did you go after a line like that? Banality? 'Leanin' on the oboe / Singin' this song'? Romance? 'Leanin' on the oboe / Thinkin' of you'? Pathos? 'Leanin' on the oboe / Just had a stroke'? Christ knows. It obsessed me.) My ballooning weight was never mentioned, but my clothes quietly ballooned to disguise it. Trousers were let out and elastic discreetly snipped; the belt on the kilt I was forced to wear to Sunday School suddenly had another two notches bradawled into the end of it. The kilt came with a famously indestructible pair of bottle-green cotton magic pants which had been in the family for decades, and had been worn by three or four generations. The 'Bottle Imp' of underwear, they were handed, with some ceremony and considerable relief, from father to son. Infinitely expandable, able to fit any man between three and eighty-three, fatal to moths, bomb-proof and eternal, if they leave the family the house will fall. They're still glowing in a drawer somewhere.

Slowly, very slowly, I stretched and grew and thinned, leaving my back covered in whip-mark striae so deep and pronounced you might think I did a gap year in a Saudi prison. (On more than one occasion I've had trouble convincing girlfriends that these scars weren't inflicted by a violent parent: 'You can be honest with me, you know. There's no shame in it.' 'No really, I was just a fat fuck.') Even more slowly, I swapped out sugar for nicotine, dope and round-the-clock anxiety. But the constellation of neurons that makes me a sugar addict will always be intact, and still clunks on like the Blackpool Illuminations at the sight of a Twix.

As they say in cybernetics, and as they should say everywhere else, the consistent outcome of a system is not its by-product but its purpose. Sugar is the most effective way of keeping the lower orders fat, addicted, distracted and controlled in number. Obesity, diabetes, docility and death are the *object* of the exercise, which is why governments are loath to cut sugar tax. Sure, diabetes costs the NHS, but nowhere near as much as longevity. And if the plebs stop thinking about sugar, fat and booze, they might start thinking about other things, like why austerity only ever seems to apply to them; so the little Spars on the estate must stay stuffed with their

12 Metric Mental

In McLean Street, we lived on the ground floor of a three-storey brown-harled tenement, entered through the light-eating maw of the close, or 'closie'. The diminutive is familiar, not affectionate. When I was small, the rear of the closie went to heaven or hell: on the left was a pleasantly bright, window-lit stairwell, and on the right, the steps that led down to the stinking bin recess, and the door to the back green. There was an omphalic pock in the concrete at the centre of the closie, a tiny two-inch amphitheatre where we'd stage gladiatorial combat between insects. Ant vs ladybird. Forkie tailie vs slater.* We couldn't interest them in it.

There was so much more early death on the street than I took in at the time. Widows and widowers in their fifties and sixties abounded. Mrs Smibert, 'Nosy', the curtain-twitcher from over the street; Mr Rees, the kindly Welshman across the closie, whose house stank of bleach and seemed to grow cleaner, colder and more spartan by the year. Mum's friend Alice in the next block died in her sleep in her late forties. Mrs Depta was already wheelchair-bound with MS. The Steels on the top floor lost their mum to a brain tumour. For the post-war urban poor, life expectancy was short, but also psychologically low, and the

* Earwig vs woodlouse, if you prefer.

latter tended to guarantee the former. No one much wanted to die, but nor did they seem terribly surprised to. Rationing had led to poor nutrition in their early years; a male population traumatised by the war had transferred the pain to their wives and families in turn, and produced a generation addicted to tobacco and alcohol; food regulation was minimal, and there was little to protect poor communities from exploitation; and in 1971, decimalisation was an opportunity to quietly inflate and price-gouge and get away with it, and everyone was rendered even more skint at a single stroke. (Pickled Onion Tudor Crisps had gone from 3d to 2p a bag overnight, I noted, but the maths couldn't be done in your head. Okay . . . so if 10p was two shillings and a shilling was twelve pence then 2p was a fifth of two shillings ah forget it.) If all that didn't get you, there was pig ignorance. Ours was, thankfully, the last generation to be sent out into the street to breathe in the fumes from the tar vats when the council was fixing the potholes, because it was good for our lungs.

Walker on the first floor was a decent neighbour to us, until his early dementia turned him into a monster. (Only someone thoroughly loathed could have their title dropped; when it dropped, it stayed that way.) It took an odd form: he would slide long handwritten letters through the door before dawn, and these would detail his every grievance, from my mother's breaches of bin-recess protocol and the noise we made in the closie to my father's late-night 'dance band-related comings and goings' and door-slammings. (Dad was as quiet as he could be, but tenement households were acoustically interfused in a way that could feel like communal living, and your privacy was mostly mentally constructed, which is to say fragile.) Mum came to dread the arrival of these thick unstamped envelopes; they were made all the more disturbing by their articulacy, which gave them the veneer of sanity – Walker had been an intelligent and well-read man. The kids would get grief from him too. I can see his florid head, thick specs and curly grey hair sticking through the kitchen window like a horrible puppet, savage with righteous fury, his mouth apparently raised and lowered by a drawbridge of spit, howling that the back green was to be used for laundry only, though it had been a traditional bairns' fiefdom forever. His poor wife, a meek soul who'd always been friendly to us, would pass us in the close head bowed and silent, as she'd been instructed. Walker's principal confusion seemed to be around the weather. He'd lie out in the back green in a deckchair in a raging storm, and be out watering his potatoes in a downpour. The man was in hell, but he was keen we join him. Mum and Dad renewed their campaign to get us rehoused, but our two-bed flat was the standard allocation for a family of four.

Around this time – I'd have been about ten – something went badly wrong with me. It seemed to coincide with my sister Louise's arrival (which Mum had announced to me, tearfully, in the kitchen; a third child was an unplanned expense) and my father's immediate vasectomy, but I'm not sure there's as much to work with here as my shrinks later insisted. The expanding headcount did at least bump us up the council waiting list, and we moved up the road to a three-bedroom house, which seemed a palatial improvement. You might just say that I'd suddenly became very impressionable – but literally so. I'd see, hear or read something, and it would stamp me permanently, like clay. BBC Two ran the dubbed biopic *Edvard Munch* over three nights, and I watched it on the black-and-white portable upstairs. Munch was thereafter – and still is – less an artist than a feeling that came over me. This was new. It was a little like one of those eternal spaces that used to open in the afternoons of my early childhood, those moods so perfectly *sui generis* and strange that they'd defy any attempt at description. But this new space had a lower, morbid, sodden, half-lit purgatorial quality, and I had trouble shaking it off once it had settled in.

Then I saw a documentary about rabies. There was some hysteria around the subject at the time, and fears that our new EU membership would lead to lax borders and the disease becoming endemic. Rabies seemed the worst possible death one could undergo, in its irreversible progress, its absolute final agony and madness. I knew I was destined to catch it. Death might still be hundreds of miles away: Death I visualised in the form of a little dog, still with its family holidaying in France; it had just run off into a field of tall grass, where it would, unbeknownst to its owners, get a nick from a rabid fox cub; the next day, the family would return to a small port with sloppy customs checks to avoid putting the dog into quarantine, and while visiting relatives in Scotland two weeks later they'd be out in Dundee city centre on a Saturday, when the sick little puppy would lick my hand as I passed it in the street. There might still be plenty of slack in the line, but I'd swallowed Death's worm, and he was casually reeling it in. Of course, I knew there hadn't been a case of rabies in the UK for years, and that I was being perfectly irrational; I told no one. But for months I thought of little else.

I also began to dream, in a counterbalancing way, of some final purge, some great cleansing, some mechanical winch that could draw out the miles of dead worm and black string and rotten sinew of which I was composed, and leave me empty and clean. Munch and the promise of my purification converged on the cover of Arthur Janov's *The Primal Scream*, which I read at eleven, having requested it as a birthday present, something my parents really should have refused. Janov's quack theory consists of cathartic discharge: you scream away until your neurosis is gone, its source being the buried, untapped and unfelt pain of infant trauma. It's junk psychology, of course, but in my case it might have actually worked, though I did worry that if I started screaming I might not stop. I also had more pre-echoes of my later madness. One weekend my Auntie Jean, one of Dad's older sisters, was looking after us all while our parents were away. Everyone was in bed. Again and again I heard the Eagles' 'One of These Nights' start up on the music centre downstairs. I kept getting up to check if someone had put it on; of course, they hadn't. I checked about once every twenty minutes, right through the night. I remember that it struck me at the time as a mystery. There was a simpler explanation.

As to what was going on at school: I was bored so

comprehensively shitless between the ages of six and nine I can hardly tell you a thing about it. It was mainly a maths issue, but back then maths seemed to take up half the day. I would grasp the principle fairly quickly – okay, carry the thing and remember to move the yeah yeah – but for the life of me could not see why it had to be fixed in your brain by a million identical pushpins when one big nail was all you needed. The main instruments of this torture were *Lomond Arithmetics* and *Top Ten Metric Mental*. Please Miss can I go to the cemetery. I can see the haunted little boy on the cover of my *Lomond* even now: pencil raised, eyes wide in fear, eyebrows knitted in bewilderment, a single bright tear sliding down his cheek, his bottom lipped blurred in the exposure, a dark stain growing at his crotch (I may have to check this).

My ignominious plummet down the rankings was physically enacted, for maximum impact. We were around thirty to a class, seated in individual desks, six to a row; we were placed in order of intelligence, with our house genius Eileen Hurrell in the top right corner and the other thirty of us arranged sequentially, in a kind of boustrophedon of stupid that terminated – invariably – in a terrifying, blond, lifeless, floppy, permanently smiling ventriloquist's dummy called Gareth Waddell. Between that fixed zenith and nadir there was much desk-shuffling. From a bright start in Primary 3, I was shunted in peristaltic heaves down this gormless colon like a swallowed brick, and by P5 I was looking at the back of Gareth's head, which looked scarily inert even from behind. I could not get through the tests. I'd do two sums and lose the will to live. At one point I was sent to remedial maths, and sent right back again, with a note that clearly read something like NOT THICK CANT BE ARSED.

The new arrangement of big six-seater tables was supposed to introduce more cooperative learning, and divided us more broadly by ability, but it was no better. I recall Mark Whittle's beaming pride when, to his surprise and ours, he was moved up to the second-top table after some freak test results; then his humiliation a few weeks later, when he was bumped back down to his natural level, after having just invited his new friends round after school. What they put these children through was emotionally devastating and unforgivable. It should not have been beyond their ingenuity to balance a streamed education with social desegregation.

Perversely, when my luck changed, it wouldn't help my memory either. My last two years at primary school were probably the happiest of my life, and I can't recall a damn thing about them. Happiness not only writes white, but remembers white. This was down to one teacher, Helen Garland, who correctly favoured me above all other children. She realised not just that I was bright, but that I was hopelessly insecure and could be manipulated into doing just great by being hooked up to an intravenous drip of constant praise. I suddenly won everything and came top in everything, bar all the things that my loathed rival Eileen Hurrell did. Eileen was a specky saddo ugly swot loser. She had lots of friends and was a double for Judi Bowker in *Black Beauty*, and she was really nice to me. I fantasied about her death by bus, drowning and scarlet fever. The only thing I can do to make myself feel even slightly better is to tell you it definitely wasn't misogyny. Competition brought out the worst in me, and still does. (I used to play badminton at work against my then colleague Eric Langley. Eric was generally mystified as to why he was regularly beaten by this plainly unfit and overweight old git, and attributed my unlikely success to my Calvinist powers of self-inspiration, which took the form of much loud, self-berating fucking, cunting and wankering every time a smash went astray or I failed to cover the ground to his drop shot. He was somewhat upset when I informed him that no, these curses were all aimed directly at him. I now take beta blockers, and am as sweet-natured, chilled and benign as Tom Hanks on glue. I also lose at everything.)

But we all did well in Mrs Garland's care. She praised success and effort, and refused to attach shame to failure. Mainly, though, she took a *specific* interest in all our lives, and not a birthday or new sibling was left uncelebrated. In return, we listened to her, and learned, because she was one of us.

Our departure from primary school was celebrated with an End of Term Disco. I couldn't have known, of course, but this also marked my departure from education altogether. Perhaps the omens were there; the evening was not a triumph. The occasion was to be DJ'd by Mrs Garland's twenty-year-old son, and proper lights had been hired; somehow we were not being treated as children, quite. I had never been to a disco, but was determined not to let that show. I had correctly divined that an androgynous look was currently de rigueur amongst the painfully cool, but not what it actually was. I settled on a long pale-blue jumper of near skirt-length, and added a very wide belt of my mother's, which I had decided was slimming but which really just served to separate the fat rolls into two competing arenas. I had also registered the fashion for male jewellery, and insisted that I wore a chain of some kind, despite my mother's scepticism. I ended up borrowing a huge, oblong silver locket of hers; in the hall mirror it looked pretty dang impressive. I also thought a sweatband or bandana would be a cool addition, but all Mum had were rain-mates and headscarves, and I couldn't find anything that didn't make me look like Hilda Ogden. Scratch that.

Arriving at the school hall, I had an immediate, almost Damascene sense of my own ridiculousness, and went from glam heartbreaker to fat clown in about half a second. The girls didn't recoil exactly, but instead regarded me with that combination of repulsion and curiosity you feel when you encounter a thing in the wrong element: a fish on a lawn, a bird on the road, a fully dressed man face-down in a swimming pool. I braved one dance, but to minimise the jiggling it was more of a stand, and only my head was moving. I tried wobbling it; I tried shaking it from side to side; I tried nodding it; I decided to keep it very still. Now we were among the flashing and whirling lights, my giant locket was certainly getting some attention, and indeed it would burn out your retinas if you caught it at the wrong angle. Thank Christ no one asked to look inside it, where they'd have seen a picture of my mother and father kissing. Luckily, the lights had left the hall with many dark corners. I grabbed three cups of juice and four slices of cake, and found one.

Many years later, I did some kind of 'My Favourite Teacher' radio programme with Helen, and had the opportunity to thank her personally for destroying any chance of a normal existence by encouraging the life of the mind. Together we looked at the school photo from that final year. As my finger moved along the row, I was unsurprised that I could remember every kid's name, but was astonished to find that so could she. They weren't *her* golden years. I doubt she forgot one kid she taught. But in my head I was also saying *AIDS living murder* (that was Mark Whittle, me, Arthur) *living junkie junkie living diabetes living living jail living missing AIDS living living suicide living.* It really was a poor estate.

13 Bus Did Flatten Batten Roo

While my middle primary school years seem to have been deleted off the drive, I can, however, tell you everything I was listening to. Kris Kristofferson's first record, *Kristofferson*, was my first object of musical study. *Kristofferson* was a great record, and had 'Me and Bobby McGee', 'Help Me Make It Through the Night' and 'Sunday Morning Comin' Down'. When I was eight, I would perform every number in a terrible American accent, and knew every damn word. Or rather I knew a word that was close to every damn word, because what I didn't know was what the hell Kris was on about. The result was less mondegreen than a kind of homophonic translation. *Bus did flatten batten roo / headin' forth it rains / veal-in-ear lay faded asthma jeans / babby calmed da-deedle-down . . . I took ma hard poon out of my durdy reed banned nana . . . I* was appalled when my dad lent the album to my Uncle Iain. I only wanted to listen to one record. What if he broke it? The so-called 'outlaw' sound and aesthetic was all the rage then, especially in Scotland and Ireland; its principal avatars were Waylon Jennings, Willie Nelson and Kris Kristofferson. My father and I looked up to them as wild 'n' crazy highwaymen whose lives were a fairground of whisky and wild women and poker games where you'd bet your guitar or your hoss on a turn of the card. (We were misled: Jennings was a radio-jingle writer hired by Buddy Holly as a backing musician. Nelson was a professional songwriter whose outlaw activities were primarily confined to tax evasion; the First Nation stoner look was a later move, though no one would accuse him of inhabiting it insincerely. Kristofferson was a Rhodes Scholar who'd studied alongside Bill Clinton at Oxford.)

Hitherto Dad's only attempt at cultivating his stage presence had involved customising his guitar; he'd bought some stick-on gold letters and spelled out his initials on the headstock, including his middle name, Leslie. Alas, from more than two feet away it seemed to read 'RIP', leading to much 'Very sorry for your loss' from the wits, which Dad just had to thole as he couldn't get the letters off. But now he outlawed up, bought some cowboy boots, a Stetson and a belt with a huge, blingy buckle that said 'RUSS', grew a Dennis Weaver moustache, binned the Stetson, and worked on his country music set. He was a very handsome guy, and he started getting a lot of gigs.

The temporary loss of *Kristofferson* meant I needed another record, though. Nothing else in Dad's collection appealed much. But watching some rapey old DJ on *Top of the Pops* one evening, I was wowed by the Osmonds' 'Crazy Horses', an eco-tirade against the horseless carriage, which featured Jay doing an early knock-kneed ride-that-pony thing; the Osmonds specialised in the kind of white comic dancing that only Cliff Richard could outdo. (Cliff did his best, God love him, but he always seemed about to break into an ah-what-the-hell, full-blooded chicken impersonation.) The Osmonds' billing back then as 'the white Jackson 5' didn't help, since one was obliged to immediately conclude that white people sucked. But 'Crazy Horses' was my first introduction to poetic metaphor ('Hmm . . . Cars *are* crazy horses, when you think about it'), and it featured a terrific wailing synth effect – a Yamaha YC-30 with a ribbon control, yes I know you don't care – that sounded like a startled car-horse skid-whinny, or at least you knew it was meant to.

I set off with my Christmas tokens and my Auntie Jean to Cathie McCabe's record store to buy an Osmonds album. They had sold out of 'Crazy Horses', so I bought *Phase III*. This sounded like a significant recording: Phase III, I assumed, of their protean artistic development. I could tell by the till girl's smirk that I'd made a terrible mistake, and my first listen confirmed as much. The title seemed rather to refer to the progression of a serious illness. Barring one sporting little number – 'My Drum', featuring the already portly Jay, who is actually far from the world's worst drummer – *Phase III* is maybe ten atrocious two-to-three-minute tunes of saccharine pseudo-rock. There wasn't even that much of Donny, who was of course the only Osmond who was up to snuff: gorgeous, could almost dance, and with great pitching, if not articulation. (Little Jimmy Osmond is Exhibit A in that exquisite tragedy of being forced into a line of work for which one has no gift. I mean, it's one thing being pressured into taking over the family ball-bearing business, or emotionally blackmailed into med school; but for a wee fat lad to be forced out on stage to sing every night when he can't is an unusually harsh fate, to which 'strokes out fifty years later in panto at the Birmingham

Hippodrome' seems, somehow, the only possible punchline. I hope he's okay.*) Either way, I wasn't sticking around for Phase IV. (Which was a shame; *Crazy Horses* is actually a pretty good album.) I could indulge my Donny-crush independently of the Osmonds, and besides, I'd just heard America's cover of 'Muskrat Love', which Wikipedia helpfully informs me 'depicts a romantic liaison between two anthropomorphic muskrats named Susie and Sam'. Terrible song that it was, it nonetheless contained some artful harmonies that I could tell were leaning towards actual art. I bought the single. Then I turned it over. The B-side, 'Cornwall Blank', was a keening, serious, dark, driving number, which halfway through took a left turn into a dreamy, bittersweet and lusciously harmonised middle eight. Oh yes. This was what I'd hoped would be on *Phase III*. From there it was a skip and a hop to the first and greatest Eagles album, when they were still a country band and let Bernie Leadon play the banjo. My Uncle Iain lent me Steely Dan's *Can't Buy a Thrill* to compensate for the temporary loss of the Kristofferson album. No, no: *this* was what I'd hoped would be on *Phase III*. Art. I kept it.

---

* He seems like a nice man. But it's clear the Osmond parents were not nice: they managed to trash not only their kids' childhoods but their wealth too, with a bunch of reckless investments that left them all bankrupt and hustling crap residencies into old age, when they should all have been able to retire at thirty.

even if only for yourself, or that it's literally only you that's checking every hour to see if a particular Slovenian hacker has coded a .nki converter for an obscure proprietary sample format. (No, I *know* you don't know what I'm talking about, but I've lost years to this sort of crap.) Many of my obsessions have been purely, horribly acquisitive; these can involve some ugly shortcuts. When I was about seven, I desired nothing more than the complete set of the Scottish football cards we all collected. One evening I was playing Graeme Esson, the flying countertenor, in a dismal game of a dismal game called Same or Diff. The game involved each of us flipping a card in the air and taking turns to call the result – 'same', i.e. two face-up or face-down, or 'diff'(erent) – and if you guessed right, you kept both cards. I was suddenly intoxicated by an obvious swindle: I didn't spin my card at all, but just dropped it flat, the right way up to win the hand, after Graeme's card had landed. Graeme didn't say anything but just let me get on with fleecing him. Worse, he let me absolve myself over and over: each time, I had to make myself believe that the wind had indeed mysteriously caught my card and blown it straight to the ground. Heavens! It's happened again, Graeme. As I was shovelling the cards into a William Low's carrier bag, he turned to go home, then looked back at me and said: '*I know what you did.*' O so did I, so did I. Begging his forgiveness, I tried to give him half back, to give them *all* back – but he refused, and left me in the hole I'd dug, alone with my spade and my hard lesson. By the time I got home the bag weighed like a dead dog. (I met him again a few years ago; I'd made a brief and ill-advised attempt at Dundee resettlement, and was buying a wok in the kitchenware store where he now worked. A voice squeaked, 'Donald!' I knew who it was without turning around; his voice hadn't ever broken. My immediate worry was that he wanted his cards back.)

Adult obsession drags the shadow of everything else you're ignoring: your children, spouse, career, health. However, the eight-year-old has few responsibilities, and there's little damage he can do, even to himself. Give it another eight years and he'll be reading Israel Regardie and drawing chalk pentacles round his wee sister, shorting the Argentine economy or working a Bitcoin scam. But at eight, there seemed no way of projecting anything, inwardly or outwardly. When rain had ended our street games, as it often did in Scotland, I spent the rest of the evening in bed in agony, curled up like a baby fern; I'd fall into the grip of a kind of nuclear boredom, and my body would enter a state of continuous slow implosion, as if I'd drunk a tumblerful of alum. I had been obsessed with sex, or at least anything that was inside human pants, since three or four years old; but my fantasy life was as yet too thinly furnished, and the Freudian wonderland of The Dump was closed to me in the hours of darkness. I dreaded being left to myself, knowing what I did to me when I got my hands on me.

I had observed from reading comics that English boys – or at least the English boys depicted in the comics that were all written and published in Dundee – all had 'hobbies', and figuring we couldn't be *that* different, gave that a crack. I had a succession of chemistry sets; a very short succession, as I soon demanded nothing less than the über-set, the vast Thomas Salter Chemistry 7: a boy-sized box of vials and pipettes and Bunsen burners, with great rainbows of test-tube chemicals, three layers deep. God knows how many dire nights of playing 'Will Ye Go, Lassie, Go' to howling drunks this had cost my father. An unthinkable health-and-safety offence in the modern age, Chemistry 7 relied on the power of sheer bewilderment to keep the child safe from itself, since any average prodigy would have been able to synthesise botulism and poison the reservoir within half an hour of popping the lid. It came with a huge book of experiments, all deliberately crap, except for the few where something suddenly went rock-hard, or tripled its volume, or changed colour, or flared up when lit. So I quickly destroyed my retinas by burning all the magnesium, and used up all the copper sulphate in an experiment where you mixed it with something else (baking soda? sulphuric acid? I have no idea) and it turned from a translucent lido-blue to a gloopy blood-red. Then I left it all set up like Dr Jekyll to impress my friends, and watched the dust grow thick.

I generally liked things that made me look clever, as I sensed they'd gain my mother's approval, but my appetite for appearing learned has always vastly outstripped that for actual learning, which only ever circled tightly around my obsessions – often in a way that skipped the rudiments and basic reading that bored me stiff. I insisted on a subscription to *All About Science*, a briefly popular science encyclopaedia that came in weekly instalments, and would build to a magnificent shelf of blue, fake-morocco-bound superior knowledge. I am still pretty good on anything between Aardvark and Adsorption, when my interest waned, although my rigorous completism meant I insisted on my parents coughing up until its run was complete. My interest also waned because the publisher's did: what had started as an informative and sincere project soon turned cursory and cynical, as soon as Orbis clocked that the partwork model was an idiotic one for a kids' publication. Kids don't join the series at Manatee–Methane and purchase back-copies. After D, the quality of the writing took a nosedive: fonts were larger, articles briefer, the drawings silly, the projects childish and embarrassing, and the expensive binders successively crappier. When the series finally ground to a merciful halt after three years, the final undersize tome ran something like P–Z and had clearly been typed up by a single bored hack. (I opened the last volume years later. The final articles are pretty much Y is for You're not reading this anymore are you and Z is for I am drunk.) Nonetheless, the possibility of at least appearing to be the repository of all terrestrial and cosmic knowledge intoxicated me, and one continues to furnish one's library to wow the important guests one neither invites nor desires. Even now, I am forever purchasing books on subjects I sincerely intend to make myself expert in, although who knows who I'm impressing. If I'd been Socrates, after I'd drunk the hemlock I would have raised my flute, paused, and then had a look on Amazon for *Advanced Intervallic Studies for Jazz Flute*.

When I was very young, we'd holiday in Kinghorn, a place

so close to Dundee on the map it might seem hardly worth the bother. But social immobility was so baked into the culture that distances were vastly multiplied; this had the advantage of making the world huge, and you could generally find as alien a landscape as you needed twenty miles down the road, if you looked for it. (Though it also led to some farcical miscalculation: on The Inn Folk's first out-of-town booking at the Dykehead Hotel, my dad and Willie called ahead to check they could sleep in the lounge rather than face the long haul back home immediately after the gig. They packed their gear, sleeping bags and toiletries into the car, pumped the tyres, bought a full tank and set off, arriving in Dykehead about half an hour later.) Before I left for London, I had crossed the border into England precisely once. One year we swapped Kinghorn for a catastrophic, sleet-lashed holiday in a Whitley Bay caravan site where – after a day of doing very little but wandering around, because we were broke – Mum and Dad would drop us off every night in a huge marquee with seven hundred kids, two table tennis tables and one pissed clown while they hit the bar. Stevie and I were followed everywhere by a poor kid with megalocephaly whom everyone else was too afraid to talk to. We both came down with colds and took to our bunkbeds in the tiny caravan, and made Mum and Dad promise never to go there again.

Kinghorn, my dad would announce every summer, was so-called because a king had fallen off the cliff on his horse while blowing his horn. I always pictured some elaborate horseback trumpet solo so achingly cool that both the king and his horse were vibing so hard they forgot to look where they were going, whereupon they plunged to their deaths. (Alexander III got plastered at a wedding then lost in the dark. The 'king' in the name is a coincidence. 'Kinghorn' is just *ceann gronn*, 'head of the marsh', i.e. it should be pronounced Kin-gorn. It lies next to Burntisland, which is not an island and about as burnt as the wet dog it smells like, being derived from 'Burnet's Land'. Fife seems to make a habit of this kind of thing.) My dad rented a chalet on the cliff overlooking the beach and the wide Forth estuary. This was – since it had no electricity or toilet – essentially a green-painted tin shed with fold-out beds and a covered coal hatch in the middle. It was either a fridge or a furnace. There was a beach, a toilet block and a shop that sold milk, bread and cinder toffee, and that was it. We had a great time. Our visits often coincided with those of a colleague of my dad's, a well-known Scottish folk singer and enchanting man known to us as 'Um-Pum-Skoosh', because he did magic tricks and that was his 'abracadabra'. The name is taken from the Fife nonsense rhyme which ends 'Eeny meeny macca racca, um, pum, skoosh'. (Many places in Britain have some playground variant on what's either an Old Saxon divination chant, or more likely the 'Yan tan tethera' of the 'shepherd score' counting system, which traces back to Brythonic Celtic numerals. There's a lovely bit in Opie somewhere where a wee girl performs her version for the researchers, but prefaces it with 'You won't know this one, though, because it's just been made up', before reciting her version of a rhyme likely a thousand years old.) I had to overprize. After an article about Bobby appeared in *The Scotsman*, visitors to the graveyard greatly increased, and this brought in considerable revenue for the local community. When the original Bobby died of old age, having rather conspicuously not pined away to nothing, a younger Skye terrier was hurriedly purchased. This explains Bobby's famous longevity. When you think about it, this works for absolutely everybody.

Finally, we'd head for the Kaaba of our pilgrimage, the Floral Clock in Princes Street Gardens. We literally went to Edinburgh to watch a clock. As Beckett would say, the time would have passed anyway, but honestly. Dad led us to believe the Floral Clock was a one-off miracle of horticultural science, and for a long time I was convinced that it somehow worked by flowers alone, a belief it was worth indulging since it prevented me from discovering how boring it was.* It's a half-truth to say we were too poor to do anything else, but we would have felt excluded from the museums and galleries, or at least too ignorant of their protocols to have dared stepped foot in one. We got dressed up for the trip, though, because Edinburgh folk always seemed far better turned out than Dundonians. We had no notion of Edinburgh's own poverty. Neither did Edinburgh; the city was then in deep denial as to its existence, and it did not suit its sense of itself. At least in Dundee we were no one's dirty secret.

---

* It's a good technique: next time you're bored, invent a magical explanation. Right now I'm looking at the trees thrash about outside the window, and I'm pretending they're doing so of their own volition. It's quite entertaining. Actually it isn't; it's colossally disturbing.

Later, we'd get better summer holidays than most other folk on the schemie, because my dad would work through them to cover the cost. Every year we spent a week in Soroba House, then one of the nicest hotels in Oban, and he'd sing for three hours in the bar every night. We took this so much for granted – 'What did I know, what did I know / of love's austere and lonely offices?' – that it's only now I realise that my dad went about a decade without having a holiday. I recall venturing an early piece of music criticism, opining that compared with Marc Bolan – it was the summer of 'Children of the Revolution' – my dad's voice was really boring. (He had a good, in-tune voice, just not an operatically expressive one; it was pitched somewhere between Waylon Jennings and George Hamilton IV. Michael Marra once told me he liked my dad's singing because it was rare to hear something so straightforwardly honest. That pretty much nailed it.) He teared up, swallowed hard and said nothing, when by rights he should have smacked me across the ear. Louise wasn't born yet, and my mum dressed Stevie and me identically, in a selection of lurid nylon shirts and hand-knitted jaggy jumpers my Granny had apparently made from sheep dags and Brillo pads. Mum told us to sip the orange juice that came with our breakfast very slowly, because it was real orange juice, and very expensive. We spent all day at the beach, or island-hopping. As usual, maps weren't heavily consulted, and on landing in Grasspoint on Mull one afternoon, Dad proposed that we stroll round the island. It was clear he'd miscalculated slightly; we'd been walking for a couple of hours but could tell the road was not tending to the left, as a circular route would be inclined to, so we headed back. This is easily explained by the coast of Mull being three hundred miles in length. The weather wasn't yet perma-screwed, so Augusts were reliably hot. I usually returned home fat, sick, burned to a shade of tomato and stinking of calamine lotion. (One year was cut short by a week when my Pappy died, and I still shudder when I think of my loud and long complaining in the car home, and my total obliviousness to my father's grief, until he broke down and reminded me.)

Our last summer in Oban was a washout, though. Dad, having read the forecast for the week, suggested I try stamps. You collected them, apparently. I took my seat at the window like a porthole of the Ark, and rode out the weather with Stanley Gibbons. As usual I was tooled up to the nines – magnifying glasses, tweezers, perforation gauges and God knows what other nerdy accoutrements I had insisted Dad buy me. I laid them out with the anal rectilinearity that so worried him and so pleased my mother, then spent the rest of the week sorting a bin liner of mixed stamps into their respective nations, cutting out little mounts for them and sticking them into the pale-blue grids in my giant album. As everyone was packing to leave on Saturday morning, I was fixing the last Zanzibarian five-cent green into place. I closed the bulging book and waited for my deep sigh of satisfaction. Nothing came. Instead there was a downdraught of despair, a great cold emptiness that broke over me like a single giant raindrop. I waited until my parents had left the room, scooped

15 Donald Is Seeking Fellow Paper-Folders

Like many physically lazy men, I am far better with my hands than I dare reveal myself to be. I am a great believer in Getting Someone In. They need the work, and I have plenty of my own. As Cyril Connolly says somewhere, we should dedicate ourselves to the 1 per cent of our skill set that is unique, not the 99 per cent that others can do as well or better. Freeing up the time for this, however, often means falsely declaring oneself 99 per cent useless. Consistency is important here: I had long affected the total inability to wrap Christmas presents, until a girlfriend, looking at the row of tiny folded animals on my desk (a few are watching me as I type this – a chimpanzee, a centaur, a duck, a flamingo, a turtle, a winged horse, a Great Dane with a horrible wee man humping it from behind), reasoned that this could surely not be so. She was right. I can wrap Christmas presents like a dream.

One day somewhere around my ninth year, Mum, attempting to save me from another week of Olympic-standard middle-distance staring, brought home a copy of Robert Harbin's *Origami 2*. This was clever, as she knew me well enough to know I would hold anything called *Origami 1* in immediate contempt. After about ten minutes I knew I'd found my career. It's hard to explain the attraction, but even now there's something miraculous and impossible about origami.

There's only really one dimensional quality in the universe: volume. Post-Big Bang, 2D and 1D are elusive. Pretty much the only stuff one regularly encounters that comes on like two dimensions (in a way that isn't contingent, like paint, or gold leaf, on some third thing) is the sheet of paper. It's a sort of impossibility, in its way: I think that's why I'm still wowed by things like very flat TVs and the MacBook Air. Things aren't supposed to disappear when you turn them side-on. But paper does, and many of my books do also. I have always had a thing for quality stationery, which somehow brought me closer to God; but origami makes you *feel* like a god, and conjures something from next to nothing.

Now: there are a finite number of good uses to which you can put your hands and a single sheet of paper. You can blow your nose, wipe your bum, impersonate Neville Chamberlain, pay for your muffin or fold one of Jack Skillman's box-pleated polyhedra. Next to singing, origami has the simplest medium of all the arts, and, better, just one rule: you can only fold, not cut or tear. It's both a crazy, arbitrary restriction and a Zen-like edict. Whatever the result, the model is still the same unbroken square, still of an essence with its origin, and can still be unfolded to its primal state. At its best, origami appears to trick the true Forms from some plane of eternal innocence. For those only acquainted with the flapping bird or the fortune-teller, all this may sound a mite pretentious. Such scepticism can be allayed in two words: Akira Yoshizawa. But I'll get to him.

After *Origami 2*, I acquired Harbin's other books – *Origami*

3, Origami 1 (grudgingly, for the sake of completism; I was sneeringly delighted by its babyish models), and then a reprint of *Paper Magic*, a much older book which boasted it had 'introduced origami to Britain', though the introduction was more discreet than Harbin's ambitious puff seemed to think. *Paper Magic*, while idiosyncratically and sometimes incomprehensibly illustrated by the young Rolf Harris, later a talented paedophile, was nonetheless a fine book. The Holy Grail, though, was Harbin's *Secrets of Origami*. I finally purchased it at Thin's in Edinburgh, then the biggest bookshop in Scotland. I recall the occasion vividly, as it came at the end of an appalling week in which Stevie and I had been left with our Aunt Bett and her husband, Jimmer the Nazi. Bett was the elder of my dad's two sisters; my beloved Auntie Jean was the middle child. Jean was a nervous, churchgoing librarian, with a finely curated classical music collection and a heart of gold. Jean had never married and lived alone, but took several holidays a year with a tattooed bus conductor called Sheila who had never married and lived alone. Bett was a schoolteacher, mad as a fox, flamboyant, spontaneous, and like her sister and brother, thoughtlessly and rigorously kind. She loved children but was unable to have them. This may have been a blessing, as they likely would have arrived via the black seed of her husband. Jimmer was a hulking redneck from the bleak farms of the Galloway uplands who'd also, somehow, gained his qualification as a primary school teacher, a thought that chills me now. They had married in secret, as I suspect Bett knew her parents would reject the match: Jimmer was a slightly unpleasant, angular style; Gershon Legman and his elegant, intelligent animals (again, I assumed this was his main gig, not knowing him – obviously – as the sexologist and inventor of the vibrator); the legerdemain of Fred Rohm, whose outrageously frivolous models – a snake charmer, a seal balancing a ball on its nose, a bunny on a die – always had some breathtakingly impressive maths and engineering under the hood; our Emily Dickinson, Argentina's Ligia Montoya – the elusive 'angel of origami' who always 'folded white', with her exquisitely detailed flowers and birds and insects; the beautiful proportions of Adolfo Cerceda's aviary. And there was the *papiroflexia* of one Miguel de Unamuno, whom I therefore got to know as an origamist a good twenty-odd years before I opened *Tragic Sense of Life*. Even now, I have a hard time thinking of his writing as more than a side-hustle.

In the 1940s – after twenty years of selling soup door to door in his underpants to subsidise his craft – Akira Yoshizawa had more or less invented modern origami, and remains one of just a handful of folders who have elevated it to an art form. But despite the claims sometimes made for it, origami is not really an art. It's a sculpting medium governed by one beautiful, idiotic rule. It's also a procedure: you can often achieve a broadly identical result to that of a thirteenth-dan origamist by carefully following their instructions. But Yoshizawa was a genuine artist working within a self-limited strategy, like Morandi with his half-dozen cans and bottles. There was, in all these books, much talk but tantalisingly little of Yoshizawa. Maybe a simple fold, or a few pictures:

Secrets had a photo of one of his famous early pieces, a baboon, in which I could detect an artistry that no one could put into a set of instructions. When I finally got hold of a few imported books, the shortfall between my careful following of the diagrams and the photos of Yoshizawa's own finished models was heartbreaking. Instructions for a Yoshizawa model were like the changes for a jazz standard: they were just a set of possibilities for interpretation, and allowed for everything from genius to shameful cacophony. Just because you could hack your way through 'My Foolish Heart' didn't make you Bill Evans. To the rest of the world, a crease was a crease. Yoshizawa folded with *gradations* of creases, and folded only as much as he had to. He folded with the grain of the paper, which was really more sculpted than folded. I remember turning a page of *Secrets* to find a photo of an origami elephant. Though it was less an elephant than an essay on elephantinity, a distillation of all that has ever been and will be elephant; it was the form that threw its shadow on the cave. I was speechless. It took me a long while to notice that the elephant was balanced on a thimble. Just as Picasso could swipe a recognisably Picassoesque bull in the dark with a sparkler and a long exposure, so Yoshizawa could take a hundred-yen note, fold it three times with one hand, and hand you back a swan that was his and his alone. It was Yoshizawa, in the end, who would kill it for me. The end was three years away; but even at the time, I had a gnawing feeling that the problem was less likely to be my inadequate technique than an impossible shortfall of talent.

I spent the next two and a half years of my life doing nothing but origami from dawn till dusk, which – a recurrent theme – began to worry my parents. I had very little need for human society. The day before the British Origami Society newsletter turned up, I would be confined to bed with anticipatory stomach ache. At my parents' panicked insistence, I wrote to the *Evening Telegraph*, hoping they could help me recruit similarly paper-obsessed chums; they made it their lead letter, and sent a lad round to the tenement to take my photograph. I was pictured (ten years old, porky, hair like a lassie, trying to look devastatingly intense) surrounded by 'a great number of models, several of my own design', under the headline 'Donald Is Seeking Fellow Paper-Folders'.

There were a few responses, but I was worried by their lack of seriousness. My mother insisted we invite these kids over anyway. I had envisioned an origami salon, where we would sit around discussing the aesthetics of wet folding and the scissor-heresy of Kasahara ('My own position, since you ask, Sandra, is that just one cut renders it technically *kirigami*, which let's face it [*sneers*] is an essentially *decorative* art form'); then, perhaps over an Irn-Bru, we would lighten the mood with a little frivolous gossip, and I would solicit their take on the strange disappearance of the Danish maverick Thoki Yenn, or the uncanny improvement in Adolfo Cerceda's work after he changed his name from Carlos Corda, following his heart attack. Then we'd round off the afternoon with some hard study, exploring whether the aggressively asymmetrical Rohm Simplex Base had at least *proposed* a non-oriental school, or whether excessive pre-creasing was antithetical to the whole dynamic vector of our aesthetic, since it involved *unfolding*; or if Jean Randlett's diagrams had merely lent a superficial elegance to a badly overstretched symbology that had failed to keep pace with recent innovations in three-dimensional modelling. That kind of thing. The kids who turned up wanted to make water bombs and aeroplanes. They brought no paper. I watched in horror as they helped themselves to great wads of my handmade Japanese squares for their botched little crumplings, and wept with joy when they left.

By eleven I could fold perfectly in the dark. I could fold in my head, and did, dropping off to sleep with some great web of pre-creasing mapped onto whatever the normal half of my brain was thinking about doing to Sally Arthur. I began to realise it could not be a career, and to understand the difference between what I was doing and what Yoshizawa was doing. Moreover, I was an official failure: I had entered a British Origami Society competition to fold the world's smallest flapping bird. The flapping bird is a basic Japanese model any origamist can fold in twenty seconds. In their sleep. With their teeth. With typically virtuosic economy, Yoshizawa had designed an even simpler and better one in half a dozen folds, but the traditional form was still the emblem of our guild. Confident I would walk away with the glory, I set about my task with some tweezers and a magnifying glass somehow overlooked in the bonfire of the stamps, and a 5×5mm square of thin greaseproof paper, which takes a crease like a razor blade. I took about three days over it, mounted it in a little cellophane envelope, and sent it off. I came fifth. The others were smaller, neater and – this cut me to the quick – 'more professionally presented'. The winner was an Italian who had folded his from a 2 × 2mm square at Padua University under an electron microscope or something, and mounted it on the tip of a pin in a tiny glass globe. If I could travel back in time and take myself aside, I would have consoled myself with the simple observation that he was a *grown man*, who almost certainly still lived with his mother. I would, however, never have allowed myself to be so consoled.

Mercifully, my brain was soon to be sluiced hourly by strange and wonderful hormones, though I was unable to break the folding habit immediately. In a terrifying transitional phase, I invented *pornigami*. It was, alas, a wholly unselfconscious outpouring. 'Vast Melons' was a pair of superb inflatable breasts with double squash-folded nipples and aureoles (2:1 rectangle, double frog base, title influenced by the *Goodies* annual); 'Shazam!' was an innocently racist fold, an Arab with a monstrous ten-foot penis, his forearms raised in a gesture of happy surprise (3:1 rectangle, stretched bird-cum-fish base); I adapted a dynamic mechanism of Eric Kenneway's, that great exploiter of tensile potential, in my action model 'Wanking Hand' (square, Rohm Simplex Base, wet-folded). I sent meticulous diagrams for these models off to the BOS newsletter and waited for my life membership by return of post. I mean, they'd have to make me a fellow, at the very least. After six months of deepening silence I quit staring at the letter box and retired to my room, not with one of my many volumes of Montoya or Randlett, but the Lingerie and woefully underrated Shower Curtains section of the Grattan's mail-order catalogue, and began my next phase of study in earnest.

I did make one return to origami in my thirties, and was horrified by what I found. Instead of Yoshizawa's symbolic approach – his rendering of the essence of a thing, the lotusness of the lotus, the swanity of the swan, the monkitude of the monkey – US folders now dominated the scene, and had introduced a style that was both breathtaking and horrible in its verisimilitude. They had misunderstood the entire premise. Origami was deep in the uncanny valley: conch shells that were indistinguishable from real conch shells; insects photographed next to the insects they depicted, and impossible to tell apart. The outcome – giraffe, porcupine, *Millennium Falcon* – was decided in advance, and computers would design the 'base' from which you could then fold the model; origami's art had met its camera. I suspect origami has had its Bach for a few millennia; maybe a new Yoshizawa will emerge to lead us back to the light, but no doubt it's the turn of ice sculpture or découpage to be the beneficiary of such cosmic whims. Anyway, my own last fold took place a few years back, when, in a bar in Rotterdam after a reading, I turned a ten-euro bill into Adolfo Cerceda's exquisite peacock, hoping to impress a beautiful girl from Kyiv. This was a model I'd learned as a kid from Robert Harbin's *Secrets*, and I loved the caption below the final diagram – 'Now wait for the *oohs* and *aahs*' – which made the palms of my hands hurt when I first read it. The *ooh* of surprise and the *aah* of aesthetic pleasure (and maybe the *uhhh* of a visceral, emotional bullseye) are pretty much all you'd ever want to wring out of an audience. When I propped the peacock on the bar, the girl reacted appropriately: she widened her eyes, she made a little O of surprise, she laughed in delight; then she flattened it out and bought two beers.

16 A Man in Uniform

The after-echo of national service still rang through the community, and many kids of my age were signed up for one of the semi-military options available. The Duke of Edinburgh's Award scheme was for weird kids; Scouts was seen as too middle class, and the sort of thing the High kids joined. The High School of Dundee is the town's one private school. I have private reasons for thinking ill of this middling institution, but it's long been held in more general contempt by the wider populace. Dundee folk hate folk getting above themselves, and in a way, the High School exists for no other purpose. (My school motto, by contrast, was pretty much *Sciebam Patrem Suum*.) The school bizarrely boasts William Wallace as a former pupil; you will recall that bit in *Braveheart* in which the blazered and satchelled Wallace – distinguishable from his fellow pupils, at this point, only by his woad – has his sense of national injustice ignited when he kicks his rugby ball over the railings, only to see every passer-by refuse to return it, a scene frequently re-enacted in his honour to this very day.

Instead, I joined the Boys' Brigade – next to Chimp Division, perhaps the most infamously useless of Her Majesty's military corps, and a rare sight at the front. I lasted three weeks. Mum bought my uniform from Alice McFarlane next door. It was too big, but I was too wide, so that was okay; even better, her son

Alan had achieved a very high rank, so it already came with a white lanyard and forty badges sewn into it. I thought I looked magnificent, and that the ribbed jumper made me look svelte. I'm not sure why Mum encouraged me to turn up dripping in unearned ribbons and medals, but the Royal Family, whom she admired, had long set a precedent for this kind of thing. I suspect she assumed I'd get away with it when they saw what an astonishing young man I was. When I arrived at the North Halls at the bottom of St Mary's Road to sign up, I was immediately taken into a side room, where it was explained, firmly but kindly, that the badges and lanyard had to be won, not merely acquired. The badges had to be removed, and they handed me a pair of scissors to cut the threads and unpick them from my uniform. They saw my crestfallen despair and gave me one badge by way of compensation: the one for needle-work. It was my last badge: I left halfway through the first forced march. The plan was to set out from North Halls, head down Strathmartine and out into the country, walk through Bridgefoot and then hang a left out towards Auchterhouse, where we'd be picked up in a bus. I was far too overweight, bored and unfit to complete this, and made my excuses upon reaching the war memorial in Bridgefoot ('Sir: I'm not sure if my parents explained, but I am asthmatic'), which was plenty far enough. I waddled home alone, while getting torn into the Tupperware box of tablet and traybakes and the two cans of Fanta Mum had given me to keep my blood sugar up.

At this point in time, I had had a best friend for years, a nice kid called Alasdair. I haven't yet mentioned him because our exploits were scrupulously unmemorable. Other than our shared distaste for adventure of any kind, I am not sure why we selected each other as best friends. But everyone else seemed to have one, and besides, the qualifications for bestie were then minimal, as our characters and interests were so sketchily formed. The one thing children do see and understand, however, is status, and that does most of the selecting for us. We were in a fairly thin subgroup in schemie terms, something like Upper Third Division Church-Adjacent Dweeb, so fate likely steered us together.*

I got it into my head that we mirrored our hobbies and interests but, like most reflectors, had failed to reflect that it only takes one mirror to do that. When I'd taken the Queen's shilling, Alasdair had joined the Red Cross, probably in an attempt at symmetry-breaking: we were eleven, and about to enter high school, whose far larger social pool would provide us both with an easy excuse to go our different ways. But seeing me now clubless and un-uniformed, he asked me to join him. The Red Cross involved a bit of oath-taking and symbolic square-bashing, but was mainly focused on first aid. Badges were for really specific stuff like wound-dressing and fracture-splinting; they were also splendidly graphic, and an

---

* Status is a completely hardwired and often class-based feature of childhood that accounts for much genuinely terrible suffering and life-altering insecurity amongst kids. But no, let's ignore all that and talk to them about stuff that obsesses adults, like sex, gender and race. (Anyone want to guess the one human cohort that actually 'doesn't see colour'?)

outsider would have been hard pressed to say whether the more heavily decorated of our number had been honoured for treating the injuries or inflicting them. Every week presented us with a new worst-case scenario, and it was really a kind of horror club. As these horrors had to be vividly conjured, one could also gain a badge in 'simulation', i.e. the art of wound design: using only pink modelling clay and paints drawn from opposite ends of the spectrum, slashes, burns, ruptures and fractures were conjured with horrible realism, and indeed often looked far worse than the real thing. By the time I left, I could do you a plausible compound fracture or a facial wound that would have you rushing for the toilet bowl, and would have make a good hire for George Romero.

We also had field exercises. First we'd be divided into A and B teams. Team B would be subjected to mass simulation – the full menu of contusions, compound fractures, stab wounds, gaping slashes, third-degree burns and internal bleeding – and drilled in feigned concussion and spleen rupture. We would all be driven in a bus to Reres Park in Broughty Ferry, a small, densely wooded square with a little hill in the middle, where Team B would hide. Team A then had to locate them, diagnose them and treat them. Finding them was easy enough. The wood was littered with mangled bodies – in the bushes, buried under leaves, halfway up trees. Indeed, at the start of every exercise the temptation to shout, theatrically, '*What* in the name of the living *fuck* happened here??' was almost unbearable. Had the question been posed, one might have swiftly concluded that a knife-fight on a 747 carrying a platoon of dwarf soldiers had resulted in a failed emergency landing into a forest of hyenas, but we were instructed to accept the scenario at face value, as something very likely to come up for which we should be well prepared. There was some brilliant overacting, as Team B had been briefed to scream and moan whenever inappropriately moved or treated. Entering into the spirit of it, I once essayed a totally straight-faced 'He's gone, Chief. We've lost him', accompanied by a grim shake of the head, but Mr Stewart wasn't having it. Arms were tourniqueted, recovery positions set, non-kissy CPR delivered and legs splinted; little kids ran away screaming and dog walkers called the police. Wee Kenny Mollison, who marched with his arms and hands straight out like a tin soldier, once got left in the rhododendrons with massive internal bleeding and a broken ankle, and we had to drive back and treat him for actual hypothermia.

The Red Cross also provided me with my first literary award, the Dundee Red Cross Junior Essay Prize, for which I had little competition, in the numerical sense, not the meritorious. Mr Stewart nonetheless stated that my essay on the demilitarisation of the Red Cross contained 'some interesting postulates', whatever they were, which thrilled me to hear; pleasing one's critics is quite the kick, I will have noticed. The cup had my name, Ronald Patterson, lightly engraved on it, and I was allowed to keep it for a year.* One

---

* My mother has just informed me that I never gave it back, and it's in the loft. I guess that means the Dundee Red Cross Junior Essay Prize competition was never rerun and I was its final winner, and likely entrant.

weekly Red Cross session fell on my birthday, which went as well as ever. Alasdair and I had been given permission to go to the Wimpy in Reform Street, next to the Red Cross offices, for our very first meal out alone. I ordered for us, with what I felt was some casual sophistication; rakishness, even. 'Oh – let me look – and . . . yes, two Brown Derbies. Why not, eh?' I could get good at this. Within two minutes, Alasdair, overwhelmed by the occasion, had made a dyspraxic fork-jab and sent his Wimpy Delta Grill spinning to the floor, chips, burger, sausage ring, tomato and all, and was in tears. We had no money to buy another. The waitresses were kind, wiped the ketchup and picked the chips off his uniform, swept it all up and brought a replacement. I wanted to die, but I wanted Alasdair to die first. We finished the meal in silence, choked down our milkshakes and Brown Derbies, and slunk away for the long bus home. Pass-aggly, Alasdair gave me a number to remember forever and claimed I couldn't. It was 343.

17 Farm of the Warrior

In P-Celtic the 'Baldragon' in Baldragon Academy means something like 'farm of the warrior', and is disappointingly unrelated either to the false god Baal or to dragons. Nonetheless, in the mid-seventies it managed to live up creditably well to its terrifying name, and the new arrivals from the gentler upper-working-class primary schools of Macalpine and Downfield gathered silently at its main entrance at the bottom of Burn Street like huddled shades before the gates of Dis. Despite reassurances from our mothers that the horror stories we'd heard – of heid-doon-the-lavvy drownings or actually fatal wedgies – were merely big boys' tales meant to frighten us, everything turned out to be true or worse. All first-years without older brothers or sisters, or unable to find an older boy to protect them, were fair game. I have heard many declare that their old school must have been at least as rough as mine. Frankly I doubt it. Few can claim, for example, that their school was merged with a young offenders' institution. The year before I arrived, Baldragon had absorbed Balgowan Boys' School, the local borstal, following the assessment that their feral cohort would be seamlessly assimilated into our own school population. They were wrong: our welcoming committee left the Balgowan lads begging to be reincarcerated.

On a regular day, chairs were hurled through windows,

legs were ripped off pigeons and shites taken in teachers' desk drawers. In line with Scottish educational policy at the time, discipline was enforced through corporal punishment: officially, the threat and practice of belting children insensible with an oven-baked Lochgelly, the fork-tongued, hand-tooled leather tawse; unofficially, anything you could get away with if no one was looking. (I know of at least one teacher who favoured the discreet blow to the gut outside the classroom door; they bragged about it. As for the PE teachers of the 1970s: what's the point. One came to expect the worst. About half of them need their own Nuremberg.) One enterprising art teacher liked to place the child inside a dark cupboard with his or her arm sticking through the door with their hand out, so the kid had no idea when the strap would fall. He would repeat this six times but take a leisurely ten minutes over it. No disrespect to the survivors of the boarding schools of England, but I'm sure if we'd been offered an alternative form of abuse we'd have at least considered it. Towards the end of my years at Baldragon, as calls for a legal ban on in-class torture grew louder, there were various awareness-raising exercises to train staff out of their old ways, though by then we'd have settled for a vague request to observe the Geneva Convention.

War it was, though. Mr Anderson, aka Fat Ando, the bald forty-year-old Germanist in the beige cord jacket who still lived with his mother, was forever pleading for the return of his belt, the theft of which was an equivalent shame to an NYPD cop losing his piece. He would bribe us with sweets; as soon as the prize was claimed, the belt would be swiped again.

Ma Scott was an octogenarian supply teacher and married to a local minister. Kindly of demeanour, floral of dress, gentle of bosom and completely full of crap, Ma Scott would tilt her head and pout her lower lip in sympathy while she belted you into an endorphin coma. My first English lesson began with us all innocently chattering away, as we would pre-class in primary school, and this continued as Mr Davidson walked in. He didn't say a word, but placed a piece of chalk on the edge of the desk, took two steps back, whipped out his tawse from some inner pocket of his tweed jacket, and with a crack that sounded like and probably was the sound barrier, exploded the chalk into dust. Silence then ensued, for six years. 'Granny' Gordon no doubt had a tragic entry in her backstory that would explain her; we heard rumours of the death of a son, or a jilting at the altar. Either way, something awful had happened between her teaching my father in St Cyrus, where she was apparently well liked and held little impromptu parties for the students, and her turning up a quarter-century later in Baldragon, where her sole human joy was the torture of the thick, the inattentive and the underperforming. (She hated weakness, so the bad lads who stood up to her went unpunished; in fourth year, my mate Alfie would just go to sleep at the back of the class, stretched out over two desks, while she grinned indulgently.) Girls and boys would spend a sleepless, weeping night before her class, then have to be dragged to the gate the next morning; they'd stammer every answer and piss themselves at their desks. Her belting technique could've been taught as a martial art, and indeed I learned something from it I would later transfer to my pool break: follow-through. You have to think speed, not power. If you think power, you're usually concentrating on the point of collision between cue and pack, or in her case between belt and sweaty little hand. Ignore the pack or the hand, and fire right *through* it as fast as you can, and the result is usually a cheerfully entropic spread of balls, or in her case a sudden contraction of them, along with a comprehensively wrecked childhood. I came across her grave in St Cyrus fifteen years back and did a wee jig on it. I feel bad now; she must have been in hell. But she had a choice, and the displacement of her own suffering blighted many other lives. At least she will have known what we thought of her, and would often start the day by opening the drawer where she kept the registration book to find the turd left there from the night before.

Violence, as we know, just begets violence the next rung down. New kids might be subjected not only to the time-honoured, practically light-hearted practices of debagging and head-flushing, but have their schoolbags torched with lighter fluid, be gassed to within seconds of death in locked cupboards in the science block, or wedgied Baldragon-style, which involved being dangled by the lengthening loops of your underpants from the second-floor balcony till they were round your ears and your balls had wisely retreated to your lungs. Mostly I escaped this as I was too weird-looking. I was the exotic frog in the food chain that folk would instinctively avoid, just to be on the safe side. This visual warning was the accidental result of my mum trying to fund a middle-class semiotic on a working-class wage: I had my grandfather's old leather briefcase instead of a schoolbag, and gleaming black brogues. She bought some proper second-hand rugby boots three sizes too big and stuffed them with newspaper; no one else wore clown shoes to PE. Her final what-the-actual-fuck addition was a Rangers FC tracksuit, not the Dundee FC one I'd requested; my mother had deemed it 'a bonnier blue'. It turns out when you wear a sign that says 'Kill me', you tend to get left alone.

Besides, everyone was far too taken up with traditional targets, like Alexander House. Promptly christened 'dug' – which likely exaggerated the luxury of his own lodgings – Alexander was probably immune to pain by the time he reached us, and so his inquisitors gleefully realised. He had watched his father tie his mother to a chair, douse her in paraffin and torch her alive, and he himself had nearly died when his head had been caught in a mechanical potato-harrow when he was scrounging behind it for something to eat. He was still sporting a white turban bandage when he turned up at Baldragon. He was immediately subjected to a programme of highly inventive daily torture, which by then he will have accepted as his fair due. He had a sidekick, Oliver Devany, another tiny dark wee boy who always had the kippery smell of stale urine. In midwinter Oliver came to school only on alternate days; he had an elder brother with whom he shared a coat. I remember the two of them pinned against the PE block, a white halo thickening on the wall behind them as they faced an apparently inexhaustible fusillade of snowballs, most of them seeded with sharp pink gravel, some of them just rocks rolled in snow. They stood close together, bolt upright with their hands straight by their sides as if before a firing squad. They made no attempt to protect their faces. Conveniently I can't remember if I took part or not. I don't think I did. Oliver's brother Willie was another ineducable disaster, but he had an almost paranormal gift for drawing animals without looking at a model. His jotters, otherwise troubled only by dirt and nosebleeds, were filled with beautiful tigers, dogs and elephants that stunned even his tormentors into astonished respect. 'That's . . . fucksakes, that's *really* good, Wullie. Uh, you cunt. Gonnae dae wiz a giraffe? Please.' He was prevented from doing his art O-level, though, on account of his not being able to draw faces, probably because he'd been scared to look at one directly for most of his life, and was heartbroken. I'd give Willie's chances of having made thirty a solid zero.

I was close to being on the receiving end myself, but my giant clown boots got me co-opted into the rugby team. There, I fell under the protection of Tam McRae; our dynamic was 'nerdy prisoner who works in the library and writes valentines for Mr Big'. Tam hated bullies, and his physical presence reminded the likes of Dougal Spankie that a mere terrible personality is never any match for *force majeure*. At fourteen he was simply a man, and a giant one at that: five foot eleven and built like a road gritter. I saw him get four strokes of the belt once; he smiled throughout. Not threateningly: benignly, sweetly, indifferently, forgivingly; *encouragingly*. The teacher was terrified. In the rugby team I inexplicably functioned as loosehead prop, a position so named as my head had been permanently freed from my torso by collapsing rucks that often saw me twanged high into the air before I broke my fall with my neck. Our team was rubbish, but we rarely lost. All you had to do was somehow get the ball to Tam, then collect the points. I can see him now, a shire horse of a man, plodding the length of the pitch through the cold morning mist with the ball under his arm, as if he were making his way back from the shops with the Sunday papers and rolls. On either ankle he wore a small boy he was dragging face-down through the mud. One fell off near the twenty-five-yard line and didn't move. He may have been dead. On reaching the try line, Tam placed the ball carefully between the posts with one hand and ruffled the remaining lad's hair with the other. Tam later went on to become the supremo of the local branch of the most admired rollerblading club in Scotland,* and manned a highly popular local community helpline which would get the call if something needed urgent sorting, but kept off the books.

Around the end of the last millennium, my brother called me from the West Port Bar.

– Where are ye? I can hardly hear ye.

– The Westie. I just called Big Tam.

– Why?

– Guess who I'm looking at right noo.

– Nae idea. Ralphie Milne.

– Nope.

– Thon lad fae Deacon Blue. What's his name.

---

* This line has been adapted on the advice of in-house lawyers.

– Ricky Ross.

– Is it Ricky Ross.

– Nope. Why would I call Tam on Ricky Ross?

– 'Chocolate Girl'.

– Last chance. Think scarier.

– Lorraine Kelly. I give up.

– Arkan.

– Who?

– Arkan. Y'know. The Serbian warlord.

– How the fuck was I meant to guess *Arkan*? Anyway fuck off.

– Straight up.

– I think he's wanted for genocide.

– Aye he is. Any roads Tam said he'd be here after he's walked the dug.

I assume Tam got there too late to spare The Hague or Arkan's future assassin the trouble, otherwise you'd have heard about it already. But the story checked out: there was a spell in Giovanni Di Stefano's versatile career when he was simultaneously pursuing a stake in Dundee FC and working as Arkan's personal lawyer.

18 Your Time Is Up

I should say a word at this point on my very limited exposure to formal music tuition. It was pretty much inevitable that my mother would start me on piano lessons, the clearest aspirant signifier of the day; this had nothing to do with music and everything to do with levelling up one's status. Piano lessons neatly implied several important things: your son was a genius; you could afford to send him to piano lessons; and you owned a piano. (Stevie was sent to an elocution teacher round the same time. Little how-now-brown-cow stuck: he is a sophisticated man, but his primary fluency remains, proudly, the language of the gutter.) These lessons will have been hard for my folks to afford, but were almost certainly offset by the near-sexual pleasure Mum will have gained from rehearsing and delivering the line 'Yes, Donald has his piano lesson this evening.' Force-taught as a child, Mum played piano herself, very nicely, even though she didn't think of herself as particularly musical, and could sight-read well. She bought the sheet music for 'Come Back to Sorrento', and played it over and over again: she had been besotted with Mario Lanza in the fifties, and this had been her howl of mourning after his early death from overeating. Mario was the cause of the one fight my mother and father ever had: my jealous dad had called him a poof, and Mum – who had just watched an

Elizabeth Taylor film – slapped him, experimentally. Rather less experimentally, my dad 'threw her across the room', to use the phrase by which she enjoys recounting the story; that is, he manoeuvred her carefully in front of the sofa and laid her down, gently but firmly. They were both mortified, and my brother was probably conceived on the spot.

I was around eight years old when I was packed off to Mrs Drysdale. She lived in Symers Street and was your identikit kindly old piano teacher, and I can recall nothing of these lessons because I was so very, very bored. She would . . . Uh. She would balance a penny on the back of your hand, and if you played the scale without it falling off, you could keep it. There's a wee anecdote. Are we done? Even writing this up, I've had to crawl back inside the soul-compacting black hole that survives in lieu of an actual memory. One day, during my half-hour of enforced daily practice, wishing I was dead or unborn or in a coma, I was poking my way through 'Bonny Bobby Shaftoe' with one finger on our crappy upright, which was all ghost keys and shuffling hammers and seasick discord. Mum wandered in. She was shocked to find me staring right through her. We agreed that I should not continue in such pain, though it was hard for her to give up on my brilliant future, and I hated disappointing her. (Not that I was permitted a guilt-free escape. For years, one of Mum's favourite and most widely mocked mantras was 'Look where you could have been if you'd stuck in at the piano' – the answer never being 'concert pianist', weirdly, but some high-status gig that I would, by now, have been comfortably occupying: bank manager, dentist, or Moderator of the General Assembly of the United Free Church of Scotland, which was, purely coincidentally, her own father's career high.)

The record player back then was a four-gear affair, and setting it to the wrong speed was a common error – and occasional amusement, if you wanted to hear how Mario Lanza might sound with a left-hemisphere stroke, or 'Come Back to Sorrento' performed by George Formby. (In a move that exactly parallels the influence of the sped-up drum loop on contemporary drumming, fiddle and guitar technique would occasionally get a boost when instrumental records were accidentally marked with the wrong rpm and played at almost double the recorded tempo.) In addition to Dad's Lonnie Donegan and Hank Williams 45s and 78s and his slowly growing library of decent folk and country albums, we also had a few spoken-word records, most memorable among them *Sparky's Magic Piano*. *Sparky's Magic Piano* blighted the childhood of every kid unlucky enough to hear it, much like the 'African culling song' accidentally collated in *Poems and Rhymes from Around the World* in Chuck Palahniuk's horrible *Lullaby*. I am convinced that *Sparky* also spun at the creepily otherworldly and least-used speed of 16 rpm. The story is simple, and heavily padded out with 'improving' classical performances of Chopin and Liszt: little Sparky falls asleep at the keys halfway through what I remember as my own Grade 0 party piece, 'The Jolly Farmer', but can't have been, then dreams his piano is alive and conscious and can play itself like a pianola. (The piano talks through the filters of a

Sonovox, a kind of early vocoder, which sounds like a human voice vibrating the piano strings sympathetically.) As I too often fell asleep at the keys, the story seemed straightforwardly cautionary. The actual composition for the speaking piano on the record is utterly brilliant, a harmonically enhanced mixture of emotional tease, faked innocence and horrible cynicism and foreshadowing. 'I'll play anything you ask me to play . . . *for now*.'* Even better, the piano – who is effectively grooming our little giggling coquette ('Sit down on my stool . . . Put your fingers on my keys') – can play Sparky, who quickly makes a name for himself on the performing circuit. He inevitably gets too big for his boots in the end – his hubris seems to be coming back out for an encore – and the piano finally shuts up shop at Carnegie Hall, to which Sparky has found a non-traditional route, and indeed the very opposite of practice. The piano announces his dereliction with the immortal, horribly cheery and gloating little up-and-down-the-scale 'Your-time-is-up-I-will-no-longer-play / for / you', which is the voice that still plays in my head even now, any time my luck runs out. Sparky keeps playing, but the result is awful, clanging, two-fisted cacophony, and he is shamed utterly on the world stage. 'Sparky, *why* can't you play? *Why?*' yells my mother, I mean his mother, inconsolably. Then she wakes him up, and he gets milk and cookies, and he resolves to be a good boy

---

* In one stroke, they had solved the honking, six-hundred-year-old problem of the operatic recitative, which should have been conducted solely through vocoders since 1940.

and to practise hard and make everyone legitimately proud. In my head, though, a parallel story continues, with Sparky laughed off the stage, having shat his pants in front of Harry S. Truman, returning home to disgrace and the taunts of his classmates, retaking fourth grade three times before dropping out to smoke meth and sell his arse on rat alley, then freezing to death alone in a dumpster at nineteen, on his birthday. The lesson it taught me was that my worst nightmare – the one with the frozen golliwog and the balloon-man song – wasn't. This was. A big thank you to all the adults involved.

But I had other, unconscious reasons for signing up to these lessons. I was range-finding. I heard music in my head all the time, but didn't have any way of expressing it; I would improvise fairly complex tunes, but I had the musical equivalent of locked-in syndrome. The possibility of being the Stephen Hawking of jazz was starting to scare me. I began to audition instruments, or rather, Sparky-style, I let them audition me. None of them would play me. After the piano was sent away to live on a farm, I became a truly terrible trumpet player. I have always operated on the principle that one grows into the role, so, adopting the part of Mozartian prodigy, I'd head off to school with my Papa's old leather music case with the fold-down flap and the brass retainer bar. This was an incomprehensible object on the schemie, and served as a fine conversation piece. When asked what was inside, I'd reply, insouciantly, 'Oh – y'know, symphonies, string quartets and that,' and head to the practice room where I'd fart into the mouthpiece for ten minutes before connecting it to the tubing for another forlorn stab at 'Row Row Row Your Boat'.

Once I moved up to Baldragon, I was switched to the trombone, and was hopeless at that too. The brass teacher, Mr Brown, was a rugose, fat and jolly drunk who spent the entire lesson in the bike shelter smoking and reading the racing odds. His teaching method was a version of the Indian classical approach, whereby you are left alone with your sitar or vina to practise your ragas fourteen hours a day, and the master puts in a wordless appearance once every three months to lightly adjust the angle of your arm, and then departs. Had I had any interest in being a trombonist, this would have worked, as I am temperamentally unable to be taught anything by anyone. (This shows. Where others have degrees and specialisms, I have a hi-res bathymetric map of the ocean of my stupidity; it looks like Micronesia from space, with little islands labelled things like 'drum machine emulator plug-ins' and 'US pool hustlers of the 1960s', and I get through life by hugging their coastlines.) I also had a job in the Music Centre in town that I'd copied from Alasdair, who was a good tenor horn player, polishing the instruments in the gloomy and haunted Brass Room. The brass band family obsessed me. It seemed to consist of several families of identical instruments of twenty different sizes that were played in no other musical situation. It was a room full of non-transferable skills, but also infinite alternative. (I still have an urge to study the euphonium, the cello of the brass band, and the most crazily underexploited instrument on earth.) Looking at their serried rows, each baritone or flugelhorn gleaming by its own light in the near-dark – they often seemed to move too, an effect of prolonged Brasso inhalation – I figured there must be a match for me out there somewhere. Because it wasn't the trombone.

Sensing my growing frustration with the thing ('The trombone is the only orchestral instrument that can be played perfectly in tune' goes the old saw, always failing to add: 'but never is'), Mr Brown tried moving me to bass trombone. For a while this went slightly better, as the parts were easy and could be covered by an averagely competent lighthouse. To my mother's incontinent delight, I was also scheduled for some TV exposure: Baldragon Brass Band was selected to represent Dundee schools on an episode of *Songs of Praise*. I made a half-second appearance, wincing one-eyed at a bum note from the horns. However, this triumph was a blip on a sharp decline. My final performance was a public end-of-term rendition of that great trombone showcase, 'Those Magnificent Men in Their Flying Machines'. This contains one of the few programmatically justified full 'bone slides in the repertoire, on the line 'Up, down, flying around, / looping the loop and defying the ground'. After 'up' and 'down', you would perform a ballsy slide – up, and then down, although the temptation to slide down and then up was almost overwhelming. But rehearsals went well and provided a kind of bonding bit of theatre between Mr Brown and me, as he could appear to conduct me in my controlled skids.

The day came, and the assembly hall was packed. We honked our way through 'The Floral Dance' and 'Eye Level or the

Theme from *Van der Valk'*, and both passed without incident. We gamely embarked upon 'Those Magnificent Men'. The moment came. Mr Brown indicated me violently, like a mad wizard, casting an 'up' spell with his baton. I panicked and immediately shanked the big glissando, lipped into the wrong octave, and raspberried it. I tried to compensate immediately with my slide on 'down'. Now: some technical information. These days, one can reach the lowest notes on the bass trombone with the induction of an extra coil of tubing engaged via a discreet valve, but back then we were purists. In those days the bass trombone had an additional seventh position, one only within the reach of basketball players, statistically few of whom are also brass specialists. But mortals could reach the bottom note by flinging the slide out to a full arm's extension, and then *additionally* flinging out a little ornamentally tooled handle, which would afford you the extra four inches you needed for your deep contra-parp.* Anyway, appalled by my up-note, I determined to really make up for it on the descent: I made a gratifying growly downward slide, like a fat motorboat speeding past your ear – then flung the handle out to end on a big Alpine blart. Only I failed to catch it, and the trombone slide shot off the end, whistled past the ear of the French horn in front of me, and clattered to the floor six feet away. This all took place over about two seconds, which lasted about an

---

* I read online that 'players found this tiring, and by the end of the nineteenth century, these handles had almost completely disappeared'. My arse they had.

19 Heinz Fry Dry Fear

At the age of twelve, around two years before I finally succumbed to it, I picked up the guitar for about a month. Alasdair and I immediately formed what we called a 'rehearsal band'. We were called Powerplant. We were called Powerplant because this was the English translation of Kraftwerk. We were me on acoustic guitar, doubling on Jew's harp, Alasdair on piano (upright; non-movable; front-room) and three more Jew's harp players whose names are lost to the haar of time. Hang on: Grant Thain, Angus McKay, Gary . . . Nope. We sounded like testing day at a cartoon bed factory. It wouldn't be quite true to say we modelled ourselves on the German man-machines; for one thing, we were hamstrung by our lack of synthesisers, which we assumed was what allowed Kraftwerk to play the same thing over and over again perfectly, though it might have been talent.* We'd play the same thing over and over again too, but it came out very differently each time. We were, though, admirers of their look. Some critics read Nazi

* Kraftwerk's anality is the stuff of legend: no external sound is tolerated in Kling Klang studios, and for decades the studio phone had the bell removed. If you wanted to talk to Florian or Ralf, you would call at exactly the appointed time, and they would pick up; one second late, and your chance was gone.

sympathies into the Kraftwerk style, but what they meant was that they looked German. Not that they all carried off the *Cabaret* Stormtrooper look with equal aplomb – Florian Schneider's expression was always more ashen-faced docker caught in his wife's knickers and eyeliner – but the point was: *band uniform.* We had a brief experiment with our old Boys' Brigade caps, mascara and foundation, but we valued our lives, and wisely opted for civvies. Alasdair had tried to pass off his brutal number 2 cut with the engraved side-parting as Teutonic affectation, but we all knew it was because his old man used to be Plymouth Brethren.

Kraftwerk didn't exactly capture the alienation of a generation, quite, but they did speak perfectly to that subset of tormented bright kids with no friends, few friends or friends they didn't much like, for whom adolescence will always be the purest torment. The 'Werk got me through some bad days, not least because all their music seemed to be pure locomotion, headed in the general direction of the hell out of here. The first album that turned us on was *Autobahn.* The title track, with its catchy refrain of 'Wir fahren, fahren, fahren auf der Autobahn', built to a twenty-odd-minute epic that seemed, to us, a veritable *Ring* cycle. (The resemblance to the Beach Boys' 'Fun, Fun, Fun' was, I read here, 'wholly accidental'; frankly, I could have worked this out for myself.) It was mind-blowing: sequenced synths, speeding-car noises panned left to right, skids, horns, laddies talking like robots. Side Two had a couple of rinky-dink things, and a bizarre synthesised field recording of birds and insects with fairy recorders and a mandolin. We played it once, and silently agreed never to mention it again. But then came *Trans-Europe Express*, which we dissected forensically. Finally, something recorded by a robot for other robots to play in the evening. Throughout, the Department of Redundancy Department was in permanent overdrive: we'd Dalek-sing along to 'The young man stepped into the hall of mirrors / Where he discovered a reflection of himself'. Or the crowning glory of *Trans-Europe Express* – 'Trans-Europe Express', with its catchy refrain of 'Trans-Europe Express': so doggedly literal in its evocation of wheels clattering over points and other chuff-chuff noises, it really did feel like you were on the train, and as I had been on a train maybe four times, this was no small thrill. 'Showroom Dummies' is actually counted *in*; given that the whole tune appears to be based on a Casio keyboard preset held down with a single finger, this might be humour, or some German misunderstanding of it.* The end of the tune daringly attempts a little semi-fiddly synth melody, but rapidly falls to bits in a kind of trad jazz for Cybermen. (Robots, just like Kenny Ball and Acker Bilk,

---

* I actually lost my German translator through a failed attempt at humour. At a poetry festival in Dresden, I'd improvised a little bit of completely inoffensive but – herein lay the offence – unscripted banter, which infuriated him, and the entire audience agreed that this was a really disgusting stunt to pull halfway through a four-hour bore-a-thon that had, thus far, been running like clockwork, *danke sehr*. I spent the interval crying in the toilets, and after the gig no one would talk to me. I later received an email saying: 'I hope you will find someone else to translate your work; I am fed up with it.'

understand synchronisation but not counterpoint.) We tried counting in, in German ('Heinz Fry Dry Fear'), and worked hard to synchronise our twangs, and even attempted a hocket, where two pairs of Jew's harps would twang alternately. With the addition of Alasdair's repeated staccato chords on piano, it now sounded like something written by the infant Steve Reich, i.e. even worse than the adult Steve Reich, but the effect was tighter and louder, a bit like two fat elves making steady and passionate love.* Alas, Powerplant soon fell apart owing to musical differences – some of us weren't musical – and I put down the guitar again.

A couple of years later, Alasdair and I tried, unsuccessfully, to re-bond over Gary Numan, since he had clearly styled his miserabilist automaton pose on Kraftwerk, via pre-Midge Ure Ultravox. But Gary made the mistake of moving, slightly, and was further let down by the bulldozed graveyard that was revealed every time he opened his gob to do his strangulated Bowie thing. But Gary's real problem was *pathos*, something that Florian, Ralf and the gang were way too cool for. 'Are "Friends" Electric?' and 'Cars' were pleading, embarrassing, Wullie-no-mates affairs. Kraftwerk made me feel *good* about having no mates.

---

* I think minimalism is a hoax. Sorry. But Philip Glass's music seems to be the product of some well-intentioned equal-opportunities scheme, and 'Variations for Winds, Strings and Keyboards' is why Reich shouldn't have been allowed near anything with a longer decay than a banjo.

20 If with His Skirt He Do Touch Bread or Pottage

Alasdair and I had been drifting apart through Primary Seven; things had never been the same since a sexually confused sort-of fistfight – the pretext was some football matter, about which neither of us knew a thing – but as Baldragon first-years we had found ourselves thrown back together as we had no other friends. Heartily fed up with each other, we reflexively joined the Scripture Union on the assumption that it likely served as a hub for our fellow Baldragon nonentities. We also joined because we were in fear of our lives. While the hopeless cases might draw most of the flak, the flak factory of the scheme meant there was still plenty left for the likes of us. We sought protection, uselessly, in God and the Scripture. Being both from 'kirky' families, it was a fatally natural move. Alasdair's dad was an angry church organist whose main sexual outlet was violent performances of Widor's Toccata, which he attacked like a cross between Little Richard and Vincent Price. Since I was seven, I had been able to recite all the books of the Old Testament in fifteen seconds flat, as a sort of desperate party piece; this had convinced some easily impressed old dears at Sunday School that this bekilted and sporranned, wavy-haired prodigy was, like his grandfather, destined for the manse. Maybe I was finally getting the show on the road.

What was really driving me was more complex. At one

level, joining the Church just continued my life-game of seeking both forgiveness for everything and the approval of my mother. Though she'd long accepted that he wasn't going to come round, Dad's rejection of the Kirk still rankled; this had left her increasingly isolated within the household. So apart from anything else, this was a pretty smooth Oedipal move. Initially, then, I'd spotted a chance to kill two birds, but I soon saw I could take out a third. After about a year of lager-shandy-strength praying and Bible study with the Baptists, my testosterone was beating its way up the beach, and I felt in my body that youthful rebellion was a contractual necessity. Atheism, weed, a porn stash and some minor vandalism should have worked fine, as it did for most of us. But I had no intention of returning my blessings, either heavenly or maternal. However, I could see that if I embraced a faith far more extreme than my mother's or grandfather's, it might also accomplish the goal of Being a Worry to Them. My unconscious must have been delighted with itself for circling that squared circle so elegantly. You'd have to ask it.

Things got off to an unimpressive start. In the playground, my 'Jesus Saves' badge conspicuously did not shield me from a bucket of dirty water emptied over my head by the egregious Dougal Spankie; I loftily forgave him and embarked on Matthew 5:38, 'I say unto you, that ye resist not evil, but whosoever shall smite thee on thy right cheek, turn to him the other,' though didn't make it as far as 'And if any man will sue thee at the law, and take away thy coat, let him have thy cloak also,' as Dougal was by then stomping my blazer into a dirty puddle. He then made me eat a pan drop that had been previously inserted into the anus of one of his orc-posse. I reasoned that I was not praying hard enough, and resolved to put in more hours. We were going to need a bigger badge.

The Scripture Union was run by a plain young woman called Mrs Jack, with no shoulders or breasts and untameable rough fawn hair that grew in four different directions. She was a kind and sincere soul, and she had a husband who put in the odd appearance. He was a sales rep for a soft drinks company, a handsome, olive-skinned, Mediterranean-looking guy; we reasoned somehow that she had been *rewarded* with him. Mrs Jack was soon pregnant, and he was soon dead of cancer, and her forbearance and lack of anger were admirable and terrible things to behold. This event – or at least the equanimity with which she reported it – shook me, and made no sense. I was close to seeing through the whole scam, when Mrs Clyne stood in for the grieving Mrs Jack. Small, dark-eyed, pale, essentially Ali MacGraw with a mess of black snakes on her head, Mrs Clyne was the last woman in the school to wear a black cloak, under which she wore white stockings and – this fact verified by a number of semi-horizontal oops-dropped-ma-pencil sources – matching suspenders. She suggested that we might like to go to an inter-school SU meeting in town with her once a week. Had she proposed we go and tend the pustules of dying jakies under the bypass, I would have responded with no less alacrity.

It was here I discovered the Prayer Group. Now: at least the Buddhists are mostly involved in some kind of genuine self-work, the dervishes are getting a little exercise, and his five-times-daily prostrations mean you rarely meet a Muslim bloke under the age of eighty with a bad back. By contrast, the Christian prayer group is just about the most useless gathering on this earth, being twenty people in a room pleading endlessly with someone who clearly isn't. Prayer meetings, we would be reminded frequently, were *not* meditation. The great evil of Transcendental Meditation was then receiving a lot of publicity, and pictures of yogic flying (basically a game of seated bouncy-bouncy with a row of mattresses) were circulated as evidence of its black magic. The devil was real, and the self was his portal; it was not to be dwelt on, enquired of or investigated further. All *thinking* was absolutely forbidden. (Meditation involves its cessation, of course, but evangelical Christians believe exactly what they like; they falsify nothing and verify everything.) We had to concentrate on Christ the beloved, block all thought with his radiance and learn to speak continuously without engaging our brains.

But it was not enough that we had saved our own souls. We had to Go Forth and Witness in the name of the Lord. We were given our urgency through the fact of our living in The Last Days. The Last Days begin pretty much half an hour after the Ascension, and afford all born-agains their biggest sexual kick. This is where they find the licence for their taboo-breaking, their behaving as if excepted from the normal protocols: it's what frees them to shake, foam and collapse on the ground, to yell like winos on street corners, and to act like children in adult company. Alasdair and I agreed with the current projections: given the signs, we were definitely talking this October, at the latest. By June, the Beast would have us all tattooed with our personal barcodes, and by August we'd be listening to the frogs bouncing off our umbrellas.

Fuelled up on imminent Rapture, I took to the air and shot down unbelievers like the Red Baron, and slapped a thousand crosses on my cockpit. I made more conversions that year than Andy Irvine. I had an eye for the friendless and the insecure, and a good line in hellfire. The fact that they lapsed or renounced after a week was no business of mine. Aftercare was the Church's job. My technique was to identify the worst fear of my target, fix them in my unblinking stare, and detail how very much worse things were likely to get for them after the imminent Return, i.e. before Christmas. Ronnie Wilson: not only will your mum never come back from Tenerife, where she is currently shagging the Grattan's catalogue man, but you will be separated from the rest of your family for *all eternity*. Alasdair Bottoms: you will be the fattest boy in hell. Stuart Buist: if you think your spots are bad now, I can promise you that the oozing buboes that await you below will cause you to look back upon this time as one of creamy-skinned perfection. For I have read somewhere that it will be so.

It was around this point that either my mum or dad probably should have intervened. The Church is safe enough for kids, if it's the sort most folk used to attend, where they believe in the goodness of belief far more than they actually believe, sing a few songs and hear a nice sermon on human decency. Adults can believe what they want, and they should be respected, if those beliefs hurt no one else. (Their *beliefs* certainly shouldn't be respected, though one should find respectful ways to convey one's disdain for them.) Children shouldn't be allowed to believe in anything but Santa and the love of their family and friends. They especially shouldn't be allowed to believe in anything as sin-obsessed as the Christian God and his satanic enforcer, and especially during puberty, when their brains are already undergoing profound and confusing change. What kind of asshole, precisely, would tell a fourteen-year-old they'd be damned for a wank, or a mouthful of cider, or the touch of a breast, or a trip to the cinema, or merely the *thought* of those things – things whose intrinsic evil was never once explained to us, beyond a jab at some practically Delphic line of scripture? I can tell you precisely: two kinds of asshole – one weak and afraid, and the other some shade of evil. But it will have been hard for my folks to judge the right moment to step in. My mum's initial pride at my churchgoing only slowly turned to concern, and she couldn't have known the moment I began to *truly* believe, which is to say go mad. Dad described himself as an agnostic, because his atheism would have hurt my mother, so he avoided the subject; that epitaph for dads everywhere.* Besides, any intervention would have

---

* I was so proud of my mother for allowing us to give him a wholly secular funeral in line with his own beliefs. The crematorium was stowed out with his friends and colleagues, and it was basically just a country music gig. We came in to Noam Pikelny playing 'Mississippi Waltz'; he went out to Alison Krauss singing 'Down to the River'.

been met with the kind of hysterically well-briefed resistance neither of them had the energy for.

Of course, the only genuinely guilty parties were the grown-ups within our mission. There were far fewer of those than the set of adult humans, given how many of the childlike – in the form of the lost, the easily led and the mentally ill – we attracted. And amongst those folk, there were men and women I persist in thinking of as 'good', even now; though they *weren't* good, because to be 'a person of faith' adjects no credit to your character, and while they may have performed some minor charities, all were in service to their 'mission', which was invariably either unnecessary, unwelcome or actively Mother Teresa-style catastrophic. But nor were they wicked. They were merely religious. No, only a handful were really culpable, and they were the same as cult leaders everywhere: narcissists whose faith wasn't even cynical, because narcs do neither sincerity nor insincerity, which are both values predicated on the existence of a soul. Nor do they distinguish between lies and truth, since either can serve the same end, which is the fulfilment of their will. Their evil plans aren't even evil, but just energy-saving pathways made visible to them through reptilian necessity.

Despite all this frenzy of witnessing, Alasdair and I were terribly aware that we were Christian Lite. I had yet to be formally converted, for one thing, and a few of my brothers were voicing concern at the speed I was taking the corners on my provisional licence. Besides, you had to take the oath of conversion before you could be Baptised in the Spirit, and baptised before you could really start to climb the ranks. I envisioned a sort of kyu/dan system I would progress through until I could turn my cheek with such devastating humility it would strike Dougal Spankie dead on the spot, like a kind of aikido for Christians.* The ceremony was conducted by the nice wee minister from the Baptist church on the scheme, in his underheated front room, over a cup of tea as weak as bathwater and a saucer of Peek Freans biscuits. I merely had to repeat a standard form of words, like marriage vows. However, I misheard, and said 'loving God', not 'living God', or the other way round. I was thereafter convinced my mistake had invalidated the whole thing. I mean, what use is a god who doesn't attend to the letter as carefully as to the spirit?

We would hear rumours of the hard core who gathered down at the Tent Mission, and some thrillingly occult goings-on no one seemed keen to discuss. They had prayer meetings that were *six hours long*. Women prophesied and had visions and frothed and bled from the nose and fell over. Men spoke in strange tongues and performed miracles and healed stuff – nosebleeds for starters, I imagine – and Alasdair had heard they got naked sometimes, which had to be bullshit, but who knows. While we were fascinated, we were happy enough for now to paddle around in the harmless shallows of our playground recruitment sorties, 'daily texts', mind-destroying visits to old folks' homes (dreaded by both parties) and daft campfire

---

* As far as I am aware, aikido is the only martial art to focus specifically on the losing side.

songs with 'actions'. Since pop music was banned, there was always a heavy demand for new songs, and a buzz would go round whenever someone had shoehorned an obscure bit of Leviticus or Haggai or Epistle to Titus into half a tune and illustrated it with a bit of 'YMCA'-style dumb-signing we could all learn. These were our chart hits, our top ten. 'Hey – have you heard "If with His Skirt He Do Touch Bread or Pottage" yet?' I found all the idiot mumming a bit hard to swallow, though, and thought continually of *Play Away* and *Rainbow*, until I realised that was the point: it was a further abasement performed before the Lord, a challenge to you to survive the furnace of your own red-faced infantilisation, indeed to emerge from it smiling and unscathed.

Many years later, I was walking with my own seven-year-old twins in St Andrews, and came across a group of born-agains proving their commitment by giving it the old 'I'm-a-Little-Teapot' semaphore outside a church. *These hands* (show hands) *that hold* (clasp imaginary tennis ball) *this heart* (point to heart) *of mine* (point to face) *have formed* (hold imaginary mug of soup) *the world* (attempt to hold planet) *since the start* (point at . . . the start) *of time* (tap wrist), etc. The boys were mystified. Jamie looked up at me. 'But Dad, where are all the *kids*?'

21 For the Love of God Amen

Yet our little band of believers was wholly content. Well, we would have been wholly content, if it hadn't been for Luke Gillis. Luke was seventeen, a charismatic firebrand and brutal bully of a boy. His eyes were a foot apart and he had a forehead so prominent I want to use the word 'prehensile'. He also had piercing BO: his armpits *sang*. (Once he told us he was late for a meeting because he had fallen asleep in the bath. I remember exchanging glances with Alasdair. The *bath*?) He tried to talk a version of RP, or, more accurately, to graft some imaginary, authoritative acrolect on top of his schemie Dundee accent. He was a man possessed of a truly terrible fanaticism. Whenever I ask myself how anyone could saw another man's head off, slowly, cack-handedly, in the name of God, I remember Luke. I still don't really know how, but I'm pretty sure I have known who. It's a matter of catching them at the right age.

A few said that Luke would have been a thug had it not been for God, but they got it the wrong way round. Luke was a thug anyway, and God merely justified his thuggery. He would toy-fight with us sometimes in the graveyard after church, and enjoyed kneeling on our shoulders until we couldn't breathe. 'Fool' he once called me at a prayer meeting, when I expressed an opinion that conflicted slightly with his. Foolishly, I replied with Matthew 5:22 – 'But whosoever shall say, Thou fool, shall be in danger of hellfire.' He took my thin neck in an excruciating Vulcan grip. 'Don't – Ever – Quote – Me.' I looked around, waiting for the company to correct him, and couldn't get an eye to meet mine. The trouble is that having made one concession to absolute subservience it's too easy to make another, and one becomes, by definition, easily led. Cowardice was our social glue. Luke, like many church leaders, was not cowed by God: this was because he didn't really believe in God, other than as a means of lending some muscle to his own coercive control. He had found himself in a bullies' paradise. (My own informal but not negligible dealings with them suggest that the cohort of religious leaders consists of around 40 per cent of the very best of humanity and 60 per cent of the absolute worst, with almost nothing whatsoever in between.)

Despite all this, or probably because of all this, Alasdair and I had a serious crush on the guy, and we vied for his attention like two giggling floozies. And so began a recurring life-game: obsessive crushes on obvious narcissists. Luke had already learned the basic narc skill of conjuring your wondrous future, and he promised he would get us into the Tent Mission Prayer Group when he deemed us ready; that way lay Baptism in the Spirit, and beyond, infinite powers. I was standing at the Baldovan bus terminus one night, and praying that Luke would materialise in time to get the bus with me to the church; he emerged from the gap in the fence just as the bus was about to pull out, which I immediately took as a sign from God and almost fell to my knees. I mean, it wasn't even a *coincidence*. Once or twice he graced me with a home visit, and I could hardly believe my luck, having Luke himself in my own front room, with his gleaming black suit and his blacker King James. (Alasdair and I favoured the Good News translation, with its fawn covers and cartoons. Luke dismissed it as childish and blasphemously inaccurate.) My mother was unimpressed, not doubting the young man's sincerity – it was impossible, given his full-cornea, unblinking monomania – but underwhelmed by his personal hygiene. I was furious with her for not loving him as we did, and another seed of distrust towards my mother and father was sown, something that would eventually blossom into full-blown paranoia. All I smelled off Luke was the intoxicant of his vastly more powerful faith. I bought myself a starless King James with my Christmas tokens, denounced the Good News as the work of the devil, and stopped showering.

We treated witnessing and prayer as a sport, and vied to outdo each other in length, style and self-abasement. I recall one recent convert, a wee old guy on the twelfth floor of the Ardler multis whom we bombarded with almost daily home visits. He must have felt like those poor refugee kids, inoculated into teabags by thirty-three competing private charities as soon as they make it over the border. After we had eaten all his Jammie Dodgers we'd leave him propped in front of *Crossroads* and retire to his spare room to pray – to pray about any old rubbish, so long as it was for longer than Luke had prayed at the weekend, or Raymond the day before.

Less fun, since it involved an encounter with an actual

reality, were our calls on Ma Gunn. These were high-prestige visits, and got you a double stamp on your card. Janie Gunn was a blind evangelist who'd run a well-known mission in the city centre in the fifties and sixties. She'd been bed-bound for many years. Her flat lay up some unlit spiral stairs off a close in the High Street. We'd be greeted at the door by her daughter, a grunting troll who wore what looked to be a dress made out of old dish towels. The dark flat immediately choked you with its sour, awful human smell. Everywhere howled of piss. Every surface was filthy. Your shoe soles stuck to and peeled off the lino as you walked. This wasn't just poverty, but folk who couldn't look after themselves. Ma lay in a deep, greasy socket in the centre of her bed; I doubted she had seen a change of sheets in years. We prayed, we bore witness, we read her favourite verses, and we sang the choruses we all knew. We'd heard a rumour that Ma had no legs either, but one day we saw them stir beneath the piled blankets, to our mild disappointment. Ma was tiny, blind and toothless, but still sharp, and knew us all by name. We prayed and sang with her, and she reminisced about her mission days while I distractedly widened a hole in the damp plaster of the wall behind me with my fingernails. Beside the bed was a bookcase with her long-unused, huge Braille Bible volumes. Her daughter wanted to sell them. I assumed her only source of income came from local winos she noisily entertained in the back of the flat; I can still hear that rising *muh–muh–muh–MUH MWAAAAAARGHHHHH!!* through the wall that had one evening concluded 'Go Tell It on the Mountain'. If

could see that our prayers not only had no effect on Global Events, but did nothing to affect even the very smallest things, stuff that surely could have been accomplished by the tug of a divine earlobe or a raised eyebrow. So not only was Luke not Shown the Error of His Ways, or Malcolm prevented from Straying from the Path of Righteousness (I gathered from a pearl-clutching Alasdair he had gone to the *pictures* with a *girl* who wasn't *saved* and afterwards they'd had a *drink*); Mary's tumour continued to metastasise, and the wars raged on.

The reasons for God's non-intervention were so doctrinally obvious as to be not worth discussing. Our trivial requests were beneath him. It was selfish of us to have asked He wasteth His time with them in the first place, and we would later apologise. We loved apologising, especially as we had so little sin to declare in those days. *O Lord forgive us that in our unworthiness and ignorance we did pridefully and foolishly* etc. The greater plan was woven into a cosmic tapestry of which he had the one decent view, and we were encouraged to take great delight in our ignorance of it. His Garbo-like mystery was his principal appeal. Christians, in my experience, spend very little time agonising why 'a supposedly benevolent God' could allow X or Y to happen, and breezily take the tsunamis, famines and genocides in their stride, until their own kid gets creamed by a drunk sixteen-year-old in a stolen Vauxhall Corsa. Agonising is mostly an agnostic pursuit.

In all this I seem to have omitted to make any mention of faith itself. This is because faith itself was a matter of almost no consequence to any of us. Faith is something required only by casual churchgoers, not true believers, as faith is predicated on the existence of a capacity for doubt. Banish doubt and you can skip faith and proceed directly to incorruptible and certain knowledge. Banish doubt, alas, and you also proceed directly to insanity.

Luke was now sufficiently impressed with our endurance-worship to get us an introduction to the Tent, and the Pentecostal group that met there. We were initially disappointed at the lack of theatre, nosebleeds or nudity, but their extremism made up for it. It was brilliant. Whole new arenas of previously unsuspected sin were delineated. You could sit in an empty room and think of nothing and still be inching closer to damnation. I got to work especially hard on Sex and the room it took up in my head. I couldn't make it take up any less room, though, so I made sure that every time I thought of something, it was accompanied by the shadow of its infernal punishment. This made it take up exactly twice as much room as before, and meant that the greater part of my waking hours was now given over to cursing myself, which was upgraded from pastime to vocation. It was a positive relief, then, to bound up those stairs three times a week into that overlit yellow room to give myself a break from my self-disgust, and have some other folk be disgusted with me instead. Of course, they weren't, but having gone to such lengths to convince myself that I was the embodiment of all human wickedness, I'd have been disappointed to find they didn't share my opinion of me. I fell in love with a beautiful, very overweight girl with black hair and milky blue eyes who didn't say anything, and

I exhausted myself lying in the dark for hours trying to not imagine what I didn't not want to not do to her. This was, accurately, a sign that change was in the air.

22 Absolutely Tragic

I took a break from my growing religious mania by hitting adolescence, at thirteen, in the school holidays, in Belfast, overnight. I crawled into bed as a child and woke up as a depilated spider monkey, smelling like a lamb bhuna and sporting an erection that appeared to have been levered upright by the Amish. We were staying at my Uncle Frank's. Frank had done well and owned a shirt factory; he had a big house in Shandon Park, next to the golf course. Frank had recently bought a fondue set, and we had just spent two days recovering from his attempt to cook raw pork in hot cheese. Possibly this had had some catalytic effect on my hormones. The visit was also memorable for the Sex Pistols' first appearance on *Top of the Pops*. The Pistols' demonic reputation having reliably preceded them, the adults were primed to be scandalised. 'Put that rubbish off.' 'No no no leave it on leave it on leave it on!' I could tell it was godless, but it was also utterly compelling. The young Johnny Rotten was as cool and scary as you'd hoped the Antichrist would be; he had a withering take on the Elvis curled lip, itself already a withering gesture, that was somehow both its weary deconstruction and the most genuine curled lip in history. He was as strange, baleful and spellbinding as a comet. What the hell is *that*. 'We're so pretty / Oh so prettyaaarghhh . . .

We're vay–CUNT!' It was the first real thing I'd ever seen on television. 'Pretty vacant right enough,' said Frank. 'But he just *said* so! It's a *declaration*!' 'Aye, pretty vacant right enough,' echoed my dad. Parents didn't get nihilism.

My own was fuelled by a sudden sense of masculine inadequacy. Childhood had insulated me from this, and overnight the excuse had evaporated. Yesterday I was passively irrelevant; today I was actively unappealing. When my cousin Catherine wasn't listening to *Rumours*, she was mooning over the ringlet-haloed, open-shirted guitar twerp Peter Frampton, like every other fifteen-year-old girl that summer. *I'm in You* had just been released; talk about knowing your market. I decided the only way to go was weirdo, so I went into Belfast and (after a thorough frisking from the RUC for incendiaries at the doors of Boots; I gathered there was a war on or something) used all my holiday money to buy the Fairport Convention compilation double album *The History of . . .* This was a pretty hard left turn at the time. *History* covered the momentous decades between 1967 and 1972, and Fairport's revolving-door personnel changes were apparently seismic enough to merit one of Peter Frame's famous 'rock family trees' on the sleeve. I memorised it, and can still tell you when Ashley Hutchings came back for a week and then left again to form Morris On or whatever. But it wasn't an entirely random purchase. I'd bought Steeleye Span's *Below the Salt*, and as a child, about a week ago, had sung along with it – louder than I knew, in an unembarrassed sort-of-West-Country accent, from inside my Mickey Mouse headphones:

'With me roo-run-rority ri-run-rority ri-no-ority-an . . .'
(Maddy Prior accidentally became a pal in later life, a fact
which still necessitates some confused double-takes.) My
dad had already bought Fairport's *Rosie* on Willie Whyte's
recommendation three years before. Although it was later
clear to me that this had been Fairport's worst album to date,
I'd grown to love it. *Rosie* does contain at least one sublime
moment. The American guitarist Jerry Donahue was then in
the line-up; on *Rosie*, he sounds like an angel who accidentally
took the lift to the wrong planet, but hung around for an hour
to save face. Jerry was unusual in that he was both a country
shredder (he later developed a hitherto undiscovered double-
string-bend technique; attempts to learn it caused enough
tendon damage to merit a class action) and possessed of a
totally adult restraint when he needed it. He contributes a
perfect guitar solo on the album's best track, a clever, pretty
Swarbrick ballad, 'My Girl', and it was perhaps the most
understated and emotionally articulate thing I'd ever heard a
guitarist play. It was a little sixteen-bar thesis. You listened,
and your heart went, quietly: Yes, that's true. (Jerry's advice
on solos was wonderful: 'I just play the nearest note I can
think of' – which you might think meant the adjacent note
in the scale, but it doesn't; it's a tiny manifesto for a musical
naturalism.)

And so, with a heigh and a ho and a faulty radio, I tried
being a folkie. *History of . . .* had a lot of Richard Thompson
and Sandy Denny, and was therefore great by definition. They
taught me about the authenticity of performance, or more

precisely about the inauthenticity of rock theatrics. Most rock singers 'feel it', hysterically, when they sing; most folkies sing *with* feeling, but not about it, so the audience's feelings are provoked, not usurped. On such a prepositional confusion the entire art of performance often founders. A sobbing singer will usually leave every eye in the house dry in its socket. (Unless you can tell they just can't help it, like Celine Dion's widowed crack-up halfway through 'All By Myself', in which case we're all lost. Her actually making the high note into the key change is less a symbol of human triumph than a straightforward example of it.)

History of . . . contained Thompson's early classic, 'Now Be Thankful', a song full of what sounds like Sufic or Templar symbology, and knowing Thompson probably is. There exists a wonderful video of a live performance of that song, from about fifty years ago, with Swarbrick in ruthlessly committed and searing voice; at one point he makes impeccably louche use of the four bars between verses to nick a draw on a roll-up, the tip held inwardly, stealth-grip style – and then storms back in at full intensity. Smoking can be *really* cool, kids. I once saw Nusrat Fateh Ali Khan do something similar. Between solo spots he'd look bored as hell, check his watch, scratch his belly, wince, yawn at the tabla player, have a think about his dinner – and when he was up to sing again, take off like a jump jet. He was able to go from bedridden to thermonuclear by flicking a switch. The trick was simple: in his mind, performance was not conceptually separable from intensity. To give it less than everything was amateurism. *History of . . .* was full of such moments of electric presence and commitment. 'Meet on the Ledge' should have been written by a forty-year-old who'd lost half his mates to suicide and the needle, not a seventeen-year-old Richard Thompson about a tree in his back garden; but genius always anticipates its own course, and in its beginning is its end. It's also why it has a habit of short-circuiting. Religiously aided self-control spared Thompson in this regard, but Sandy Denny had no such resources.

The voice has always been my favourite instrument, and it's Sandy's fault. What makes Denny's voice great is the amount of information it encodes. The outward perfection of the singing apart, each sung line also arrives layered in micro-inflection and nuance; these infinitely various quantum fluctuations of breath and pause and vibrato render her a kind of lexicon of human feeling in microfiche. Almost any line of Sandy's, isolated and studied, flowers and flowers like an emotional Mandelbrot set: you feel you could zoom in on any point of a spectrogram of her voice and never find a bare fundamental, and that every spliced moment would reveal a travelling ripple of harmonic partials. Such an absurd *capacity* for feeling – always denied the catharsis of its full expression, which would have killed the art – would have been too much to carry straight, so Sandy was mostly drunk, and died of the indirect consequences.

By the end of my Belfast trip I was listening to 'Crazy Man Michael' and 'Who Knows Where the Time Goes' twenty times a day. For years afterwards I was locked into a Fairport album called *Rising for the Moon*, often overlooked in the canon because it's exactly half absolutely terrible ('There's no excuse for torture – *that* you ought to know,' sings Swarb in 'Let It Go', if only he had) and half the best Denny solo album ever recorded, with four or five anthology pieces. 'After Halloween' alone got me through the second-worst break-up of my life.* If my grandfather had wanted to stand next to Paul Robeson in heaven, I would request to be comfortably seated at the dusty end of Sandy's Fender Rhodes. In purgatory, though, where they have a bar.

About three years later, *The John Peel Show* informed me of the death of Denny – it was an offensively throwaway mention – and I wore a black armband to school the next day. My slight acquaintance Eck Prain was also wearing one. 'You heard?' I said. I was surprised. Eck had a black mullet and a denim jacket crowded with heavy-metal patches, and his knuckles were still bleeding from an early pre-bell round of Scubby Queen, a horrible card game where your losing-trick forfeit was to be rapped on the back of your hand with the edge of the whole pack, as hard as the victor could, the object being to draw blood. I hadn't had him down as a folkie. I greeted him, and we fell into brief conversation.

– Oh man. Sandy Denny eh.

* Now that I think of it, the first-worst was the same woman twelve years later. *OK Computer*, since you ask, specifically 'Let Down', its best track. No question. *OK Computer* is a personality test. A mate of mine once claimed 'Karma Police' to be its masterpiece, and I've never been able to relax in his company since.

– . . . (momentary confusion) Oh yeah. 'Battle of Evermore' man.

– Er yeah man.

– Terrible isn't it.

– Terrible. Absolutely tragic.

– Oot like a light.

– Never had you down as a fan.

– *Really?*

Eck drew my attention to his jacket with a downward sweep of his palm. Despite the obscurity of the gesture, I left impressed at his unexpected sensitivity. At break, I saw *another* guy wearing a black armband; I was starting to feel that I maybe hadn't been very special to Sandy. By the third armband, though, I sensed something was up. It was: John Bonham had just died. I had physics with Mr Forbes next, a teacher we regarded as something of a cool genius because he was obsessed with the Phaistos Disc and the various conspiracy theories around its translation. (Something to do with bull cults, apparently.)

– Never had you down as a Led Zep fan, Donald.

– No, it's for Sandy Denny.

– But she died two years ago.

– . . . Yes. I know that. Uh anniversary.

Mr Forbes looked dubious, but let it pass. I slipped off the armband in the toilets, put my head in my hands, and waited for the invention of the internet.*

---

* I once had a five-minute conversation about 'The Prelude' with a

composer friend of mine. We complained of its longueurs and praised its brighter passages, we whined about its turgid lines and its boring repetitions, and so on. 'Some memorable themes nonetheless, though.' 'Oh, absolutely . . . Some, uh, strong themes there.' Then he hummed one of them. At which point I realised I was talking about Wordsworth and he was talking about Wagner. One wonders how much human disaster was similarly produced. I always felt the Treaty of Versailles had a certain air of Pope vs rabbi about it. (It has just been suggested to me that, terrifyingly, not everyone may know this one. Okay: the Pope decides to throw all the Jews out of Rome. The Jews resist. A summit is called between the Pope and the eighty-year-old chief rabbi as a last attempt to resolve their differences. Since one speaks only Italian and the other only Hebrew, they decide to communicate in hand signs. First, the Pope holds up three fingers; in reply, the rabbi raises just one. The Pope makes a circle with his hand in the air; the rabbi points firmly at the floor. Lastly, the Pope produces a bottle of wine and a communion wafer; the rabbi answers him by taking an apple from his knapsack. Then the Pope sighs and throws up his hands, crying out, 'I concede. The Jews can stay.' Later, the Pope meets with his bishops to report the conversation. 'Well – I said to him, "Look. The true God is a trinity – Father, Son and Holy Spirit." The rabbi said, "Perhaps for you; but the God we both share is also really one." Then I said, "The true God is all around us." Then he said, "Maybe; but that means that God is also here with us, right now." Then I took out the communion wine and wafer, to show him how Jesus died for our sins. Then he took out an apple to remind me of Adam and Eve, and that all of us are sinners together. What could I do? He argued subtly, and I had no reply.' Meanwhile, at the synagogue, the rabbi was explaining what happened. 'So the Pope says, "You Jews a-gotta three days to get outta here." I said, "Go screw yourself." Then he went, "No, you a-go bye-bye now." I said, "We're staying right here, boychik." And then we had lunch.')

23 Oombara Coombara

Home from Ireland and back at the mission, I was now armed with a perma-erection to underwrite my fundamental sinfulness. If *this* wasn't something to apologise for, I didn't know what could be. The endless prayer meetings were led by the kindly Jim Sprunt, a giant baboon of a man with a hook nose so big he had trouble drinking properly, and had to pour liquids into his face from one side. Jim had initially made his name as an exorcist, but now had the forlorn and underemployed air of a too-successful pest controller. The accompaniment to our sung praises was provided by a (clearly gay, I can see, now the mists have cleared) bouffanted beanpole called Brian. He had a twelve-string guitar, the first I'd ever seen. It sounded like . . . a twelve-string guitar, which is really enough, if you've heard one. Two guitars emerge from the shape of one guitar, one a heavenly high ghost of the other. They can be slightly out of tune and be even more beautiful, as the detuning creates a chorusing effect. This is fortunate, as they are *murder* to get in tune, and therefore usually aren't. I made a mental note: one day I would play a twelve-string guitar.*

I was more desperate than ever to be baptised, and my

---

* I did. They are murder to play.

second-class status was really bothering me. After the Baptism
in the Spirit, real power was conferred. You would receive one
of the charismata, which were the gifts of either Tongues,
the Interpretation of Tongues, Prophesy, Miracles, Healing,
and so on. Dave thought one was Invisibility, but he wasn't
well. Baptism in the Spirit, though, depended notoriously
on God's inscrutable whim, and attempts to rush him into
anything tend to be counterproductive. Some members of the
group had been waiting for years, and those individuals were
effectively sacrificed to underline his divine capriciousness.
(Again, it hadn't occurred to me until now to think how *cruel*
this was, given the whole thing was made-up bollocks.) The
seemingly endless stint as Under-Christian is also crucial
to building up the frustration needed for the dam-burst of
hysterical gratitude that convinces the baptised of the reality
of their experience. I think the group registered how useful
such young and zealous recruits could be, though, and I was
earmarked for early promotion.

I rolled up one Tuesday night to find they'd booked the
star preacher on the circuit – an appealing, dumpy little guy
from Aberdeen (affectionately known as The Wee Pope, in a
touching demonstration of their genuine lack of interest in
sectarian matters). His shtick was pretty much identical to the
others', just much louder and more quivery: where some would
shake from their lack of conviction, he shook with an excess
of it. He spoke quite normally, but when fully inflated with
the Spirit sang in a high-pitched, heavily vibratoed monotone
that drooped at the end of each phrase, like a ghost from

Scooby-Doo. We started prayer, and were an hour or so into our private chunterings when I heard him walking amongst us. The footsteps stopped behind me. 'And who-oo-oo-oo is this young ma-aa-aa-n?' I heard him ask Jim Sprunt, and I knew it was my night. There was then a laying-on of hands, which meant a few folk laid their hands on me, and Lo, the Paraclete descended among us; I was then, as Luke would say, filled with the Holy Spirit like what were the apostles at Pentecost, and I did speak with the tongues of the heavenly orders. I stood with my arms frozen in that classic attitude of big reception, like Bellini's *St Francis in Ecstasy*. Grace descended; I wept, I shook; my cup did runneth over. Later, at the boiling up of tea and setting out of biscuits, I was hugged and congratulated, as if I'd won something. Which in a way I hadn't.

When the queues for the charismata form, everyone except the genuinely mad (Invisible Dave) or the power-mad (Luke) lines up for Tongues. The Gift of Tongues is technically identical to that fire that descended at Pentecost, which allowed the apostles to wind the clock back pre-Babel and talk to all men in their own language. You might speak, it was said, in Polish or Malay or Catalan, or maybe even the big one, Middle Aramaic. *Everyone*, of course, aspired to Middle bloody Aramaic, though even back then it was a point of common scholarship that Jesus would have spoken at least as much or more Greek. Since no one had a clue how it sounded, it was frequently claimed. I did once hear someone attempt Spanish, hilariously, and it really was all *dónde está la estación por favor*, with a bit of ying-tong-tiddle-I-po what-the-hell thrown in. No one ever wanted to speak Sanskrit or Navajo, i.e. anything heathen or primitive. Mercifully there was a get-out, a relatively dignified solution, and almost all of us flung ourselves at it. One might also speak in The Tongues of the Angels.

Angeloglossia were, on the strength of our performance, a whole bunch of mutually incomprehensible dialects with a lot of bilabial plosives. They clearly had a Babel of their own up there. The clouds must continually resound with the Angelic for *You huh?* and, amongst the wags, *That's easy for you to say*. Some, however, were very beautiful and sounded just like real languages, and indeed may have been, if not of this planet; they had a consistent music and phraseology that must have converged, here and there, on something real *somewhere* in the cosmos. I knew that I had just heard in *santanderi tro mestfira li menor li menoschka tre perrissa* a snatch of a laundry list, or match report, or love poem, from whatever passed for a Transylvanian enclave on some Rigelian exoplanet, or from a cloud of sentient flying wombats deep in the Beehive Cluster. Others were plain echolalic gibberish, and sounded like the ombly-jombly-wombly bits in Edward Lear, and it was hard to keep a straight face. Whatever it might have sounded like, my own private language was a fairly satisfying affair, as my tongue was liberated – weirdly, beyond any freedom I could permit it in private – to make all the lovely syllables I had ever dreamed of. It was, in the midst of the most psychologically damaging experience of my life, wildly cathartic; I still think there is a sound secular therapy in there somewhere. Luke's tongues, on the other hand, were another matter. Luke spoke in the dialect of some brain-damaged infernal troll. It mostly consisted of two words: *Oombara coombara oombara coombara oombara coombara* . . . I was both terrified and embarrassed for him. I was amazed no one had ever pulled him aside to tell him to either shut up or make more of an effort.

There was one beautiful thing, though. After the interminable bearing witness, after the endless prayers stapled together from the same handful of stock phrases, after the prophesy of such arse-covering vagueness it made Nostradamus sound like a shareholder presentation, after the comic attempts to heal the sick (I remember a pair of crutches falling away from one poor bugger, in slow motion, like the support cranes on an Apollo rocket; for one glorious half-second it seemed that he would stand unaided, before he hit the floor in a puddle of limbs, as if the puppeteer had suddenly remembered a lunch appointment), after the gabble, jabber and gibber of tongues . . . After all that, someone would start to sing. It would begin with one person, always a woman, singing one long note, to which everyone gradually ascended like a slow, lovely air-raid siren; then we began to harmonise, every man or woman still singing in their own strange tongue, but the vowels lengthening until we were singing together, one supple, fluid, rippling vowel, shifting through its formants like the spectrum through the skin of a salmon. It was a symbol beyond anything we were equipped to understand, but it gripped us powerfully. It sounded very close, I discovered later, to Free Church psalm singing in the Western Isles, where the precentor sings a line of Gaelic, to have it echoed and elongated by the congregation, the difference in timings creating harmonies that, had they not had the appearance of accident, would have been disqualified as sensual excess, and possibly have led to dancing. Their psalms roll out in shifting, delayed layers, like one cold Atlantic wave slowly breaking over another. But here, we harmonised too, and beautifully so.

Long after I extracted myself from the Church, I heard that Luke had himself been thrown out for heresy, having unwisely claimed for himself the gift of healing and suggested to several incurable paraplegics that only their weak faith stood between them and a trial for Lochee Violet. Whether this was true or not, I warmed to him all over again. For one thing I was delighted that you still *got* heretics, in much the same way I was delighted to find, in a wee sweetshop in Thurso last year, that you still got McCowan's Egg & Milk Chews. I gather they let Luke back in after a month or so, though, as heresy isn't what it used to be. (How on earth could Giordano Bruno or Jan Hus have been expected to make their reputations from ten minutes in the sin bin?) A cursory google for Luke reveals a man still apparently devoted to his faith, and to community projects in those parts of the world which will, I guess, forever remain catnip to white saviours. I've tried to forgive Luke, and tell myself that he was facing down his own demons back then; for all I remember him as an adult, he was only a boy himself. But he was a narcissist, and they're all incurable. It's so sad, because narcs never get any sympathy: they do too much damage. But behind their lies and rage and gaslighting is fear, and behind the fear is a terrible, crushing shame, and at the root of their shame is often the worst and most abusive kind of parental neglect. The narcissistic trait is also statistically more heritable than Huntington's. I found an interview with him online. Nothing had changed: he had the same bomb-proof certainty and cross-hair singularity of purpose (a shark's most characteristic attributes shouldn't be ours), the same insistence that the world take precisely the form he required it to.

I wish I could say that I learned my lesson. But too much of my life has been spent working as a narcissist's 'supply' (we've already met a few narcs, and a few more will put in an appearance). One would like to declare oneself cured, but that would merely lead to a lack of vigilance. Most of us, to at least some degree, are vulnerable to their charisma and supreme confidence. Most of us like to be charmed, to be confidently led, to believe in the golden future they hold open for us. (Those 'sunlit uplands' Boris Johnson claimed we were bound for is a narc's tell: in our online support groups, we call it 'future-faking'.) But almost everyone enjoys being in their circle, because they're often hands-down, dinner-and-a-show, wonderful value: funny, flirty, inappropriate, rule-breaking, irreverent, straight-talking, clever, inspiring . . . We don't recognise their disorder because we don't want to. Only those who've survived the hell of being in a close relationship with them can see through *all* narcs, immediately, simultaneously, and know that their supercharged self-assurance is one of their biggest giveaways. A quiet confidence is to be respected; this is often just the product of a loving home, an acquired expertise and a respect for others. But here's some advice: when you hear someone express nothing *but* certainty, you should avoid them, challenge them or, if necessary, nullify them. (These folk usually just consist of a paper-thin, wildly overconfident act disguising a crust of fear, over a mantle of shame, wrapped round a core of nothing, where a parent should be.)

Some narcs are geniuses (they can specialise themselves into remarkable expertise), and are not only useful but crucial to the advancement and perhaps even survival of the species. Others are phenomenally dangerous. Some are both. They come in all political stripes, though their actual *beliefs*, as distinct from their insights, are either provisionally held through hour-to-hour expedience or totally non-existent. All are bullies, who need you to stand just there, no left a bit, yes just like that, thank you. Most are sentimentalists (this provides them with a simulacrum of a feeling self); most suffer an existential crisis when they are not the centre of the room, and detest or destroy anyone else who draws focus. None are fully human in the way you or I understand it. Others are simply not reflected within them. The myth is that 'they have no empathy'; *au contraire*, they have empathy in abundance, as they need it to get inside your head. What they lack is what immediately follows empathy in a way you and I naively imagine is continuous with it: compassion. For a narc, this certainly does not follow, as other narcs are the only people they regard as real. The rest of us pass as ghosts, function as instrumental extensions of themselves, or as mannequins to be wrestled and wrangled exactly to where and what they need us to be.

But the real tragedy of the narcissist is this: a personality disorder *is not a mental illness*. This means they are by definition untreatable, and very difficult to care about, once unmasked. Many narc-survivors wouldn't care if their narc died, as they are soul-murderers. And if you think this is overstatement, O my innocent friend, you have clearly been fortunate enough never to get acquainted with some of their cooler tricks: 'trauma-cycling', the love-bomb/rejection/love-bomb/rejection routine which floods the brain and body with dopamine, then cortisol, in an alternation so predictably dependable it becomes addictive, so even the terror of the cortisol comes with the promise of future reward; or their triangulation skills, where a rival third party is frequently invoked, should you get slack in your attentions and duties to them. (You are often performing the same function for the third party.) No narc should *ever* accede to positions of power or influence, where actual compassion is crucial to good decision-making; most especially, all should be debarred from any political activity beyond the think-tank.*

Of course, from another perspective Luke was merely an avatar of his god; the Church attracts many of his kind. God is a narc, and the flock are his supply. He ticks most of the boxes.

---

* The real epidemic of performative narcissism is hosted by the alt-right and leftist subcultures of YouTube and TikTok, where the mentally ill have parlayed their delusions into microcelebrity; the result of this unregulated nightmare is the brainwashing of a generation. That humanity could seriously invent the internet and then 'leave it to see what it does' may be, if not our crowning stupidity, at least our defining one.

Grandiose self-importance: check. Lives in a fantasy world of unlimited power and influence: check. Demands constant praise: check. Exploits others without a trace of shame or guilt: check. Gaslights, intimidates and bullies: check. Trauma-bonds through a cycle of fear and forgiveness: check. Has a staggering sense of entitlement: check. Triangulates: duh, check. Future-fakes: triple-check. Does not technically exist: check. And on the evidence of Pentecost, he's probably also very good at accents (an obscure entry on the narc tick-list, but watch out for it). But I could still weep for his patheticated young supplies, those teenagers you see on TV on Sunday mornings, one hand on their heart, one hand raised in vow, eyes closed, smile frozen, and that slow, perverse *shaking* of the head in what they think is deep affirmation but is no more than the disavowal of their own agency.

I saw through Luke in one reverse-Damascene flash, but the acceptance that God wasn't real was longer in coming. I don't remember leaving the Church, because I detached myself like a piece of gum. I attended less and less, I prayed less and less, and read the scriptures less and less. I slid away and lost my faith by degrees. I prayed and wept to Christ alone in the toilet to please make his presence known unto me, and thought I saw signs, sometimes, in the clouds, in the trees, in the scratches on stones I came across. I achieved ecstatic states, and in those I sometimes woke up to the strangeness of the world, a trick I would deploy later when I started to write poetry. (You learn to flick a switch and strip away the name and human utility from your shoes, or that chair, or that flower; it then returns

24 Your Representative

One should make it clear that at Baldragon Academy, amidst all the carnage, a Scottish education was doggedly pursued and indeed regularly delivered. You might emerge from Baldragon with a heroin habit, tears tattooed on your face, pregnant, dead, or all of the above, but you might have added to that a Higher Latin, an opinion on the South Sea Bubble and some basic facility on the clarinet.* We all assumed the school captain, Joe Howard, was destined for high office: he was rugby captain, already a superb classicist, and a B♭ bass virtuoso in the brass band (no mean feat on an instrument so low that its presence was merely felt in the arse of your trousers, like an earth tremor). From fourth to sixth year, he delivered every end-of-term inspirational speech with the kind of Periclean force that had even the neds choking up with pride and resolving to do even worse next term. Three weeks into university, he dropped out. At Eton, the golden-boy shtick doesn't really cost you any effort, but Joe had been swimming upriver for

---

* Things are different in Scotland now, and these days educational policy is more clearly aligned with England, where the poor have long been expected and indeed given every possible encouragement to fail. The point is hardly uncontroversial, but until the brightest children of the poor are again removed for separate schooling, it's all screwed.

years and was already exhausted. He abruptly had half his face tattooed – that clear sign that someone is taking themselves permanently out of circulation – and turned to dope, drink and dealing. (He kept his good accent, his decency, wisdom and independent scholarship, and was an expert on the Ottoman Empire and a fine church organist. He's dead now, obviously.) Plenty thrived, though. Baldragon won the UK-wide inter-school quiz *Top of the Form* one year; the captain lived upstairs in our tenement and ended up designing the Crick Institute. Many terrible habits were encouraged, but ignorance wasn't one of them. Mr Davidson of the exploding chalk, for example, revealed himself as a decent Ezra Pound scholar and hipped me to some obscure Sandy Denny recordings. One might be spat out at sixteen with one's career path set to 'unemployable stoner', but at least you were skinning up on Joan Didion and Kathy Acker. It was an age when at least half the clichés about the Scottish democratic intellect were still broadly true, and there was more cachet to be had in not being able to read a book at all than in being caught reading a bad one.

We were only segregated by sex when it came to PE and the tech/home economics axis, but girls mostly, and sensibly, kept to themselves anyway. The boys – the odd Tam McRae apart – were developmentally retarded by about four years, and not worth their time. Occasionally liaisons would be formed between a mature (i.e. usually thick) fifth-year boy and a third-year girl, of course, and there were always a few scary lasses from the more feral sectors of the Kirkton estate keen to breach the mucous membrane. I recall Alice Cooney asking me if I wanted her to 'grease my boab'; I absolutely did not want her to do that. Otherwise our interaction with the female population was confined to the agonies of long-distance yearning and the odd brief contact – a borrowed pencil, a whispered test answer, fingers touching over a retrieved shuttlecock – where one's existence was briefly and joyously acknowledged.

Kay Jack now works as a consultant obstetrician in a hospital in Manchester. I just looked her up on Facebook. Judging by the name and height of her son, I'm guessing that her husband is Russian and huge. Kay was queen of the most prestigious female clique, which numbered such luminaries as Jill McCartney (poor, overweight, beautiful, kind, vast of bosom and heart), Rhiannon O'Mara (blonde, classicist; we thought her also vast of bosom, but a late post-party report came in that this effect had been prosthetically achieved) and Stacey Stein, a small Gillian Anderson lookalike, dark-eyed and raven-haired, aquiline-nosed, high-achieving, and to our slow-witted astonishment sexually precocious, though not with any of us. Rumour had it she had a twenty-year-old Björn Borg-clone boyfriend who would meet her at the school gates in his Fiesta. We made a rapid reappraisal of our chances, and felt like the wee boys we were. But Kay Jack moved among them like a caryatid on castors, like a three-masted ship, its long bow doubtless bearing a figurehead of the likeness of Kay Jack. Kay was tall, impossibly upright in her bearing, and with the kind of facial symmetry that seemed to indicate God's personal oversight of the casting process, though admittedly symmetry was at more of a premium in a school where merely having one eye on either side of your nose was considered a good feature. Love might have blinded me to Kay's faults, which her vast Siberian husband may confirm are legion, but frankly I doubt it.

In fifth year, I was often told I looked like Jesus. The hood on my duffel coat was permanently raised, indoors and even in high summer; within this inky cowl my gaze was myopically and enigmatically unfocused, like Robert Powell's on the cross, as I wore my glasses only half the time I needed them. (I would also hail strangers and ignore friends on the street, which further added to my mystery.) I'd grown a wispy beard and my hair was worn very long and straight. It was naturally curly like John McEnroe's, but I hated the curls: I had developed a hair-flattening technique which involved encasing my entire head in Sellotape while the hair was still damp and letting it dry within the transparent helmet. This would work for a day or two, and the glue gave it a high sheen. Less messiah-like was the hankie I would sometimes fix over my nose with my glasses – I had a cold for two years straight – to catch the stream of clear snot that poured freely from my nostrils. It was, at least, a look too unique to be called merely a bad one.

One day Miss Abercrombie, a sexually liberated, witheringly sarcastic and very cool woman who was banging Mr Larbert in the brass band cupboard during playtime and had shagged at least one sixth-year after the Christmas school dance, asked for volunteers to serve as student representatives on the School Council. Kay put her hand up. So did I. As the least representative student in the school, I was hardly the man for the job, but I immediately saw the opportunity to walk Kay home one evening a month. Her house stood in its own high-walled garden, as mysterious and impregnable as Kay herself. Yet we would stand outside her gate and talk for hours. She may have been indulging me, but I doubt it; she lingered too long. She had large, clever and rather mannish hands, a slightly orange perma-tan (her father owned a couple of newsagent's, and they holidayed abroad at a time when few folk did), spoke in a fag-enhanced contralto and was possessed of the most beautifully regal face, which somehow managed both a certain *hauteur* and a total absence of judgement or condescension towards anyone. She was smart as hell and rigorously focused on her studies, but also horny for physically mature bad lads, which will have emphatically ruled me out. (She had enough self-knowledge to know it was a phase, but one which couldn't be skipped; for one tiny moment in their lives, these spunk-propelled morons get a crack at the alpha girls – but unlike them, imagine it may be forever. They never properly recover.) She forgave my wildly desperate efforts to impress and entertain. Some basic skills were honed: I learned that mere enthusiasm – say, my extended paean to the last Art Bears album ('Dagmar Krause is basically doing for Brecht what something did for something something,' I partly recall, with horror) – was not enough to hold someone's attention; I learned that a man who listened, and who could show that he had listened, was a valued thing; I also learned that if I casually claimed an expertise, I had to back it up if evidence was suddenly demanded. (Maybe all I learned is that some things are way easier to bluff than others. One can plausibly pass oneself off as being gifted in aura-reading and Swedish massage; juggling and gas oven repair, less so. It turns out.) I also learned that I straightforwardly preferred the company of women. I was probably as in love with Kay as I've been with anyone, though very much doubt I was alone.

After I left school our paths rarely crossed, but I carried a travel-sized Olympic torch for her for a good long while. I met Kay once again, on the purgatorial fourteen-hour London-to-Dundee bus after I'd moved south. I'd have been twenty-one, and she will have been studying in Manchester. Unbelievably, we found ourselves seated next to each other. We talked about our lives: she was thinking of specialising in obs & gynae; I was working as a guitarist on the London free jazz scene. I talked about my ongoing and broadly successful efforts to make my instrument sound like a bag of spanners; she used the word 'endogenous', conversationally. We should have been light years apart, but hit it off as well as ever. She fell asleep with her head on my shoulder. I didn't dare move lest she wake and adjust her position, so didn't sleep a wink; I prayed we'd miss a turn-off and that the journey would never end. But I was still 'too boiled and shy and poker-faced to make a pass', and that was that. I will persist in the belief that, if I had, it would have been kindly rebuffed, because my life has seen tragedy enough.

25 Nowhere Fast

I finally succumbed to the guitar at the age of fourteen. Few things in my life have begun with such a sense of helpless inevitability. US pool tables . . . No, that's about it. Not that my pool game is any great shakes. But it will be. I worked for several years as a music teacher in London. I had a guitar student, a Basque girl called Edie Bidarte. She was a strange, deep and wise soul who had spent several minutes dead on the road after a motorbike accident, and hung with a very strange group of twilighters who spent their evenings liberating suicides from purgatory, where apparently they get stuck. She talked about it so matter-of-factly that it was hard not to just simply believe her. Edie was a hopeless, flat-fingered student, and I advised her to pack it in, but she kept on turning up for class. She'd say, 'I *know* I'm terrible! But you gotta start sometime. You *do* know that Pablo Casals was five crap cellists before he was Pablo Casals.'

I realised I'd only been avoiding the guitar because I was trying to not be my father. I got over myself, picked up his Yamaha acoustic and slapped a DeArmond pickup in the soundhole, like John Martyn. My father was delighted, but he'd been steering me in this direction for years. Knowing that the Patersons can't be taught anything – not through any arrogance, just a congenital inability to pay attention – his pedagogical approach was just to leave decent instruments lying around, and if I had any questions, he'd answer them. (I did the same with my kids, and it seems to work well.) Starting as I meant to go on, rather than learn something actually useful like a C or G chord, I tried to find a shape that sounded cool. From fifth to top string it went – not that I knew this yet, but I can see the chord now – A, G, B, another open B, F# – and I sat strumming this vibey, ambient suspension for hours. I'd been tripping out on a track called 'RFD' from the not-that-great Quiet Sun album. I made up two more stupid chords, and in another fake-it-till-you-make-it move that outdid even my Mozartian youth, I put an ad in the Dundee *Courier*, between 'Orraman Wanted' and 'Top-loading washer for sale', for 'Avant-garde jazz guitarist seeks like minds'. Thankfully no one replied.

Soon I was thinking of little else. The minute I got home from school I'd sling the guitar strap over my head, and there it would remain, through tea, TV, supper, trips to the kettle and the toilet, until bedtime. I'd grope for the guitar as soon as I woke, and practised in bed, flat on my back. I'd walk round the estate with the thing permanently round my neck, even if I was going to the shop for milk. I learned a couple of blues scales. Dad was prematurely proud and keen to show me off. (All fathers fantasise about playing on stage with their sons. Tragically, no sons fantasise about playing with their fathers.) I made my reluctant debut at the Edzell RAF base, hacking through 'Truck Drivin' Man' and backing Dad on 'Ghost Riders in the Sky'. RAF Edzell was at the time used by the US Navy, an exotic and handsome cohort whose irresistible appeal to the natives had to be formally accommodated somehow, and left the already deeply weird town of Edzell a notorious hotbed of swinging, long after they'd left.

While I figured out some theory myself – I have a systematising kind of brain – I didn't have a clue what I was doing. However, for many years my dad had subscribed to a magazine called *BMG*, formerly *Banjo Mandolin Guitar* – 'The Oldest Established and Most Widely Read Fretted Instrument Magazine in the World' – and he'd kept every copy. *BMG* dated back to the pre-World War I age of banjo orchestras, when the mandolin had a large classical repertoire and the guitar was a kind of parlour eccentricity. Editorially, *BMG* was supremely conservative, and for years had regarded black-and-white minstrels as something of a leftist plot to steal gigs from Pierrot bands; as for rock and roll, it was a virus from outer space, and it would one day vanish as mysteriously as it had arrived. But if you could navigate your way past columns on why the Electrical Plectrum Guitar would never usurp the Eb Zither Banjo and the sheet music for 'Darkie's Lament', you could find some wonderful stuff on harmony, theory and technique. *BMG* was also worth reading for the columns and reviews; by today's standards the writing was Conradian (the great English guitar composer John W. 'Jack' Duarte wrote a regular and generally brilliant column, dripping in sarcasm), but I didn't know Conrad from a hole in the ground, and I just assumed all magazines were written like that. I still read back-copies for the pleasure of reminding myself what criticism looked like long before social media, when your honest appraisal of a sub-par recording or a brutal assessment of a rival would not result in a dogpile on Twitter or doxxing on Facebook, and there would be no consequence for your honest speech – unless someone was prepared to take two days off work to go down to the town hall, scour the electoral register, find your address, take three connecting trains to Loughborough and then walk two miles to punch you in the head. In the pages of *BMG*, no reputation was spared. 'Finally, we turn to yet another disc from the young Paco de Lucía, who continues to disappoint. The album opens with some wretched *bulerías* which, for all their fleet-fingered execution, confirms the suspicion that our prematurely balding *Wunderkind* has had his soul removed by surgical procedure in exchange for empty facility. One has encountered more *duende* in a can of lentil soup,' etc.

Most of all, though, I wanted to play *fast*. Almost all apprentice guitarists desire speed above all other technical accomplishments, for speed wows the ignorant. (For some reason the gold standard on almost all instruments, including the guitar, remains not the Paganini *Caprices* but 'The Flight of the Bumblebee', and attempts to dispatch the wretched thing in record time, especially on the violin, have long been a staple of daytime television. All such chancers operate on the common principle that the faster you play, the less scrutiny will fall on each individual note, and these performances less resemble music than attempts to file the instrument into sawdust.) After about a year of solid practice I could rip up and down my scales pretty well. Although I switched permanently to playing fingerstyle at about twenty-five – I was harmony-obsessed, and besides, it brings you physically a step closer to the instrument – I first formed the dubious apprentice habit of cleanly articulating every note with a pick, which makes as much musical sense as tonguing every note on a trumpet, i.e. none. I was following the example of my then obsession, an awful, shades-and-open-shirt jazz guitarist called Al Di Meola, who'd then released *Land of the Midnight Sun* and *Elegant Gypsy*. Al has long been regarded on the shop floor as the David Brent of jazz, but at fifteen I took his advice very seriously. Now that I watch him, Al's technique isn't something you'd ever want to imitate. The idea is to make it look as if your hands are hardly moving; his look like Mr Bean practising air piano.*

But then I suffered the mortified joy of discovering the British virtuosi John McLaughlin and Allan Holdsworth in the same week, and saw that I had to start cutting down on sleep. *The South Bank Show* had a special on McLaughlin's acoustic Indo-jazz fusion band Shakti, because TV in the seventies was like that. McLaughlin and L. Shankar, the young violin prodigy, sat cross-legged facing each other, stared into one another's eyes and started up the ballad 'Two Sisters'. Having had no previous inkling that such music existed in the universe,

---

* Frank Zappa was onto him in 1979. There's a fade-out jam on a song in *Joe's Garage* where Frank goes: 'Just like an elegant gypsy!' and then throws in a couple of Al's going-nowhere, knitting-machine dribble-runs.

I burst into tears on the spot – involuntarily, like someone had punched me hard, for no reason: why did you do *that*? (I later read of John Fahey's hearing Blind Willie Johnson for the first time, and recognised it immediately – the weeping, the confusion, the nausea; Fahey describes it as a 'hysterical conversion experience'.) When I came round, I realised it was all in the feeling, the timing, the phrasing, the articulation, the nuance. McLaughlin might have been known for spitting out notes like an AK-47, but there was a lot more to his technique than speed, and he played with a huge feeling it served only to articulate. As present and correct as all these things were, 'Two Sisters' wasn't about the notes, or technique, or intellectual sophistication, or musical rivalry, or any of the other things music was quickly becoming about. It was about what it *said* it was about, two sisters, and the music was in service utterly to its theme and to itself. I started to wonder if I'd ever actually *heard* music before. (The held gaze of jazz musicians is unique to the genre. It's intimate, but not sexual; you're listening too hard. You do it to lock on to the same digital frequency, the point being to then have as intense a conversation as you dare; this can't take place unless your senses of nuance and timing are in alignment. Outside of its tea-for-two incarnations, in jazz there is generally little small talk.)

My dad then took me to see Allan Holdsworth in a concert arranged by Big Rab, who was then bringing some world-class musicians to Dundee. Rab sold these gigs in the time-honoured fashion of lying to the *Courier* about their Dundee connections; as long as it went via the news desk, no one questioned it. 'Famous Jazz Man Bennie Wallace Is Heir to Wallace's Scotch Pie Fortune'. 'Famous Polish Jazz Man Tomasz Stańko Surprised to Discover He Went to Primary School in Mid Craigie'. The gig wasn't a classic – no one was looking at anyone else except in anger, and it sounded like it – but I was blown away by the band's staggering lack of professionalism, the opposite of the slick prog acts I'd been listening to. If someone embarked on a long solo, someone else would go to the bar. The solos were endless, so the bar did good trade; the band got drunk, and worse. Holdsy correctly felt he hadn't had his best night – though I later learned that he *always* felt that, even when he had – and ended up hammered, and sobbing at the bar over his poor performance. But I just didn't get it. Even on this evidence, he was clearly a better musician than anyone for a thousand miles in any direction. I understood this when I later read an interview with Frank Zappa; Frank said he only hired musicians who thought they couldn't play. This usually indicated they were merely in a losing competition with their own absurdly high standards.* I

---

* Zappa believed in acquainting musicians with the limits of their ability, lest pride make them slack. I collect initiation stories, and among my favourites is Steve Vai's tale of his audition for the Zappa band. Frank had asked him to learn some punishingly difficult material in advance – and then didn't call any of those tunes at the rehearsal. Instead he threw Steve charts that he hadn't had a chance to look at, all of them black with notes. Then Frank played a tricksy guitar lick, in no earthly scale. 'Play this. Okay. Now add this note. Now play it in 7/8. Okay. Now keep it in 7/8, but play it *reggae*. Now add this phrase

bought some jazz theory books and gained another half-hour a day by playing on the toilet.

I also got competitive. Martin Hyatt was the best guitarist within three schemies, and was notable for his rhythmic prowess and the weird way he said the word 'mattress', with the accent on the last syllable. Luckily, few sentences had to deploy it, but still. He played in a band with Billy MacKenzie's wee brother John, and other bits of the Associates. I quickly got faster than Martin, who had a huge Roland JC-120, which in those days made a hiss like a chippie fat-fryer even on zero volume, but compared with my HH PA head – less a guitar amp than a way of declaring a general emergency – still sounded like plugging into St Martin in the Fields. It was then I dimly realised that amps are part of your instrument, and that the HH might be the problem. (Many jazz musicians remain in denial all their lives, and regard amplification as a necessary evil, or, indeed, the enemy.)

Then there was Steve Rizza. Steve was handsome, bearded,

---

to it. Now add *this* note up here.' Frank kept making increasingly absurd demands, until he finally asked Steve to play something that was a physical impossibility, for any human, anywhere. Steve said as much. Frank sneered, and delivered the now-legendary line, 'I hear Linda Ronstadt's looking for a guitar player.' At the end of a nightmare afternoon, Steve, just twenty years old and thoroughly humiliated, started to pack up. He apologised, and thanked Frank for the opportunity, and said he felt he'd best go home now. Frank said, 'Huh? You're in the band.' Steve hugged him. The precious things should be hard to obtain.

reputedly heir to a famous Dundee ice cream fortune, lived in a posh house in Broughty Ferry, and could play at astonishing speed, Holdsworth-legato style. I picked my speed up again, but there always seemed to be someone faster than me. But no sooner had I approximated Steve's bpm than I discovered another guitarist on the local scene, whose name I will redact but who was known at the time as 'Brrrrrrrp-Fuck' on account of the sound he made when he was practising. (He went on to patent a new kind of plectrum for playing at warp speed, made of glass or something.) It was the tiniest flapping bird all over again, and shame and failure loomed.

It dawned on me, slowly, that I really had to stop treating the guitar as a sport. I decided I'd better join a real band, any band. I auditioned for The Abortions, a gratifyingly short-lived affair, though it would be funnier if I could tell you they were still going. I was auditioned by a pink-Mohicaned, multiply self-pierced septic punk from the Dryburgh estate and a mysterious guy in shades and a trench coat. (I am fairly sure this was Steve Falconer, who later changed his name by deed poll to Bread Poultice, of Bread Poultice & the Running Sores. A part of his on-stage shtick was to announce that he'd now 'play guitar in the style of Jimi Hendrix, with my teeth', which he would then remove and use as a plectrum.) I ripped through a few Mahavishnu Orchestra riffs on my shit Chinese Strat as they listened in respectful silence. I joined in on a two-chord, one-minute number called, I think, 'She's a Fucking Nutter'. They were the soul of kindness. 'Uh – wih really like yer playin', man, but it's more o an image thing, if ye ken what wir sayin'.' I was wearing full school uniform and black NHS specs with one leg repaired with pink Elastoplast, which they had initially interpreted as a punk signifier, though they now seemed up to speed. I then got in tow with an odd and doomed lad with a wispy moustache who really wanted to form a covers duo called Horse. He already had a wife and kid at twenty. He was a nice guy with a good voice, and he played well, but he creeped me out for reasons I could not explain. I see now that it was because he'd arrived pre-defeated, and I was afraid I'd catch it. He also lived in McLean Street, and regression terrifies us. One of the nastiest things about humans is the way we too quickly quarantine those we think are losers, which absolutely guarantees their losing. I went back to playing with my dad, only much, much faster.

26 Stairwell to Heaven

When I was a wee boy, my father used to take me to Largs Music Supplies in town to look at the guitars he couldn't afford. The guitar department lay in the basement at the foot of a wide, red stair, and was somewhere between a funeral parlour and a reptile house: two twilit, red-carpeted corridors arranged in a U, the guitars displayed in bright glass cases flush with the walls, where they reclined in proconsular luxury against waterfalls of peach and strawberry silks. They bore impossible prices, half a year's wages, and were as distant as another life. Who bought them? It was a mystery. How badly I wanted these guitars for my dad, those Gretsches, Gibsons, Guilds and Martins, those cathedrals of ebony and ash and maple. We'd walk along that underground street, stopping at every window to admire some bit of abalone purfling or polished rosewood, until we reached the counter at the turn of the U. There my father would talk quietly and sometimes darkly to Mr Dunn about his hire-purchase payment on whatever downmarket box he was playing that year.

He did own the first Yamaha acoustic in Dundee, however – a surprisingly fine FG-180, which I eventually bought from him; he couldn't have afforded to upgrade to another guitar otherwise. The idea of selling my kid a guitar seems bizarre now – it would certainly seem so to my own kid, for what's mine is clearly his, to judge by the stupid hipster tunings he's always leaving my guitars in – but in those days, working-class families bought and sold from each other, to seal the money in. Later, I almost ruined the Yamaha by following John Martyn in the grievously misguided practice of sanding down the soundboard until you can see the light through it. This makes the instrument louder, but weakens it fatally. Many who followed this briefly fashionable advice woke one morning to find the guitar had just imploded under its two-hundred-odd pounds of string tension. I saw an instrument do this once, sucked instantly into its own soundhole; it looked like *The Scream*.

Dad often recounted the non-anecdote of the time he ordered a cheap Harmony sunburst mandolin and didn't tell my mother, hoping he could sneak it into the house unseen. He was tormented over his deception. It was delivered while he was at work, in a plainly mandolin-shaped box; on returning at teatime he decided not to try passing it off as a toy coffin for next door or whatever, and to face the music. Only there was confusingly little music to face, and the story would end there, with a little sidenote on my mum's generosity and capacity for forgiveness. But what Dad didn't understand was that Mum was then developing a serious hire-purchase problem, and racking up a formidable tab at Goldbergs for soft furnishings he was too music-obsessed to notice: my dad could rise from a pink sofa in the morning and plonk himself down on a green one in the evening without remark, if his copy of *BMG* magazine had arrived in the meantime. My mum had plenty guilt of her own, and being no gaslighter wasn't inclined to displace it by guilt-tripping anyone else. (In 2016, immediately after he received his dementia diagnosis, my dad's first move was to go straight down to the vintage guitar shop in the Perth Road and put a serious ding in his superannuation with a beautiful Faith steel-string, far and away the best instrument he'd owned in his life. He had his speech prepared – 'I am no longer in full control of my senses' – and a doctor's note to back it up. Hero. Of course, my mother didn't put him through it, and let the matter go without a word.)

But those beautiful guitars let us know we were poor. Largs was good at this. The upstairs floor, Largs Electrical, was the *mise en scène* of my one class-shame poem, whose occasion I'll describe shortly. I used to think I'd written only one class-shame poem because I had nothing more to say on the matter. I later realised I had plenty more to say on the matter, but I wasn't going to say it in a poem for what would inevitably be the entertainment of a largely middle-class constituency. I mean no sneer by this, because these are now my people. One excepts the fake leftists of the liberal middle class, who are definitely not my people, and whose efforts to remain both guilty of and in charge of everything drive me to distraction. On the other hand, I have little patience for those essentialists who still claim to be somehow *constitutionally* working class when their postcodes, properties, incomes, tastes and education now clearly scream otherwise. (Class is more like country of residence; when you emigrate, that's where you live now. My mother's agony was down to her being sent back, in her mind at least, from Brooklyn to the shtetl.) This is a hard thing for transitional classes like mine to admit, since they want to exist in both classes out of retrospective solidarity and present ambition, but you pays your money. Anyway, as Margaret Thatcher knew when she put all council property up for purchase by its tenants, the *actual* working class is a class by default, and while it's fine with that, it would generally prefer to be another one. The first thing most folk did in the eighties was switch from a council rent to a mortgage, and stick a giant white-painted cartwheel by the door and a stone lion by the gate.

As for that poem: my Uncle Iain, Mum's younger half-brother, lived for many years with my Nana and Papa in the manse in Tayport. His wage at DC Thomson all seemed to go on quality hi-fi, which was set up in the drawing room where Papa would counsel his parishioners. The room had seen much whispering and weeping and praying over the previous three decades, and had a hushed and sepulchral air that made it seem as if it was actively listening. After a family dinner one Sunday, Iain took me and Dad through to the drawing room, while the invisible kitchen fairies worked their magic. The Wishbone Ash album he played wasn't quite my dad's sort of thing, but he was astonished by the fidelity, which was very high, and had apparently dialled up the band straight into a Tayport bay window. We had a Philips 'music centre', an all-in-one record-cum-cassette-cum-radio-cum-teasmade with a smoked-plastic lid that had cost Dad a packet, and which he now realised also sounded like shit. He asked Iain what was making the difference. Iain described the speakers (vast), the amplifier (separate, valve-driven) and the stylus (elliptical). My dad's ears pricked up: that might be the one bit he could afford. Largs had a hi-fi store upstairs, and we went in to ask after an elliptical stylus. The head of sales enquired as to what kind of tone arm we'd be fitting it to. While my dad described his smoked-plastic music centre – Dad was a nervous talker, and always explained everything in irrelevant detail, and at far too much length – the guy's smirk grew and grew. 'Sir – if I can just pause you there – I'm afraid it sounds as if you'd have to *substantially* upgrade your equipment.' I could tell he was delighted with how that sentence had gone. I resolved to one day be delighted with how some of my own sentences would go too, especially the ones which lingeringly described his kidnap, torture and slow death. My dad tried to save face and bought some new needles he had no use for, and then – to quote me on the matter – we drove home slowly, as if we'd had a puncture.

Nonetheless, my father's loyalty to Largs over the years helped me land a part-time job in the guitar department at fifteen. The place had changed to an ugly, strip-lit, stack-'em-high emporium. The guitars were now all on open display, as they were no longer worth stealing. Mr Dunn was still at the helm, a deeply straight but kindly old guy in pinstripes, from the era when sales wasn't a consonantal rhyme for sleaze. Then there was Nigel, the coming man. Nigel was a moustachioed Geordie in a terrible moire suit apparently woven from two shades of nylon, raspberry sauce and algae, which made him look like a giant bleeding frog. Nigel was all twinkly charm, and could've sold Gary Numan a ukulele or the Rev. Ian Paisley *The Dubliners Songbook*. Invisible among the Saturday staff was also one Ged Grimes, later to re-emerge as the bassist with every Scottish stadium band of any note, though Ged started in a Dundee band called Danny Wilson, who had a UK smash with a divine pop song called 'Mary's Prayer'. Ged was the real thing, and therefore completely off the radar. (Danny Wilson, named for the Sinatra film, were led by Gary Clark, a genius of a musician who had sprung fully formed from the mottled thigh of the Douglas estate. I sat in with him anonymously a couple of times at The Breadalbane Arms, aka The Bread, where most of us had our first pint while we were still in shorts. Gary was already a pro at sixteen. His only impediment to superstardom was that, while possessed of a voice like Marvin Gaye, the guitar chops of Jeff Beck and the songwriting skills of a Bacharach, he looked like G. K. Chesterton in dungarees, and no amount of imaginative lighting and jaunty berets could disguise this fact. He now spends his life in a windowless bunker in LA churning out bangers.*)

At that age, real talent tends to go completely under the radar. We were wowed instead by Steve, a seventeen-year-old, tall, elfin-eared, raven-haired, feather-mulleted unisex dreamboat. Steve had been drawn by Cocteau in an opium fug, with the other hand on his dick: the roe-deer upper lip, the nose-job

---

* No, I just googled him: he's back in Dundee, working on a musical of *Nanny McPhee* with Emma Thompson. It'll be great.

nose, the distracted myopia, that particular kind of narcissistic melancholy that seems designed to convey only that its wearer would, on the most inscrutable whim, fuck anybody or anything – or indeed not fuck you for a million if you were the last fuckable thing in the universe. His impossibly glamorous weekends were a torment to me. He was into 'experimental sex', and loved to taunt me over my virginity, which I wore on my sleeve like a black armband. I would labour over the careful arrangement of the strings and capos and plectrums just to defer a little longer his usual opener of: 'So what did you get up last night.' Like that, without the question mark. Me? Hell, I had arpeggiated the largely useless minor$\Delta 7\flat 13$ chord in seven positions and all keys, until I could see the fretboard pattern like a giant molecule as I fell asleep, and its intervals merge with whatever shape I was dreaming about folding Miss Walker (Latin) into. That's what I'd done, and I was keeping it to myself. 'Not much. And yourself, Steve,' I'd ask – although here the question mark was omitted more in sapped resignation than indifference to the reply. At least he made no pretence he was doing anything other than rubbing it in. Steve had spent the evening in a Jacuzzi in Carnoustie with identical twins and a dead puppy, or in a lift with three girls from Harris Academy and their PE teacher, or in his mum's bed with his aunt while his uncle beat off in the wardrobe, or – sick of the world and its need of him – on his own, with a mirror, some poppers, a noose and a jar of meat.

– Still a virgin, Donald?

– Yup, Steve. Still a virgin.

Immaculately coiffed and manicured, his skin bearing the light sheen and fragrance of some unisex posing grease, the cool oozed from Steve. He stole packets of strings and whole tubes of plectrums, flagrantly. He played in a post-punk band called Steve and the Somethings. (Punk went post- faster than anything. We couldn't wait to get it over with.) Eventually, after much pleading from us, he played us a demo of a tune called 'We Got the Cans in the Cortina', being a lyric précis of some lager-fuelled weekend sexual anabasis. It was an ugly thing, with Steve affecting the then obligatory Ian Dury accent. The Dundee accent is similar to Cockney in that there are few terminal consonants, and sentences are often just one long fluid vowel chopped up by glottal stops. Thus a statement like *I ate all of it, didn't I* – a common enough response amongst the Dundonian lower orders to most food-related enquiries – becomes *Eh ai' aa' o' i' di' 'uh*. Had Steve been from the estates he would have managed it effortlessly. However, had Steve been from the estates he would also have been one of the stunted indigenous pizza-faced poor, i.e. not Steve. Being from good white-collar stock in Broughty Ferry, the chorus came out like *We gok da kens inna kaw keenaa*. Some horrible monosynth 'riff' buzzed away throughout, like a wasp stuck in a jam jar. Then Nigel bravely pointed out most of the tune had been lifted straight from The Kinks' 'You Really Got Me'. Steve's white grease appeared to run a little, and proposed the ghost of a blush below; but he hardly missed a beat as his lovely upper lip curled like an exhausted wave, and he berated us for being so slow to rumble such a crude plagiarism. Somehow we were left looking like the stupid party again. Nonetheless, I felt a strange creeping sensation I had not known before, which therefore took me a while to name: superiority.

Amongst the mass-produced East German clunkers and Taiwanese coffins that lined the walls were a couple of superb instruments, still unsold from ten years earlier. Looking at them translated me again to that old dark underworld Largs used to be, that gloomy lyre emporium where folk would strike their Faustian deals, literally putting their health or marriage on the dotted line. Above all, I coveted a lovely cherry-red Guild acoustic. It cost £450, a wholly fantastic sum. At quarter to five every Saturday, when the whole shop was still ringing from the last choked power chord from the last assault on 'Paranoid', I'd plead with Mr Dunn for 'a wee go' and retire to the back room, bearing the Guild like a Beefeater with a sceptre. There I'd do nothing more than play a few notes, and listen back to them.

Good acoustic guitars, in my book, are all wide and deep and loud. Not for me those tinny, buzzy Nationals, or the Maccaferris that were designed to cut through on a pre-war radio. There is an exquisite rule, though: loudness is reduced as the action is decreased, the action being the space between the strings and the fretboard. An action of one millimetre is as easy as air guitar, and in the hands of a decent musician feels like playing a kazoo. Alas, it also sounds like one, and is effectively a rubber band stretched over a matchbox. At two millimetres the character of the instrument starts to blossom, but the strings also offer a fair resistance. Higher still, and the guitar can fully write its own acoustic signature, and becomes its own auditorium, a self-amplifying miracle. By then, though, it's a perfect agony to play. The hard-core high-action brigade are mostly French 'gypsy' guitarists with fingers as weirdly overdeveloped as Roger Federer's serving arm – these guys could flick a nail through your head – or US redneck bluegrass flatpickers with huge Martin dreadnoughts who string their guitars like pianos, keep squash balls in their left pockets, coat their fingertips in superglue, and bugger each other angrily in the woods. The cherry-red Guild, though, was set up on the middle-way principle, an angel of a guitar fallen amongst the world of men. Every scale sounded as clear as a mountain stream, and every chord was so much fairy campanology. Steve heard me practise and screwed up his pretty nose. 'It's all just *runs*, isn't it.' It was indeed all just runs, but I knew what they had cost me, and so did he.

One Saturday, Steve didn't ask his usual question, for which I was grateful; but then I grew curious at his own silence, so I asked him if he was okay. He was vulnerably greaseless that day and clearly fighting back the tears, so I didn't push it. I never learned why but intuited from Nigel's brusque shake of the head that I shouldn't pursue the matter further. All I could guess was that some aspect of his regular Friday night saturnalia had somehow gotten beyond his immediate control. I shuddered to think. Steve recovered his aura of cool soon enough, but thereafter was a bit broken, which made me grieve for him. As insufferable as he was, I liked him perfect.

To say I had few social skills at this time would be too generous. I had negative capability, and every conversational gambit was the mere conjecture of a shipwrecked Venusian. I had heard somewhere that slagging folk off was good, because men liked to unite round a common grievance, and that swearing was good too, but hadn't heard the bit that said the alphas have to choose the target and set the tone. I would regale the male staff and most of the customers with much comradely f-ing and c-ing, and was soon taken aside by the worldly Nigel, who was kind enough to sketch in the first few rules of human society. By then, though, I'd left myself with too much ground to make up. Anyway, the shop floor was killing me. These days, there is a universal ban on playing a handful of songs in guitar stores: from Minsk to Albuquerque, you will be hurled into the street should you broach 'Smoke on the Water', 'Sultans of Swing' by Dire Straits (a single bluff of a band name that at least has the merit of saving time) or the dreaded opening bars of 'Stairway to Heaven', which at least you can shut down before it gets started. Guitar salesfolk pride themselves on a three-note response time here. ('Bing bing bing . . .' 'NO. JUST NO.') This was their guitar-store heyday, though, and all one heard from nine to six. The other weekend hazard was the afternoon drunks, who were always emboldened to try the most expensive gear. Big Rab reported a conversation between two plastered jakies; one had plugged in a Les Paul and was painfully wrestling it into some semblance of EADGBE. Then he cranked up the amp and prepared to let rip.

– Right. Noo Ah'm gonnae make this guitar *talk*.

– Aye. And when it does, it's gonnae say 'You're shite.'

Although I could shift a mean plectrum, the bigger sales were passing me by. Guitars were sold the way Nigel sold them, through what seemed to be some kind of close-up-magic misdirection, or the way Steve sold them, by playing the first four bars of the dreadful 'Theme from *The Deer Hunter* Otherwise Known as Cavatina or He Was Beautiful', then shooting a conspiratorial look at the buyer – raised eyebrow, lopsided half-smile, a kind of inaudible microsnort – whereupon they both tacitly agreed the fifth bar was below him, and does this guitar work or *what*. I knew, though, the fifth bar was also beyond him, and he knew I knew. Mr Dunn also knew I knew, but requested, reasonably, that I *also* learn the first four bars of 'Cavatina', from Steve. Demonstrating shite three-quid Chinese guitars by a violent burst of one of my favourite intervallic studies (I had still not actually learned a *tune*) was not likely to impress a mother who only wanted it so her wee girl could learn the chords in *The Grease Songbook*. As I would have eaten Steve's tapeworm before I'd have taken a guitar lesson from him, I flatly refused, and sealed my fate. Mr Dunn soon informed me that Central Office had directed him to lose staff, and as I had been there the shortest time, it was with great regret, and all that. I believed him, and so suffered no great loss of pride.

Foolishly returning the following Saturday for a chat with the guys, I was at the foot of the stairs when I caught the sugary-sick strains of 'Cavatina' again, and quickly registered the performer was at least ten bars into it. I turned round and went home, trying to remember if they'd used it in that bit where Christopher Walken shoots himself in Saigon. Because they should have.

27 Un-American Activities

One of the hardest things to explain to your kids is The Work of Art in the Age of Mechanical Reproduction but Before Your Dad Had a Cassette Recorder. For much of the seventies, one strongly sensed that one's copy of an album wasn't a copy of anything. There was one of it. It could not be duplicated, and only replaced at great expense and inconvenience. It could be borrowed, which was fraught with danger, with assurances and sureties often wrung from the borrower. As for its purchase, you couldn't afford to get it wrong: the candidate disc would be weighed up for weeks, meticulously researched in *Melody Maker* and *NME* reviews, then subjected to all the stages of courtly love: mooned over, dreamed about, sniffed, warily auditioned, checked in the shop for its immaculate virginity. It was then played until it would play no more, its every note and word burned into the mind, its lyrics and artwork and sleeve notes subjected to exhaustive exegesis, every track's fade-out turned up for some human leakage, and its one long groove manually spun backwards for anything you might have missed.

But then Dad finally got his 'music centre', that aforementioned seventies mega-appliance that assembled every noise-making device short of a CB radio into one handy seven-foot unit. They seemed to pride themselves on their insane technophilic complexity, and had a knob or button or slider for every possible function, because more was more. (I mean: who in the history of the race ever wanted to turn Dolby *off*.) Their built-in double cassette recorders meant not only that *The Peel Show* could be preserved for later review, or an inferior version of your record spun off, but copies of copies made too. The magic aura of the original vinyl was, however, a long time in fading. Even after cassettes were commonly shared, the album was still the priceless incunabulum. Each one represented an investment in not just your own cultural stock, but your cultural meaning; they *embodied* your tastes. Your Spotify playlist only indicates them.

I had steadily turned away from the smoothed Rs and note-perfect studio aesthetic of American music towards the UK and Europe, and had been teetering on the edge of entering what would have proved a catastrophic prog phase, i.e. a prog phase. I was listening a lot to Premiata Forneria Marconi's *Photos of Ghosts*. Italian prog-rock bands were then markedly superior to their UK counterparts, and PFM could even play jazz, sort of. But it was still prog, and therefore heroically daft. Something had also gone badly wrong with the lyrics. I assume this was down to a tonal miscalculation on the translator's part; it sounded like King Crimson had accidentally hired Richard Stilgoe and just decided, unwisely, to brazen it out. Even I felt stupid singing along to 'Tea and biscuits secretary's legs / Luncheon daydreams over curried eggs', especially in an Italian accent.* On the other, admittedly only slightly different, hand – I learned the words to every Van der Graaf Generator and Peter Hammill album I could afford. By heart, it turns out. My brother and I sang all seven and a half minutes of 'Still Life' in the car the other day, in Hammill's Olivierian baritone, horrified to find we knew every word. The lyrics could not be described as underblown. 'Citadel reverberates to a thousand voices / now dumb. O what have we become? What have we chosen to be?' But while Hammill was terrible, he was also great, and the only progger the punks would publicly endorse. (John Lydon used to sneak into the back of Van der Graaf gigs, and if you listen to 'Ship of Fools' on the *Vital* album you can see why, because it sounds like the sky being ripped in two.) The reasonable objection to all prog is that it is too bombastic and ridiculous for anyone to possibly mean it. Hammill was bombastic and ridiculous, but he meant it, and violently so.

One morning I was in Groucho's (the iconic Dundee vinyl shop, only recently closed), swithering between two albums. One was *Rock Bottom* by Robert Wyatt – I'd recently read a brilliant article on Wyatt by Ian Penman in the *NME* that I'd cut out and stuck to the bedroom wall – and the other was a Gentle Giant album, *Free Hand*. I occasionally watch Gentle

---

* In the name of diligent research, I've just listened to 'Mr. 9 'till 5' again for the first time in forty years. I commend it to you urgently. It's fucking brilliant. Maybe it's finally time for my prog phase.

Giant on YouTube to remind myself that our fates often depend on the caprices of an instant. They were nothing if not hugely entertaining. A band of absurdly high musical ability, they had no idea what to do with it whatsoever, and so made the interesting decision to make some of the worst music in human history. Even for proggers, they looked unusually clueless. They were led by a chunky lad in a white jumpsuit with an overtrimmed beard from a police reconstruction, who bounded about the stage like a fat toddler on a sugar high, one hand on his hip, the other practising baton twirls with an invisible pencil; the drummer was in a football strip, the keyboard player in a silver cape, the guitarist in yellow children's-TV dungarees, the bassist dressed as Stalin, etc. Despite all their multi-instrumental virtuosity – they were the kind of band who could suddenly regroup as a credible string quartet, just to play sixteen bars in the middle of some twelve-minute elf-worrying epic – they still achieved moments of quite splendid overreach, like breaking into hideously approximate four-part a cappella fugues that sounded as if Man United had been somehow taught to sight-read. Unlike Hammill, whose songs were at least about death, eternity and the Decline of the West, their songs focused on pressing matters like 'the corrupt nature of the music business'. I had money for one album that month, and would have felt defensively obliged to be into *that* shite for at least a year.

Instead, my hand drifted over to Alfreda Benge's faux-naïf pencil-drawn seascape that formed the magnolia cover of *Rock Bottom*, and stayed there. Into the white plastic bag it went, and I carried it home on the bus, as carefully as a goldfish. I had learned from Penman that *Rock Bottom* was the first album Wyatt had made after the terrible fall that broke his back and left him paralysed. (Party–drunk–toilet–indiscretion–escape–drainpipe seems to be the synoptic account.) 'Sea Song' was its opener. Okay: let's give this a go. The bold major chord of its wobbly organ declared that this was going to be a straightforward kind of song. The second told you it absolutely wasn't. It was the dominant chord a tone above, which then resolved to its own tonic, meaning that the first chord hadn't been the tonic after all, but the subdominant. I mean . . . you don't do that. Essentially the song started after it had already started, like a story that began 'But that night he decided he had best leave the door unlocked.' Huh? And then we waved goodbye to that first chord, never to be heard again, as the chords slipped below the waterline and fell away, one after another, down some weird, plagal, sinking route until they came to a rest on the seabed, in a key a flat fifth down from the one the song had started in, which is to say in its shadow-key, as far away as possible. This was before Wyatt had even opened his mouth. What then unfolded was an impossibly lovely, weird affair. The lyrics seemed to be half maritime eroticism ('Partly fish, partly porpoise, partly baby sperm whale / Am I yours? Are you mine to play with?'), half wry English demotic ('Joking apart, when you're drunk you're terrific / When you're drunk, I like you mostly late at night; you're quite alright . . .'), whose poetry lay, like Cavafy's, in their alternation of register between high and low. The album also had my first proper jazz on it, with London players from the South African expat roster, like the trumpeter Mongezi Feza, and a smattering of the usual Canterbury left-fielders. In 'Little Red Robin Hood Hit the Road' there was even a spot from an actual poet, the Scottish surrealist Ivor Cutler, talking some mad blethers in his 'Come Missa Tally Man' voice about tripping up cars with a hedgehog, although the Wyatt lyrics that preceded it were the superior poetry, and – as I would later learn – matched Geoffrey Hill's Mercian Hymns in the active imagination of their detail: 'In the gardens of England dead moles lie inside their holes. / The dead-end tunnels crumble in the rain, underfoot.' The whole thing floored me like an anti-prog ray gun, and *Photos of Ghosts* went back to Groucho's for the credit note so I could buy *Rock Bottom*'s follow-up, *Ruth Is Stranger Than Richard.**

I spent my fifteenth year in my black bedroom, wearing my huge Mickey Mouse headphones, trying to extrude a beard by sheer force of will, and endlessly skinning up on *Rock Bottom*'s

---

* Wyatt stopped drumming too soon to ever receive the acclaim of the technically superior John Marshall, who replaced him in Soft Machine, legendary jazz drunk Phil Seaman ('Just drop me off in the Cally Road Danny.' 'We ain't done the gig yet Phil.'), the personally appalling and frankly overrated Ginger Baker, or the somewhat overpraised biddly-bosh-bump austerities of Dave Mattacks (sorry), but to my ear he was miles ahead. At times he resembled nothing so much as an untutored version of the young US prodigy JD Beck, another staggeringly exciting drummer who gives the impression of being able to play completely out of time within any two immaculately in-time strokes.

cream-coloured square foot. I brooded over every word and note like a twelfth-century Kabbalist bent over the Torah. My favourite bit of 'Sea Song' – next to Wyatt's demented whole-tone piano solo – was its ecstatic coda, an endlessly repeated rising chord sequence over which Wyatt improvises a beautiful wordless vocalese in his vulnerable Cockney falsetto. I began to get forensic about nuance, and dropped the needle over and over on tiny phrases in ever-shortening loops, trying to figure out why a particular note always raised every hair on my arm. I knew it was all in the context, but unlike everything else in the universe, some of these notes seemed to have *intrinsic* meaning.

Also, the record contained a couple of mistakes. It was the first time I had encountered such a thing. They were the result of Wyatt reaching for a note or a phrase that he simply couldn't cover; and he'd left them in, because that's what he wanted us to hear. It began to dawn on me that a little audible failure is a sign, a guarantee even, that an artist is consumed by something greater than merely the desire to impress us, and that they're working at, and therefore sometimes just beyond, the limits of their ability. I heard, too, how Wyatt singing in his native accent lent the music an almost uncomfortable intimacy. Not only could nothing be further from the over-produced, note-perfect jazz-rock and prog I had been obsessed with; never had I heard such a violently un-American activity, and never was a resident of that Dundee council estate more proud to be English.

I was also listening to the good bits on Mike Oldfield's *Hergest Ridge* and *Ommadawn* (even now, I'm shocked at how good the good bits were, given the clean-cut, cheesy neo-classical shirtless weirdo he emerged as after he graduated from the scream-yourself-broke Exegesis cult), along with Steve Hillage, the great hippy guitarist and later electronic dance music pioneer, who also sang with his weedy Home Counties twang left in; they led me back to Gong (Daevid Allen's jazz-psychedelic-chaos-Anglo-French collective), and then every band formed in Canterbury since 1967, then Kevin Ayers, and finally back to Wyatt again, and a forensic study of early Soft Machine. I ploughed backwards through the Softs' discography in the hope of uncovering some Holy Grail of a . . . phrase, a chord, a note that lit the fuse on that strange, self-aware turn in English music and could explain its eerie soul.*

* I probably found it, in the key change in the fifth bar of a haunted little number called 'Memories'. I recall my frustration at being unable to lay my hands on any of the Wilde Flowers recordings made when Wyatt and (Soft Machine bassist) Hugh Hopper were still at school; however, the demos later became available. Among them was a chilling discovery: an even earlier recording of Hopper's talismanic song 'Memories', the 'Gloomy Sunday' of English alt-rock, which Wyatt and others were still re-recording forty years later, sometimes as an instrumental; I assume they still are. 'Memories' is one of those songs that gives the impression of having existed forever, and that Hopper had merely channelled it, either accidentally or in an attempt to escape its curse. The song seems to attract the doomed. (It certainly doomed several rock guitarists, who found a shameful death between the cracks of its angular chord changes; the usual tactic of picking a blues scale and praying for the best won't get you too far.) A few US hyper-hip types like Cedric Bixler-Zavala of The Mars Volta recorded it, but if you want evidence of its cursed nature, here's the weirdest piece of pop

28 A New Jerusalem

For a solid two or three years, our social group had a guru, Alex Thom. He was older – twenty-one to our sixteen – and worked in the Wimpy in Reform Street. He read Castañeda, Lautréamont and Dalí (we all *read* Dalí back then, if you can believe it), smoked a crazy amount of weed and supplemented his bottle-washer's income with bootleg compilation cassettes, for which he hand-drew the covers. I owned a very popular Nick Drake mixtape called 'Torpid Afternoons', which many believed to be a real album. Alex was always covered in food stains, something he obscurely attributed to 'being a Capricorn'; he had red-blond, slicked-back hair, huge Francis Rossi sideburns and a de Gaulle nose that he talked through honkingly. He wore dirty green trousers and he had a huge arse. We thought he was really cool. He did have immense charisma, and would monologue thrillingly on music, sex, the spiritually enhancing properties of drugs, and the more lurid conspiracies of the day; in short, everything we could possibly have been interested in.

Post-Church, I missed being in a cult, and was therefore ripe for recruitment. (I sometimes wonder if that ever changed; a number of my adult relationships might accurately have been described as cults of two, in which one person possessed the truth and the other quickly learned to agree with it.) I especially missed the paranoia, and the obsession over hidden signs. As a Christian I had burned up many hours over Revelations, trying to figure out the identity of the Great Beast or the Whore of Babylon, or the exact date of The Return. Now I was taken up with the runes of the Phaistos Disc, which at the time we believed was a written record of a multidimensional language created by Atlanteans, whose deciphering would help us form part of a new race of superhumans, which was a damn sight more exciting than the Minoan Tesco receipt it probably was. I had also been deeply immersed in the work of the popular extraterrestrialist and brazen chancer Erich von Däniken, author of *Chariots of the Gods?* ('No'), even though so many of his claims were so dumb as to arrive already self-debunked. How could primitive man have such detailed knowledge of the skeleton hidden below his own flesh, without the education of alien scientists? No idea, Erich, oh hang on yeah death. Alex suggested a rather less stupid reading list, and whatever you think of *Beyond Good and Evil*, it was a notch up from *Gods from Outer Space*. Some kind of education finally got under way, because I sure as hell wasn't finding it at school, which I had ceased to attend.

Alex was a self-diagnosed artist, and had invented a new one-man movement called Supraliminalism, which always took him two attempts to say and whose manifesto was hard to fathom, but which produced the kind of art that might have resulted if Genesis P-Orridge had stolen your granny's voucher for the craft supplies shop. It all had a vaguely shamanic ring to it: I recall a cow's pelvis stuck on a toilet brush handle, painted half red and half blue, then hung with tassels and plastered with bits of lace doilies. Alex was permanently furious at the refusal of the mainstream art world to acknowledge his work. The word-of-mouth excitement around Supraliminalism that Alex had spread as far and wide as himself had somehow not reached them, and the path to his door remained unbeaten. He was especially furious with the Scottish Arts Council, whose evil cartel had not only declined to fund him but had 'deliberately' returned the cow's-pelvis sceptre doodad in pieces, although what the hell he thought he was doing posting stuff directly to the Scottish Arts Council in a shoebox is anyone's guess.

Alex, though, could be hugely entertaining. I remember one party where he turned up dressed as a minister, and spent an hour reading from the Old Testament in a way that would have got any actual minister arrested merely for the crime of reading from the Old Testament. He began in a solicitous and kindly tone, his head tilted in pastoral concern. 'Today we will begin our lesson with Numbers 31:17–18: "Now kill all the boys and all the women who have had sexual intercourse. Only the little girls may live; you may keep them for yourselves."' You wouldn't think you could or should get a huge laugh out of that verse, but you can if you get the target right. The Christian God was, I finally accepted, quite the massive arsehole. And so on, through the Levitical injunctions on mixed fabric, haircuts and menstruation, through all the various exhortations to murder, rape and cannibalise, to the batshit drug visions of the prophets. Alex's crotch-spritzing finale was a reading from Ezekiel, which he rendered spontaneously in the vernacular:

Noodles later, and reported that Sutherland was, as we'd hoped, very far away; there was indeed much empty and uninhabited land there; fresh water and rabbits seemed plentiful; and you should shite while crouching and facing uphill to avoid it going straight back into your pants. Empowered with this knowledge we made plans for our New Jerusalem, and began to arm ourselves with the skills our elite community would need to repopulate the earth. Chief among these were techniques for the recruitment of women, of which our chapter seemed to be notably short.

Alex was fixated on keeping everything in his control, though, and like most narcissists got terrified when it slipped away. He was mortified when I started seeing Mary Douglas, whom he'd been carefully cultivating. Mary was four years older than me; the maturity gap between a sixteen-year-old boy and a twenty-year-old girl technically put the relationship in grooming territory, but my facial hair and world-weariness disguised the child I was. She was short-haired and pretty, with an odd little off-centre frown mark; she was also socially indeterminate on account of her family moving towns about once a year for reasons unspecified, and spoke in no known accent; she was as alien as a Traveller. Mary was fascinated by my self-loathing – I was suffering from Elephant Man-level dysmorphia at the time – and was maternal enough to want to alleviate it, though not enough to want to do so by maternal means. I was also a virgin, which bewildered her. Mary was staggeringly experienced, but much of this experience seemed to have come via other family members, and she couldn't really distinguish the voluntary from the forced, let alone the merely coerced. Some families are like that; their normal is your hell on earth. Alex was furious, as he considered Mary a pillar of his harem, and had a terror of his influence waning. He called a meeting with me, and loftily agreed to share her; he actually used the word 'share'. Evidence of this arrangement would occasionally emerge. ('Relax, Donald. The penis is scientifically the cleanest part of the body.' 'Who told you *that*?' 'Alex.' 'Jesus.') We lasted maybe six weeks, and she finished it, suddenly. True, I was a bit intense, and will have declared my love far too early – a bad habit I've had all my life, since the intensity leads me to muddle the moment with eternity. (I eventually learned to dial back on the first-date declarations, but a key vulnerability remained: as a reflector, all anyone has to do is declare love, and it shall be returned, wholly sincerely, even if it's within five minutes of our meeting. Low self-esteem can result in a kind of 'echoism', and while not one of the more fashionable disorders – we care far less about the harm folk do to themselves – it's perfectly dangerous, in its own quiet way; and if you know the myth of Echo, you can quickly work out the personality types to which we are attracted.) But Alex had been briefing heavily against me. I could guess the kind of thing he was telling her, given what he'd earlier demanded I share with him. I was fairly devastated.

By slow degrees, our little band came to see through Alex. He was great value, but a devious bullshitter. Once seen through, he began recruiting the next group of acolytes. But he was, before his spells stopped working on us, one of those inspiring narcs who manage to do as much good as harm. I once had a conversation with a Dundee acquaintance who'd been part of the Thomite group which succeeded ours. She would not hear a word spoken against him, and invoked his name as one of the most profound and transforming influences on her life. One wouldn't have deprived her of the experience, nor want to taint her memory with the larger picture. Who ever really wants *that*?

29 Party Fears

In the early 1980s, Dundee social life was a kind of weird orrery revolving around the blazing, self-consuming sun of Billy MacKenzie, the Associates singer and bandleader, and your status was more or less entirely determined by your proximity. Billy was a great deal more than just the best pop singer of his generation. He had the attractive power of a 3-tesla MRI scanner, and if there was as much as a paperclip of susceptibility on your person, forget it: you'd find yourself sliding across the room as if you were on castors. YouTube hosts some delightful video evidence from the era. One interview seems to take place in Dundee on the *Unicorn*, the last warship in Britain of wooden construction (a very Dundee kind of artefact; we also invented the reverse gear and the non-adhesive postage stamp). The female interviewer is so overwhelmed with the sheer charm and beauty of the man, she spontaneously kisses him mid-interview.* In this scheme

---

* The MacKenzie family seem to have been authentically cursed. Both parents died young, and Billy took his own life in '97. (There are no happy suicides, but Billy's was uniquely depressing: an overdose, surrounded with his memorabilia, while sitting in his kennels in Auchterhouse with his beloved whippets.) His brother Jimmy OD'd four years later. John died in a fire in 2010, and in 2013 his sister Lizzie fell to her death from a second-floor window. Billy's decline

I was a moon of a moon of Pluto's, but grateful enough for the little third-hand gravity that at least kept me vaguely in orbit. Through Alex, we could claim a loose affiliation with Ray Ross, who had the approximately chiselled look of a bassist in an ABC support band, and was a minor decorative light fitting in Billy's entourage when he would show up in Dundee, which was often, as he was a terrible homeboy. Ray's actual gig or purpose was obscure. He'd have been an animateur, if there'd been anything to animate; I suppose the correct word is 'socialite', but that seems an odd word to use in a town where whelks could be served as party food. Mainly, Ray's thing was being Ray, which was no minor undertaking. The New Romantic vibe then was very identity-fluid, because we all knew that gender, as it is currently framed, wasn't a thing. It was that simple. The war back then was on 'stereotypes' (O how quaint that sounds), and second-wave feminism had liberated both sexes to treat their gender as fluidly expressive, not insecurely performative, or just be as butch or camp as

---

was so perfectly coterminous with his career's, the latter might have saved the former; however, nothing went right after the catastrophic, vainglorious miscalculation to do without Alan Rankine, a musician of actual genius who knew just how to make the cut, polish and setting that the peculiar gem of his voice required. Afterwards it still shone, but amongst rocks. (One late partnership involved a pianist apparently incapable of anything more than bare triads; the emotional effect was of a skulled half of cheap pre-flight vodka in a bleached airport toilet.) With nothing to star in, born stars don't know what to do with themselves but blink out.

made you most comfortable. We didn't have social media to gaslight each other into conformity, and it was always a surprise to see who folk turned up as in the evening, because very little advance warning could be given. Amongst the trendy and generally unconfused youth of 1982, you did what you liked, shagged who you liked and wore what you liked. Girls or boys would walk out in mascara or a boiler suit or a bra or a football strip or a wedding dress or a hard hat or any combination thereof, and the world was far better and brighter for it. Ray dressed exactly how he felt, and his torso often felt differently from his legs or his head, which left him the random product of three flick-books that had just happened to stop that day on fedora–corset–camouflage pants, or Noh play–school uniform–tutu, or whatever. I was far too afraid to experiment beyond the odd and instantly regretted sweep of eyeliner, however, and mostly ventured out in the schemie uniform of jeans, Hi-Tec trainers, punk tee and Palestinian keffiyeh, a versatile item for the Scottish climate, which could be rapidly reformed from scarf into hat, balaclava, umbrella or emergency tent as the situation required.

(Back then, gender was just an aspect of individual personality. Billy, Annie Lennox, David Sylvian – all played with it, taking it to be the expressive tool it was. Where the stereotypes remained most solidly in place in the early 1980s – to the infinite disadvantage of women – was in the poorest corners of the estate. Where, of course, they still do. But the left couldn't give a damn that their *dernier cri* – the request that identities must be fixed, preferably as early as possible, that I'd have recognised as deconstructionist, if I'd known any more about Derrida than I learned from Scritti Politti lyrics. It was something about the inability of language to express anything at all, owing to the emptiness of its signs. I was definitely securing Susie's agreement in the matter, though sadly more through practical demonstration than logic. I believe she was very slightly hypnotised by my ability to talk metaphysical shite without blinking for minutes at a time, but somehow not enough to act on the subliminal message that she should sleep with me. I could not be faulted on my intensity, but I was learning that it wasn't enough. I used to meet her at her shared student flat, in a close off the High Street. I was in full flow one evening, in her prettily decorated, patchouli-scented lamplit bedroom. 'But the mere ability of language to immediately gainsay its own assertions proves its *intrinsic* instability – *or does it?*' 'Yes, I see what you did there' – when I felt my fingers touch a familiar shape in the wall behind me. It was a distinctive, Ireland-shaped gouge. O God. No way. This was the same room where I'd prayed with blind Ma Gunn four years earlier. It had clearly been gutted and completely renovated, but even so. I had so thoroughly suppressed those years, I hadn't even clocked that this was the same flat, up the same stairwell of the same close. Suddenly I could hear my own stream of holy garbage again. Not that I immediately abandoned it; I thought Susie was weakening. She certainly looked weakened. But one evening in the Tayside Bar, Ray witnessed this pitiable charade from the wings, and stepped in to put Susie out of my misery. With a twitch of his nostril she was gone, with her pants. It was back to the drawing board.

The next phase of my versatile failure to appeal was a brief incarnation as singer-songwriter. We had plenty of fine models: Martyn, obviously, Joni, Nick Drake, Joan Armatrading, Paul Brady. In the strong field of my troubadourial shortcomings, I was a notably useless lyricist; I was no poet yet, but had a poet's talent for lyrics, i.e. none. With the exception of Burns and – nope, that's it; poets, as the control freaks of the language, generally have no idea how to leave any air or light or space for music. I vaguely sensed this, and tried to subtract anything that could get in the way, but this seemed to leave nothing at all. I talked to my dad about it. He said he'd attempted to come up with a song on several occasions, but he'd get as far as 'I was walkin' down the road . . .' and immediately run out of steam. This produced a full-body wince. I had literally just started a song with the words 'I was walkin' down the road'. I had added, redundantly, '. . . trying to write me this song', but I had no idea where I was going, or indeed bound, as we singer-songwriters say. I kept singing that bit in the hope I would find out. Eventually, I had something like: 'I was walkin' down the road / Trying to write me this song / But I'm lookin' for the code / And Ah'm getting it wrong.' (*You're* blushing? I'm trying to fix a hose to the exhaust.) This wasn't going well. My voice was okay, just about, but I had unwisely imitated John Martyn's delivery, and sounded like a bearded wino with a head cold singing in his sleep. At least it had the advantage of rendering me completely unintelligible. 'Iiizhwokkin dunna roe / dryna rye me disszhaww / buddum loogn furra coe / dunnum gerrinit wroh . . .' I got quite a lot of feedback, as I inflicted the song on anyone who foolishly drifted within a yard. I thought they all sounded marvellously encouraging. 'You've really got your own thing there!' 'Well. Didn't expect *that* . . .' 'Are you going to do more?' 'You should keep working on that one!' Ah God I can hear it now. Anyway, I managed to reach the correct conclusion unaided, and loudly declared that I was hanging up my warbling boots and sticking to the guitar. My pal George said, quietly, 'I think that's a good idea.' Oof.

In these years John Martyn was venerated, of course, and along with Joni, was one of the few artists on whom one was permitted no opinion: his greatness was incontestable, not least because he happened to be Scottish. He was hard to see live, not because he was actually hard to see live, but because he often cancelled at the last minute, or more usually the minute after, owing to concussion, blood loss, drunken incapacitation or mere caprice. No serious Martyn fan doesn't have at least one story that goes: 'Yeah, we waited two hours and then he came on [totally pissed/with a head injury/with a stab wound/with a broken arm] from [nutting the lighting engineer/a fight with his dealer/punching a wall], sang one number and [fell off his chair/couldn't play a note/started screaming at an empty seat in the second row] and that was it.' A pal recounts one gig where John had stormed offstage after ten minutes, because something. He and his friends sloped off to the pub round the corner, to find John sulking in the snug, behind three pints and three chasers he'd set up to line his stomach before he settled down for a drink. With suicidal bravery, given that 'death by Martyn' was actually a thing, my mate challenged him on his unprofessionalism: 'Bud, we'd been waiting all year to see you,' etc. Miraculously, they'd caught John in a lachrymose and guilty mood (technically, 'that day assuming the form of a lachrymose and guilty person'), and he seemed genuinely upset and contrite. He then pulled out his guitar and did an hour's set on the bar stool to an audience of about ten, who swayed, blissed out, wept and sang along, and which my acquaintance recounts as easily the best gig of his life.

More typical was my own experience. I got a call from Dad one Sunday morning. Dad had a Sunday-lunchtime gig in Arbroath, at a dark, friendly little bar called Tutties Neuk, near the cliffs. Hamish Imlach had been working there the previous night, and had brought John along with him. John had apparently threatened to do a short set in the middle of my dad's stint, and Hamish had promised to introduce me. I rushed out of bed, ran down to the bus stop at the Spar, got the 22 into town, ran to the St Andrews Street bus station, got the next bus to Arbroath twenty miles up the coast, then ran the last five hundred yards in level sleet to the pub. The journey took me maybe two and a half hours. When I got there, John was still pissed in bed with the barmaid, and would not be roused. It's not much of a story, but it illustrates John's uncanny gift not just for general let-down but bespoke personal disappointment. But our expectations of him were

30 Aieeee Banzai

Until I was about thirty-five, I had only once held down a day job. To be precise, I held it down and drowned it in a bucket, though it took around ten months for the bubbles to stop. My plan was to leave school and play guitar, and I put this into effect at fifteen, which is a year too soon. Dad was supportive, and by then I was working the clubs with him anyway. My mum was having none of it, though, and insisted that first I needed 'something at my back', which she somehow always made sound like a mattress to break a fall from a window. But I was unfit for any form of labour, having done nothing in my last two years of school but practise exotic guitar scales. Boredom was, as ever, at the root of it. I had learned too much in primary school, which meant the first two years of secondary were redundant; I had no one to please, either. By third year, when there was a lot to learn again, I'd lost the habit and the will. I figured that if I really needed to know something, I'd teach myself. Nonetheless, I remembered enough from primary to get me through my O-levels. Then I sat five Highers (Albert A'Hara begged me not to sit my Higher Greek; I have no idea why I turned up, just to post what was officially the worst mark in Scotland), and failed everything apart from English. As I had been earmarked, at least by my dad's side, as the First One in the Family to Go to University, the failure defined me:

I was more like the First One in the Family to Not Not Not Go to University.*

DC Thomson liked to keep it in the family; if I had to be employed, it was the most obvious route, since my dad and my Uncle Iain already worked there. So at sixteen I signed up just as unthinkingly as my grandfather had signed up for the coal mine, and applied for the post of trainee sub-editor. In those days DC Thomson published most of the UK's better-known comics, all still named for long-obsolete pre-war superlatives – *The Beano*, *The Dandy*, *The Topper*, *The Beezer*; primers in internalised misogyny, like *Twinkle* and *Jackie*; a number of sex- and God-fearing knit-this/bake-that/clean-thon women's magazines, where no one ever got pregnant, periods or mammograms (one had heard rumours that the wife of a high-heid-yin had demanded that the entire run of *My Weekly* be pulped for the crime of featuring a line drawing of a pregnant woman); various couthy Scottish magazines about mountains, ceilidhs and country lore; the Dundee *Courier & Advertiser*, a bedsheet-sized and hugely popular local paper, and the last in the UK to maintain the practice of putting small ads on the front page; and the *Sunday*

---

* A few years back I was discussing my academic disasters with my friends Sean O'Brien and the late Australian poet Peter Porter. Porter, a fellow non-graduate, remarked that if I stuck around long enough, someone might bung me an honorary degree, out of pity, if nothing else. (Porter used to get one every ten minutes, and would go to the toilet and return in a mortarboard.) 'They'll have to give him his honorary Highers first,' said Sean.

cast down in the DCT inferno, but Editorial was bad enough. *Commando* relived the World War II Allied campaign over and over again, with identical results. On my first day, I was taught how to expire as a member of the Imperial Japanese Army – which is to say, how many Es were in *Aieeee!* – and handed a book of tanks and planes, which I was tasked with learning to identify. My work was simple enough. I was to read the story synopses that were sent to us, and identify the likely contenders for publication. This was a waste of time, as the only publishable efforts were all by one man called Montgomery. I think the synopsis box may have been an elaborate subterfuge just to keep him off the payroll. If they were not by Montgomery, they were light rewrites of earlier *Commando* magazines the current readership was too young to remember, where 'Stick It to Fritz' became 'Take It to Tojo' and you swapped the ordnance and did a manual find-and-replace between 'Achtung' and 'Banzai'. I had to proof and check the final magazine for factual accuracy, i.e. I had to look over the artwork and make sure Rodriguez had not stuck in an ME-109 when he should've had a Focke-Wulf 190 because 'Knees of Steel' or whatever was set in 1942 (I refuse to check the accuracy of this statement, on principle, for I do not care), and that Ibanez had not drawn a spaceship, because he was even more stoned and bored than I was. Pioneers of hard-nosed outsourcing, DCT had figured out in the 1970s that Spanish cartoonists were a bit stuck for work under Franco.

The home of Jackson Strang, the editor, may have blossomed and bloomed with his redeeming features. In the workplace, however, he was a bully, an old-school sexist and a pretentious nincompoop; he could have easily made the office a convivial place to work, but instead preferred to run it like the kind of military operation of which he never let us forget he'd had first-hand experience, having served in Italy and North Africa. (To his genuine credit, though, only Nazis were allowed to be baddies, never regular German soldiers; Rommel, of course, was practically venerated.) Strang was given to what he thought of as sergeant major-style apoplectic fitting, and broke his foot one day kicking a metal bucket across the room. I broke a rib trying not to laugh. We had to proof his correspondence, a wholly unnecessary exercise as it was always ostentatiously error-free; he just wanted us to read it. 'Dear Monty, thank you for "Poofters in Khaki", which has now been packed off to Hernandez for his leisurely attention and will appear in June as "Y Is for Yellow"; otherwise anticipate minimal changes. I'm sitting here in the orangery, listening to Horowitz play K271 on the frankly indifferent Fazioli I believe Beecham liberated from the Hallé when . . .' We all thought he was a complete tit. One wishes one could explain to all such bullies that the silence that gathers around them is never respect.

Apart from *Jackie* and *Twinkle*, I saw miserably few girls in Editorial. They'd be sent off to the typing pool, or to operate the photocopier, or to train as 'balloonists', which is just what it sounds like. Balloonists had a set of speech-balloon templates which they drew on the artwork. That was the whole gig. Not the lettering; just the empty balloons. It was by directing women into this kind of zombified labour that DCT manufactured evidence of their fitness for little else, which in turn vindicated its policy of paying them considerably less. (There were strong precedents here. Dundee's wealthy class had been built on the cheap labour of women: all men were sacked from the jute mills at eighteen, when they would have been entitled to a male adult wage. The men stayed home to look after the children, and were known by the metonymic 'kettle-bilers', i.e. 'boilers of the kettle'. However, it had the unforeseen effect of establishing a matriarchal working class, and at least in their full control of the household budget Dundee women were a reasonably empowered and notoriously fearless constituency, even if Dundee's Gini coefficient was one of the worst on the planet.) The economic hit to the female workforce was elided by the tradition of company intermarriage; indeed, I took the decision to get out as soon as possible the day I opened the *Argus*, DCT's in-house publication, or, more specifically, the wedding section. 'Mary Drysdale (*Twinkle*) married Dave McCluskey (Lindsay St. Process). Alice Grant (Balloonist) married Stuart Jamieson (*Dandy*).' And so on. For pages. I sat next to a nice guy called Stewart, who was twenty-six, lived with his mum, wore the same aubergine suede jacket every day, was into photographing hopelessly unattainable women in a slightly dubious could-you-put-your-leg-a-wee-bit-higher way, ate a custard-filled fudge donut for his lunch and gave the impression of someone who intended to do just that for the next forty years. Phil was an ambitious, ruddy-faced *en brosse* eighteen-year-old who'd already done a journalism course and was destined for higher things. He was pleased with his punster skills, and touchy as hell. He had a crush on the bonny lass from *Jackie* who made up the horoscopes. (We all contributed. Mine were never used, all being along the lines of 'Libra: Tuesday may bring a sharp and unexpected pain; call a doctor? Wednesday: A close relative will make you feel uncomfortable with a bizarre confession,' etc.) Jason was six foot six, about five stone, had the world's most half-hearted moustache, and was gay and didn't know it yet. He had a girlfriend but, as he explained in a splendidly camp Dundee accent, 'Wih jist sit aboot speakin' aboot her claes and her hair and that.'

I should emphasise that, compared with other parts of Thomson's operation, Editorial was like a renaissance workshop. The big problem was a workforce with far too little to do; and no one had less to do than Print Process, where my brother Stevie worked for ten wretched years. DCT's might have suffered from many institutionalised -isms, but no one called them a bad employer. They were benignly paternalistic and paid well, if not equitably, and had a superannuation fund second to none. They were cheap as hell, but wouldn't dream of shrinking the workforce just because of modernisation. Besides, the management were so remote from the factory floor that no one had told them it took two men, not eight, to man the new machines, and no one was going to either. Driven crazy by years of enforced idleness, the printers formed a surreal and deranged guild. On his very first morning, Stevie saw two auld lads giving each other the time of day. 'Hullo,

Wullie – how're ye doing – what did ye have for yer tea last night – did ye see the highlights on Scotsport?' All perfectly normal stuff. Then Stevie noticed they were fondling each other's balls. Stevie was often illegally employed as a human pull-through; he was covered in brown paper, with a long rope tied to his feet, and dragged under the machinery to clean it. At least half his head was the wrong colour for years. Jokes were less jokes than ritualised exchanges, the dead husks of jokes. Every day Stevie would sit filling in the *Guardian* crossword in his tea break; every day, at the same time, this guy would come up behind him, lean over and say, 'Seven Up's lemonade,' even after Stevie had hit him with a hammer. My dad sat next to a guy who had adopted a pigeon, whom he'd christened Walter; every day, for months on end, the same wee bird would come to his window, where he'd feed it, water it and speak to it. One morning, with no word of explanation, he brought in an airgun and shot it. Birthday and stag-night raggings made the Skull and Bones look like the Rainbows. Grooms would be stripped, tied to a pallet, have their balls covered in indelible blue bronze ink (a tattoo is easier to remove), then be paraded through the street. One lad, two days before his wedding, was slipped a mickey and tied to a seat on the Dundee–London train, with a valid ticket for the full journey in his top pocket. (Sobering up in King's Cross the next day, he decided that he liked it down there just fine, called off the wedding, and didn't come back for six months.)

Over at the Lindsay Street Process, my dad worked as a colourist, meaning he coloured things in. He sat at a desk full of men who also coloured things in, like a table of fairly well-behaved six-year-olds with pituitary gland issues. His only job was not to go over the lines; his sole training session had consisted of the single instruction: 'Sky's blue, grass is green, denner's at twelve.' You were allowed a certain latitude with the backgrounds, but Dennis the Menace's jumper had to look like Dennis the Menace's jumper. This meant that the little artistic licence you *could* take was often taken to the extreme, and *The Beano* was awash with psychedelic sunsets and purple brickwork. There would be weeks without work, and this led to the infamous three-hour toilet breaks where Dad developed his speed-reading technique. He'd open his thriller and move his eye down the middle of the page, reading both ends of the line at once, and skipping all extraneous description and love interest. Being a fine musician, Dad had a life outside of DCT's, which is to say he had a life. But many of his workmates seemed hollowed out, or completely simplified by self-caricature. Like Jack Dare, who'd tell us the same racist joke every week. 'Aw the black lads in Dundee know me, y'ken. I walk past and they all say, "Hullo Dare!"' One should stress to the young that if you'd told us at the time that this was racist, no one would have known what you were talking about. No one, bar possibly the one black lad I knew, the magnificent Keith Abara, who was trialling for Dundee FC. And obviously Keith talked in a local accent far broader than mine. It was indeed rare then to encounter *anyone* in Dundee who did not speak just as you did. One night, my brother staggered drunk into the Chinese enthusiastic support of Enoch Powell.* In Dundee, though, I was keenly looking forward to the time when I could find some actual racism to rock against. By the time I did, not only did I hate rock, but the racism turned out to be no fun either. In London in the late eighties, I was half of an interracial couple for a few years. (The white half; just to make that clear.) It was a much more equitable time back then, and if we held hands in the street we got spat on by both white and West Indian folk at bus stops, which is really weird because Robin DiAngelo told me racism only runs one way. I assume in my case it must have been personal. When I brought my girlfriend up from London to meet my folks, I was relieved to find that the all-white estate just hadn't had any *practice*. Nearly all the prejudice she experienced was anti-English, on account of her thick Midlands accent; at least all bar that of my übercunt Uncle Jimmer, of course, who regarded her with a tilted-head curiosity, like a zoo animal. (Anti-English sentiment was far stronger prior to the resurgence of the Independence movement, in which it has, counterintuitively, evaporated, bar three blood-and-soil idiots we can identify by name. Not least

---

* At the time of writing, I hear Clapton has joined forces with increasingly relevant former has-been Van Morrison to record a terrific anti-lockdown song. I gather Eric is none too chuffed with Covid vaccines either, and claims that the AstraZeneca almost saw him go from Slowhand to Nohand: post-jab numbness in his extremities left him fearing 'he would never play the guitar again'. That the world might have suffered the permanent loss of those eight stolen Buddy Guy licks is almost too much to bear.

because most sensible folk up here suddenly realised that we desperately need English immigration.)

Ron 'General' Grant, another of Dad's benchmates, was a perfect enigma. He had the most spectacular underbite, which meant that his mouth would often fill with rain, and that he could only eat his sandwiches by pressing the bread into his lower set, like a pastry cutter, then chewing the jaw-shaped piece. A man of almost mythical dullness, less a human than a kind of Beckettian one-man endurance theatre, birds would fall asleep and crash into trees as they passed over his head. I can recall only one snatch of his conversation. He was sitting in the back of the car, reading the adverts from the Dundee *Courier*, and for no reason whatsoever listing aloud the stupid names of all the bands who were playing the social clubs at the weekend. 'The Penny Dainties.' Silence. 'The Dressed Herrings.' Silence. 'The Tiny Tots.' Very long silence. 'Fell catchy name.' (You had to be there, I think.) He had married well above his station, to Mrs Grant of *The Greek Gods*; she was notorious in the street for forcing Ron to take her dresses to the Marks and Spencer returns counter every Monday, after a weekend's wear. When Ron suddenly and incomprehensibly carked it in his fifties, she created a minor scandal when she kissed Ron's coffin at the funeral.

Meanwhile, over in Editorial, specifically in the toilets, I was getting higher and higher, although that's the wrong directional metaphor. The Dundee hash supply – so long leaf-green, fragrant and redolent of a long Dutch summer – was now black, tarry, and stank like dogshit. It was getting stronger by the week, and its effects shifting decisively from things starting with narco- or ending with -tropic, to things starting with psycho- or ending with -pathic. The week's work, which could have been dispatched in a single morning if I'd knuckled down, was taking me a month. I'd start dreading the next day about an hour into the day before. I'd take the stairs up the eight-floor DCT skyscraper because it took a little longer than the lift; I'd pray for the traffic lights to turn red just to delay the bus by a few seconds. I started screwing up, consequentially and deliberately. Deadlines were missed. Piss was taken. The dramatis personae of 'The Big Snatch' (I know, I know), for example, consisted of the names of every major supplier in Dundee. The hero was Flt. Lt. Dave 'Baccy' Baxter. The real-life Baccy Baxter was delighted with his alter ego, and would hail me at the door of the stash-flat with a Terry-Thomas 'What ho, Binky!' and reoffer his torpedo-sized doobie with a combative 'Hed enough, Fritz, or will Tommy give you some more?'

I had survived one awful and entirely deserved bollocking from the deputy editor, George Low (real name, a kind and fair man who went on to edit the magazine for years afterwards) – and, unable to think of a way out, I started making myself ill. My brain was desperate to keep my body in bed just so it could read a decent book, and devised a fake kidney complaint that kept me off for several weeks. In the process of establishing that there was bugger all wrong with me, strange dyes were injected, while my pelvis was almost snapped in a kind of rack device so the X-ray machine could get a decent fix on the problem, then a Pentax was rammed up my urethra.

31 Black Sheep

Looking back, it seems inevitable, given the half-dozen planets rolling into position from their variously tilted orbits; some of them huge, lumbering, unseen and distant, others little rainy things, but all of them, one by one, adding their gravity to the tidal draw on my brain. Despite the immediate ecstasy of my release from DC Thomson, I was mortified at the way I had let down my mother, and God: for all that I disavowed his existence, I still had a terror of the eschatological consequences of masturbation, for one thing, and basically couldn't. I regarded myself as sinful, evil and contorted, and held forth on my own Quasimodo-like deformation often enough for it to worry my friends, who saw nothing but a normal-looking, slight, wispy-bearded hippy. I was skinning up from the moment I rose (at 2 p.m., invariably) until bedtime, every day. The arms race between Scottish dealers had accelerated, and the strength of the local supply continued to double each month. I once lit up a massive doob at a Latin class reunion, hosted by Albert A'Hara's young understudy, a gentle, kindly lunk called Ken who looked like a schoolboy Boris Karloff. At the *dinner* table. I was keen to let the Junoesque Rhiannon O'Mara know that I was now a very bad boy. Ken was too stunned to protest, and just sat with his mouth open as I dragoned the smoke through my nostrils and flicked the ash into a parfait dish with the dregs of my Butterscotch Angel Delight. My folks were staggeringly naive about it and let me blame the thick funk in the bedroom on joss sticks; I even skinned up in front of my father in the car, and told him it was hand-rolling tobacco. I projected my guilt over duping them into a vague sense of their wariness of me, which was, of course, steadily growing anyway.

I eventually confessed my habit, as I knew that my mind wasn't right. It was the single occasion I can recall my father reacting in a way that was solidly unhelpful, and I'm still bewildered at how badly such a good father dealt with the situation. He was devastated. Despite their serious brush with the sixties, his class and generation had an impeccably uncritical regard for doctors, for government and for the law: all were correct, always. Drugs were not only uniformly dangerous, but uniquely shameful. So long as you kept your mixer the right side of turpentine, they would far rather you'd pissed yourself into an early grave than enjoyed one lungful of anything illegal. Dad had already gone his mild version of postal when he'd found the hemp plants thriving amongst the rhubarb patch in his allotment, handiwork swiftly and accurately attributed to Big Jim Dowie's son next door; but no one seemed to judge Big Jim with more than pity when he blew up his marriage and destroyed his health on home brew. His house was a swamp forest of burbling demijohns, in which he fermented increasingly experimental sources of sugar, from tomatoes and cabbages up to and including job lots of tinned fruit salad and out-of-date Christmas mince pies. For a while Dad made wine himself, but his impatience meant that it never cleared, something he regarded as a merely cosmetic refinement; we dreaded the glasses of opaque fruity sludge he'd press onto guests, who'd nod and grin back at him through their welling tears. Dad, a notorious lightweight, had been cajoled into a wine-tasting at Jim's one Saturday afternoon, the plan being that he'd sample a little from every demijohn on Jim's stairwell. Five steps up – 'the prune step', he later recalled – he had to sit down. We were called to oxter him home. He threw up in the hedge before we made the front door, and didn't get out of bed until Monday.

Jim would throw out the lees on his back green, and we'd sit and skin up and watch the drunk sparrows and pigeons fighting under the greenie-poles before they collapsed, their legs pointing to heaven. Jim was an amateur Burns and Scottish history scholar, his mind and judgement rotted and ruined by alcohol. But he was pitied, not ostracised. The confession of my hash habit saw Dad refuse to utter a word to me for days. I hadn't expected immediate absolution, but his silence was a terrible shock, and another gap opened up between us. I went from the vague feeling that my folks didn't have my best interests at heart to wholly distrusting them. This would intensify, by steady degrees, into a conviction that they were trying to kill me.

Weed, however, deepened my relationship with music. It spatialised it. Stoned, I could enter a record as one would a strange city, to wonder at and lose myself in. It also smuggled me into jazz, a country where I still barely understood a word anyone said. Big Rab then ran a record store on the corner of Commercial Street, and he helped supply the phrasebook: you'd go in for a Steve Hillage or a Brand X album to find Art Pepper or Pat Metheny or Charles Mingus blasting from the speakers, and go: Oh. Okay. *That's* obviously better. Determined to check out other guitarists, I had shyly courted a record of John Abercrombie's for weeks: *Arcade*, on ECM. I bought it unheard, because it had a fabulously understated glaucous moire cover that seemed to be completely unrelated to the title. These guys must be *serious*. I took it home, placed it on the spindle, and regretted it immediately. I couldn't make any sense of it. It sounded shambolic. The haunted, melancholic tunes were played only to be immediately dismantled, and the harmony was alien, dissonant and angular; what went on in the middle of each track sounded like pure chaos. I set it aside, confused. Was it some kind of . . . arty hoax? Then one night I skinned up and gave it another go.

It was precisely like one of those stereogram pictures that look like hell's wallpaper, but when you learn how to focus a foot *behind* its surface it suddenly clicks into three dimensions, and fills with birds and flowers and horses and clouds. O – *there's* the music. I had been listening all wrong. The musicians weren't playing for *me*. They were playing for each other, and I was eavesdropping. They echoed, underpinned, spurred on and made space for each other. Abercrombie followed a tune in his head only he could hear, with no thought for whether he could even *play* it, or whom it might impress (again, there were *mistakes*, left in to underwrite its human intimacy); Richie Beirach began each piano solo with the intention of taking the most interesting journey he could over the rolling, dramatic landscape of the tune's harmony; if the musicians had a purpose here, it was simply to convince you of the irrefutability of their emotional case. There can be only a few moments in one's life when the great cogs groan and creak into motion and everything is permanently reordered; another was reading Borges' *Labyrinths* for the first time in my twenties, and rising from the couch only to immediately fall over again, because someone had rerouted half the wires in my internal switchboard. But I was afraid that if I listened straight, I would lose it all. It soon became inconceivable that I wouldn't skin up as soon as the needle dropped.

I also began, in a way I couldn't explain, to really hate my father. I couldn't explain it as there was absolutely nothing to hate. Part of this was just the normal kind of individuation that most adolescent boys have to put their fathers through, and part the projection of every adolescent inadequacy I couldn't bear in myself; I think I was unconsciously worried, too, that his limitations would turn out to be mine, and that I'd never leave the scheme, never mind Dundee. But the extent of my visceral disgust bewildered me, as I knew that I loved him; the feeling fed exquisitely into the post-Christian fallen-by-the-wayside narrative that I was a fundamentally evil individual. In an attempt to provide an irrational feeling with some rational excuse, I'd latch on to anything, any evidence I could find of his (my) inadequacy, his neediness, his pathos, his gaucherie. The trouble was that Dad perhaps provided a little too much to work with. I winced at his noisy eating, and once mentioned it sarcastically, which wounded him to the point of tears, and me worse. I decided that I found his playing bland and his singing voice weak; I hated the nerves he displayed when he spoke in company and related some non-incident at pointless length, or, worse, attempted a joke: I often thought I might die before he reached the inevitably fluffed and mistimed punchline. I despised Dad's ongoing project to 'conquer his nerves', not appreciating the extent to which it was actually putting food on the table. I found his attempts to 'get into jazz' ingratiating. (They were genuine; and I'd also forget that it had been him who'd introduced me to, say, Tony Trischka, five minutes after I'd decided it was cool.)

Worst of all were what I saw as his attempts to brown-nose my friends. At midnight, Dad would clatter back in from his gig with his guitar and PA to find us all camped in the living room, talking crap and getting high and drinking tea. Then he'd hover in the doorway in his cowboy boots and RUSS belt trying to make conversation for what seemed like weeks. This was a perfect agony to me. In his mind, he was just trying to avoid the gulf that opened up between him and his own father; though there was a neediness in it too, and arguably he might have been strong enough to be sensitive to my own discomfort – loudly conveyed in my wincing, sighing and eye-rolling – and joined in just a bit less. But the guy had also spent his evening singing to total strangers for the money that was paying for our teabags and biscuits, and didn't want to feel he was returning to another roomful of strangers in his own home. My friends were all very fond of him, especially my pal Iain, a very skinny bassist generally invisible behind a cloud of bong steam, who functioned as our crew's principled contrarian. 'I think it's nice, Russ yapping away with us like that,' he coughed. 'My dad wouldn't.' It really was just me. But I couldn't wait to put distance between us; and when I finally left Dundee at twenty, my need to propel myself far away from my father made up for any shortfall I had in courage. In future years, if I ever needed another reason to hate myself, I could always look back to that time with authentic shame, as I do when I type this. But I couldn't help it. I really couldn't. Besides, I was about to discover there was another way to leave home.

32 It'll No Be You Then

It's possible, I guess, that had it not found its perfect occasion my breakdown would not have been triggered, but I'm certain I'd have soon contrived another one. There was doubtless some degree of artistic necessity involved in my Descent into Madness. As much as I hate to admit it. I have spent my life trying not to feel like an artist, partly reflexively (their minimal contribution to home economies makes them a working-class liability, and while the arts are not actively discouraged, your upgrading them beyond a hobby is often considered an act of slow-motion suicide), and partly on account of having met far too many artists who aren't, and from whom one would ideally like to distinguish oneself. I'm a little too fond of quoting Chesterton: 'the artistic temperament is a disease that afflicts amateurs', especially when it comes to poets. One might make an exception for Rilke, but the rest of y'all can quit whining. Madness, yes, but poetry gives us no special dispensation for our bad behaviour, concupiscence, solipsism and recreational hypochondria. But some of us do sense, intuitively, that a few nights in the belly of the whale is the price of entry, and that without The Turn in Hell, one's work will forever lack the single piece of underpinning knowledge it requires to remove it from the dimension of *time*. To write a decent poem, I believe you need to have absorbed the truth about the fundamental ghosthood of the human condition, our 'double-realmed', twin-citizenship status of being both now and eternal, alive and dead. It has the effect of allowing you to experience your living tongue as a dead language, which is to say it gives you the necessary distance you need to make it strange. It is, in essence, a second bite of the apple, and an even riskier stolen mouthful than the first. The immediate effect on the structure of the self is profound, but the length of your trip downstairs is crucial, lest one remains cast out of oneself for good. In hell, you get to discover that the dissolution of the self is *not* that thing folk claim happens in meditation or on mushrooms, when one can learn to make the ego absent, or asleep: there, it can be conjured back up with a snap of the fingers when it's later required – as it assuredly will be – to re-enter the world of others, of work, love, dinner and television.*

What I experienced instead, on that fateful day in a squat in Step Row, off the Perth Road, was more like the arrival of the bailiffs, the ego's dismantling by a brutally efficient team of hired contractors: its being ripped apart, shredded, disarticulated into its sixty competing and incompatible component selves, none of whom turn out to be you. It turned into a seemingly endless horror whose lack of centre didn't even allow you *ownership* of the experience; to this day, I don't know how much I'd have to hate someone to wish it on

---

* Though I've read accounts of 5-MeO-DMT ingestion that sound alarmingly similar to what I underwent, and suspect it performs a similar trick on brain chemistry.

them. It comes with a strange attendant empathy: since one is nothing more than the locus of pain, one does not want it to arise again, in the universe, anywhere, nor for any feeling soul to be associated with it, possibly on the random chance it might be yours. But at the end of it, you realise there is no master voice to listen to, no higher power beyond that which you construct; the problem then becomes finding the *will* to actually construct it, to go out in search of its quiet counsel within the jabbering crowd. There is no guarantee you will succeed. I think many fall, stay fallen, and never leave the institution.

But in the middle of all this, maybe two-thirds of the way into my hospitalisation, I heard a horseman's word, of sorts; an old secret, whispered and vouchsafed, which went something like this: *You do not exist and you are already dead.* Once you know you aren't really here – that you're a verb, not a noun, a process, not an operation, the road, not the destination – it means your potential is no longer limited by what you believed yourself to *be.* Unfortunately, your immediate task is to decide if you can handle the pain of being anything at all, given the knowledge that hell can exist right here, right now, in the park, the supermarket, the bedroom.

I know, I know: I've been talking very abstractly. I'm putting off saying what actually happened, because it's going to involve reliving it. What happened was this. I didn't trust my mum and dad anymore; who knows what they were putting in my dinner? I could certainly feel its effects. I'd started to make excuses for getting my own food after the rest of the family had eaten, though this often involved not eating at all. I'd been over to score some hash from a flat in Seafield, one of several dosshouses we then revolved around. They all stank of patchouli and weed and were all interchangeably squalid, bar one luxury addition: everyone had very high-end hi-fi. Doug Scanlon had a Linn Sondek, standing in a basin of gravel to absorb any vibration, and set on a concrete slab; this was run into a little black preamp and then a classic NAD amp, then out to a pair of giant Wharfedales. It had an SME pickup arm and an Ortofon cartridge, which had a small hot spotlight trained on it to improve the conductivity of the wires; seriously. The records were gently tipped out from their paper sleeves, and ferried to the deck between two fingertips. There they were wiped, circularly and clockwise, with an anti-static cloth. Amongst folk who could barely remember to wipe themselves, the care taken to ensure every string-squeak and off-mic cough of *Hot Rats* or *Dark Side* or *Trout Mask Replica* was transmitted with absolute, well, fidelity, was remarkable. Someone had skinned up a twenty-skin R101 of God alone knows, and handed it round. The album on the turntable was a weird old Larry Coryell and Philip Catherine record, *Twin House*; there's a track on it called 'Homecomings', which Catherine and others recorded many times. It's a minor standard, a beautiful tune based around a steady, tense arpeggiated figure that seems to want to resolve but won't, creepy and haunted as hell. (If I hear it now, I run for cover.)

I took a few draws and passed it on. I think I later established that it was PCP-laced Afghan mixed with some brown heroin to see what happened. What happened was that I was walking back from the squat with Alfie, along the river side of the Perth Road, to catch the bus back to the estate. We'd drawn level with the half-moon garden that has a stupid little model of the Magdalen Green bandstand. I noticed that I had trouble computing its size, and I couldn't tell if it was just the actual bandstand viewed from a distance. Then I was aware that I was talking. It made a kind of sense, whatever it was, but I was just listening to someone talk, who was me. Meanwhile, a daft bit of Scottish music-hall patter my Papa would often recite was racing through my head, on a loop. *Says she to me, is that you? Says I, who? She says you. I says me? She says aye. I says no. She says oh well it'll no be you then. Says she to me is that you says I who she says you I says me she says aye I says no she says oh well it'll no be you then saysshetomeis-thatyousaysIwhoshesaysyouIsaysmeshesaysayeIsays—* And then I experienced the first of the panic attacks with which I was soon to be regularly assaulted. It began as a circling, self-feeding fear, a fear of fear, a fear of fear of fear, that accelerated like the flywheel in a gyroscope, tightened on me as its epicentre, then made a kind of whirring lift-off: the sudden disappearance of the mouth and tongue, a terrible lightness underfoot, a weird bounce in the heels, and a tight band vicing one's forehead. And then a view of yourself from above and from one side, and a feeling that you were choking and about to die; and then the mortified calm horror of complete, perfect depersonalisation. I could no more get back into my body and influence its speech or movement than turn on the lights of a house I'd been locked out of; although the better metaphor is that I'd been bound hand and foot and thrown into the back seat of myself. I was allowed to watch and listen, but had to trust entirely to my newly revealed automaton to take care of everything else. Which, miraculously, it did; it walked, it boarded a bus, it declared, with comic understatement, that it did not feel right; it managed some rote social exchanges; it somehow got itself home and crawled into bed.*

The experience, and its subsequent repetitions, also affected my view of my waking hours forever. I now know, miserably, that much of our living is almost completely somnambulant. That we are talking is no sign of our being conscious. Humans talk as birds twitter, and often even less; as leaves rustle. Once home, it took perhaps six hours for the halves of my cloven self to fuse again. The night was worse than the day, though, as I lost even my back-seat driver. My one dream was my falling and falling and falling from an unimaginable height; as I fell, I began to fragment. (A few years later I would know Larkin's

---

* I have had only two other panic attacks to rival this in adulthood. They were decades apart. Both occurred at the moment I realised I was falling in love; both occasions involved two individuals who, it transpired, had broadly identical personality disorders. As all survivors will testify, deep encounters with these folk involve the complete loss of your own individuality, the effective destruction of the self, which they require to connect you as an instrumental extension of their own need. Strange, isn't it, that the body should always know deep down what's on the wind for us; but it often does, long before the conscious mind has caught up.

lines from 'The Old Fools' as its accurate depiction: I was flying apart in the darkness, and if this wasn't death, I don't know what could be.) When I woke up, I couldn't assemble myself into any coherent personality, let alone get out of bed, and could hardly speak. Mum called Dr Carswell. Dad had taken me to see him when I'd had one of my earlier rabies-related flip-outs at thirteen, where he gave a broadly useless pep-talk that Dad, bless him, tried to selectively quote for weeks after. 'But as Dr Carswell said, puberty can be a very confusing time.' But he was also a good professional who knew where his expertise ended. He seemed to come with a tick-list. Are you sleeping? Both no and all the time. I wouldn't call it sleep, exactly. Are you experiencing feelings of dissociation? (I remember thinking he was lucky I knew what that meant, though looking back he was merely treating me as intelligent.) I confirmed that yes, this was pretty much all I was experiencing. He sent me for an assessment at Ninewells, the huge general hospital on the other side of town, the same day.

I didn't really understand the urgency. It was very strange. Dad had the car to go to work, so I went alone on the bus, very shakily; I assumed that I'd receive some pills, and that the NHS would treat me at its usual indifferent pace. My experience of the NHS thus far had been (and remains) hopeless for the routine, but I hadn't yet seen that it was amazing in an emergency. The consultant questioned me about the panic attack, and my general state of mind. I opened up about God, my sinfulness, the drugs, the aura I was seeing round objects and the indigo tendrils I could see connecting them, and explained that while I wasn't mad – I'd read a lot of Arthur Janov and R. D. Laing and Jung, so I knew what mad was – I heard a lot of competing voices in my head, yes like you're talking to me now, and I had trouble working out which one to pay attention to but it was okay mostly, as their conversation was benign and mundane; I told him about how I was pretty sure Mum and Dad were trying to poison me. He was kind but very firm, and he told me I would feel a lot safer in the hospital, and to go home and pack a bag of clothes, toiletries and books, enough for one week. (I really did fall for it; of course one only needs a week's-worth of clothes.) The news was received a little hysterically, with Mum and Dad frightened to death for me. My sister Louise, then only six years old, cried and clung to me. Dad drove me back to the hospital, and I was on Ward 89 by nightfall. The diagnosis, which I didn't read until years later, was 'acute adolescent schizophrenic episode'.

33 Straight Box

This is a hard thing to write about. Not because it was agony, which it was, but because it was non-linear. In the mental ward, I had essentially the same day over and over again; such narrative quality as this episode has relates to the graph of how that day went. It went, over four months: bad; better; much, much worse; even worse than that; bad; slightly better but still bad; home.

Despite the fact that Ninewells had opened in the seventies, I still somehow imagined that the mental ward would be housed in a Victorian Gothic wing with barred windows, clanking pipes, uretic tiling, steel gurneys with one dodgy wheel and obscure brass plumbing hinting at novel water treatments, but I was confronted with one of two six-berth hospital wards, clean, yellow and bright, shipshape and modern, whose south end was one broad window looking down over pretty Invergowrie Bay and the broad Tay estuary to Fife. All the beds were crisply and uniformly made, bar one around which the curtain had been drawn. The ward stank of cigarettes, but back then everything did. Passive smoking was what we called breathing. (I burned thirty No. 6 a day back then, which was, for an asthmatic, a pretty dedicated effort. By twenty, I was alternating draws with three-blast huffs of Ventolin, and realised it was quit or die.) Ward 89 was for male mental patients; we were divided from Ward 90, the women's ward, by several rooms we all shared: an occupational therapy room with a ping-pong table and little else, a small dining hall and a TV room permanently tuned to the worst available programme. No, nothing to see here. The Bedlam hellholes were all in our heads, and each had furnished his own.

The nurses were brisk and kind, and explained the ropes, of which there were few. Here are the mealtimes; tick what you want to eat tomorrow on this form; all we expect you to do is make up your bed; here's how to do a hospital corner. That was it. Arnie was the first patient to walk over and introduce himself. I knew him from my childhood. He was a popular Dundee pantomime dame, a fat, potato-headed man-child. He still had the cadence and timing of a clown, but was emptied out with chronic depression. He delivered every sentence as if it were a joke, with a little subdued yodel at the end, but it wasn't. Blebs of metallic sweat swelled and broke constantly on his great bald napper. Arnie would often be unable to get out of bed, and would be separated from his cigarettes so he had to. There was a beardy young academic called Andy, with whom I traded notes on panic attacks. 'What is it with the bouncy heel thing?' 'I know, right? Do you get the hatband?' 'Yeah. The no-tongue thing?' 'Yip. Tingly hands?' 'Tingly hands.' This helped us both. Clinical descriptions of panic attacks back then focused on the panic, but the physical symptoms were often the most terrifying thing about them, and it was good to learn ours weren't unique. Then there was a Largactil shuffler called Bob, tall, balding and glassy-eyed, who made his blank-faced orbit of the long circular corridor to the rear of the ward hundreds of times a day, and was never out of his pyjamas. I took to measuring the time by his passing moon. There's Bob; must be ten past five. He was having weekly ECT, and couldn't speak a word. This had left him incontinent too, and he had to be dissuaded from drying his trousers on the radiator, which stank the place out like a kipper.

I was seen the next day by a tubby psychologist with a bad moustache, who immediately offered me a cigarette as an excuse to light another for himself. His hands shook as we spoke. I saw him once more as his patient, then a lot more as a co-inmate, since he was on the ward himself a month later. This inspired little confidence, and correctly: no one knew what the hell they were doing, really. Some drugs sort-of-worked, but the most reliably effective treatment was the ward itself, which often simply removed folk from the source of their distress and left them to sweat it out in peace, by which I mean a hell free from other distractions.

My bed was opposite a guy called Max Stout. Max was haunted by his miserable divorce and his terrible pun of a name, and was in absolute denial over the severity of his illness. He was a music teacher, and encouraging of my guitar-playing – in which, bizarrely, he claimed he heard Sérgio Mendes, but I don't think 'popular music' was his thing; it was probably because I changed key every two bars. At the time I was working in forty-seven different guitar tunings, à la John Martyn and Joni Mitchell.* We had an acquaintance

* As I learned later just before I dumped it, this approach means

in common, and I'd gone to school with his cello pupil Ally McCulloch. He was obsessed with Ally's natural musicianship, fine features, luminous pale skin, blonde hair, white blouses, starched pleats and virginal purity, and he held her up to be all that was good and untainted and true and beautiful in the world, i.e. not his marriage. I didn't disabuse him. Ally was a brilliant musician, but as soon as she clocked out of school she went the full New Romantic. She had both nipples pierced, was invariably at the front of the queue for the latest experimental drug, was liberal in her affection towards both sexes and dressed like a Ruritanian fan-dancer. I let Max rave on and on about her Madonna-like radiance; it was clearly helping his recovery.

I was also made aware that I had precisely sixteen weeks to improve. After that, one was considered a long-term prospect, and would be removed to the psychiatric hospital, Liff, formerly Dundee Royal Lunatic Asylum. Along with the orphanage, the jail and the morgue, Liff was one of several locations that might be invoked by a despairing parent. 'You're gonnae hae me in Liff!' A couple of my co-internees had

---

that your between-numbers patter had better be brilliant, especially now that the standard joke – 'Next, some Chinese classical music: this one is by Tu Ning' – is mercifully unavailable to us. Such endless twangathons do not favour the taciturn, and the final reckoning will show that I have spent literally sixteen hours of my life breathing through my teeth while I listened to Dick Gaughan tune up. On the other hand, the palaver of his alternate tunings turned Leo Kottke into a kind of Clement Freud of American Gothic.

already been in Liff for longer tours of duty, and had absolutely no desire to return to the front. You were lumped in with folk with far more severe illnesses, and because the population was far larger, treatment tended to be a little less individually customised. One wardmate recalled the dreaded approaching trundle of the ECT machine as it made its way down the ward, one bed at a time. One of the treatments meted out to the unruly was 'straight box', being ECT with no anaesthetic or muscle relaxant. This tended to ensure compliance, one way or the other. Liff incentivised us to get better, or at least to appear better. One patient, Davie, a garrulous taxi driver from the Fintry estate, was notorious for being constantly readmitted to our ward. I gained his confidence by covering for him when he sneaked out to the Bayview in Menzieshill for a fly pint.

– So . . . How come you never end up in Liff?

– Miraculous recovery around week fifteen. Anyway, it's no' me that should be in here. It's the wife.

– She's depressed?

– No' exactly. But the wummin's no' weel.

– So you fool the doctors?

– First time I didnae have to. Sheila's mad for the bingo. Six nights a week. For a while I took t' hidin' her purse, so she couldnae get near the Green's. One night I comes in fae the taxis and she's gone berserker. Trashed the front room, looking for it. Unbelievable. Slashed the couch, smashed the fish tank, aa mah guppies and ma Siamese fightin' fish floppin' aa over the carpet.

– You must have gone nuts.

– Didnae lift mah hand. Like I say, she's no' right. I went into the toilet t' cool down and consider mah position. Meanwhile she's downstairs callin' the polis. So they turn up at the door ten minutes later, and cool as ye like, she tells them *Eh* did it.

– And they believed her?

– Well I flipped ma lid at that point, which made her story look pretty convincin' . . . So she signed for an emergency section while PC Murdoch* stood on mah heid diallin' the hospital, and I ended up spendin' the night in here for assessment. Of course Sheila wis straight doon the Mecca before the wee white van had pulled oot o the street.

– Christ almighty.

– At first I'm like – got t' get oot o here. I am a name not a number! But the morn's mornin', I get talkin' to a couple o the lads. Then a bonny wee nurse came and brought 's a cup o tea. The cake trolley comes roond. So I'm sittin' up in bed, lovely fresh linen, wi mah French Fancy, mah cuppie tea and the *Courier*, and I'm thinkin' . . . here, *hangonaminute*. So when I saw the consultant I says, *Aye, it's . . . it's like a raging . . . FURNACE inside me, Doctor. Maybe it's better it's aw coming out now* . . . So they kept me in for twa month.

– Was Sheila apologetic when ye came oot?

– Oh very contrite. Lasted about six weeks. Then right back t' square one again. Bingo frenzy, burnin' through the housekeepin', chewin' ma heid . . . By which time I'm thinkin' . . . I've aye hated that wee nest o tables. That terrible picture

---

* Scottish. Affectionate and generic name for 'urban beat cop'.

o the greetin' bairn yer brother gave wis. Thon plaster o Paris statuette o Flora MacDonald. So I just took an axe t' them one night, called the polis masel', and telt them I wis haein' another o mah queer turns.

– So ye've a ticket in here any time ye want?

– State o the hoose, though.

Liff, though, wasn't the ultimate sanction. No one dared invoke the name of Strathmartine, the asylum just without the city limits, for mere rhetorical effect. It terrified us. As a kid, on Sunday constitutionals with my dad through the village of Bridgefoot, we'd pass by the back of the hospital, and peer through the high-wire double fence into the vast estate with its slow-moving denizens. Dad enjoyed scaring me. 'There's things in there, son, that are just *heads*.' I mean, there probably *were*. Formerly a kind of orphanage-cum-bin, 'The Baldovan Institute for Imbecile and Idiot Children', it was now an all-purpose repository for whatever the town had decided it couldn't deal with or would rather forget about. The catatonic, the vegetative, the full menu of chromosomal and DNA misfires, the psychopathic – and back then, miserably, older kids and adults with Down's syndrome. It was where you ended up when either all hope had gone or your case had been decreed officially hopeless. True, there was a wee bit of waterboarding and live inhumation to keep order, it later emerged, but it was otherwise a well-tended and pleasant estate, with its own kitchen gardens, dance hall and swimming pool. But that wasn't the point. Strathmartine was The End.

34 A Knock from Below

Most folk began on the ward claiming a misdiagnosis. But you very much *do* belong there, and you will soon know it. Archie the auxiliary, a kind man from the scheme, recognised the denial phase, and sat me down in the OT room for a smoke. 'Gie up fechtin' wi it, and get yersel intae a routine. You'll get better.' So, as estranged from myself as I felt, I did what he said. I ate, I read, I played my guitar, I slept. I could see that my freefall after the panic attack in Seafield had at least allowed me to establish the bottom of the pit. For a couple of weeks I'd just lain there, but now there was a thin stream of sunlight from above, and I could make out the dull glint of the handholds and footholds above me. I began to plot the route of my escape. But as the Serbian aphorism goes, 'Just when you think you've hit rock bottom, you hear the knocking from below.'* The second fall was much further and quite unannounced. It was also a lot harder, as not only did the first pit turn out to have a second pit below it, but I fell from halfway up the one I'd been climbing out of.

After a fortnight of observation, which is to say of

---

* The Serbs are underrated aphorists. 'Now the government is using the carrot-and-stick approach. First they beat us with sticks; now they beat us with carrots.'

absolutely nothing, I was put on imipramine. I seemed to improve overnight, and my consultant was delighted with the uptick in my mood, and rather pleased with himself that his speculative prescription (they all were, of course; we were still ten years away from Prozac) had hit the target. I was writing music again, and making plans, and talkative; if anything, a little too much so. My mother, Aunt Bett and psycho-Nazi Uncle Jimmer had been up to visit, and we'd sat chatting in a cafe within the huge hospital concourse. I'd already started packing for my return at the weekend, and had popped my guitar in its case and gathered my laundry. Mum asked what I fancied for tea that Friday. All I wanted was Findus Minced Beef Crispy Pancakes and Neapolitan ice cream. Hospital food tasted of nothing.

Ninewells Hospital boasts some remarkable, mile-long corridors; one of them, a service gangway in the basement level, is one of the longest in the UK, and nurses use it to train for marathons. I had started the long walk back to the ward with Mum, and was looking ahead to the vanishing point of the corridor when it started to slowly tilt downwards. It moved through 90 degrees, until I was staring into a mineshaft. I suddenly became very light-headed but simultaneously leaden-footed, as if my centre of gravity had sunk to my ankles. I asked her if we'd taken the lift, because the floor was sinking. The descent accelerated, and I separated from myself again. O no no no no. Though this time I felt a clean cut, a scission that I knew was irrevocable. I don't recall getting back to the ward, but I went straight to bed, at five in the afternoon, as sleep was the only possible place to hide. Through the night I received visitors at my bedside, as I was talking and shouting. Arnie the panto dame came over to ask if I wanted a smoke. My dead grandfather, Pappy, sat on the chair beside the bed for a while, but his glasses were smashed and his hands were bleeding. He was shaking as if he was crying, but he made no sound. Archie the auxiliary checked on me a couple of times, his face lined with concern. Then there was a woman in a floral dress with a horse's head who didn't move but whose position changed in a series of still exposures. Morning came, and it was worse than the night. The light was radioactive and the air smelled like dentist's gas and the pain. The pain was. How to explain it. The pain took the form of a kind of endlessly imploding terror, simultaneously shrinking and expanding. (Imagine a rapidly collapsing star being constantly zoomed in on, so its size appears to stay the same. Now imagine you're the star.) And the voices were back. They weren't louder, but they were now clear and confident. They overlapped, but I could tune in to any one of them. They either spoke completely nonsensically or monologued very clearly on the subject of evil; psychosis tends to stick to genre. I wasn't going anywhere. My parents were called and the situation explained to them: the drug had retriggered the psychosis, and I was, in the doctor's words, a very sick boy. I stayed on the ward for another three and a half months.

Imipramine is an ancient tricyclic with some impressive side effects, one of which can be the exacerbation or duplication of the symptoms it treats. In my case, it resulted in panic disorder, suicidal ideation and a schizophrenic break. They wanted me on another drug as soon as possible, but you can't come off imipramine immediately, and the dose had to be stepped down. I was committed to around two weeks of taking a drug that was killing me, like a Polonium-210 of the soul. It was countered, immediately, with a huge dose of thioridazine: I was on 600 mg daily, rising to 800 mg. This should have felled an allosaurus, but I was wired like I'd been plugged into the national grid. These days thioridazine is only prescribed as a drug of last resort for schizophrenics, since instant death was a popular side effect: it essentially put Lars Ulrich in charge of your heartbeat, with all the manic enthusiasm, rank incompetence and stick-dropping potential that implies. I tried to end the days as swiftly as the nurses would let me, and would plead to go to bed at four in the afternoon. I wanted very badly not to wake up again. (I'm surprised to recall that I did not pray, although I had promised to myself about a year before that I never would again. But if I knew nothing else by now, it was that I was alone.) Then I'd come round at about nine in the morning, and it would all start over. God God God I'm still here. I'd crawl into my clothes and curl up on the bed.

In that time I had no centre. I don't know who it was that answered when I was spoken to. I couldn't locate myself anywhere, and wasn't having my own thoughts. My mind had been rented out to strangers, and they were breaking all the good things. My friends stopped visiting as I couldn't make it out of the ward, let alone small-talk. They were kids themselves and didn't know what to say. Only Iain still turned up, out of a thrawn and principled loyalty I've never forgotten.

One afternoon I was lying on my bed, holding my knees. Bob, the Largactil shuffler, walked over to my bay. He wasn't shuffling. I had only ever seen Bob on his corridor circuit, and had never heard him talk; I had assumed his case to be hopeless. But he'd been restored to himself. It turned out he was an educated and self-possessed middle-class man from Broughty Ferry. He laid a hand on my shoulder.

– Just thought I'd pop over and see how you are.

– Uh

– Things really do improve.

– Uh

– Just hang in there, okay.

– Uh

– We'll see you at the other side.

– Thank you

In the meantime my agoraphobia meant I couldn't leave the ward to get my meals; not that I could eat a thing anyway. At the end of the fortnight's wait for my system to clear of the imipramine, there was little improvement, and I was scheduled for ECT. A couple of days before, though, they put me on Nardil, a sledgehammer of an old drug that had been around as an antidepressant since the early sixties. Nardil was a big orange pill that came with a long list of dietary restrictions; anything with too much tyramine could trigger a fatal hypertension. The voices in the mad agora receded. No, they didn't; that isn't true. What happened is that I found one voice in the muttering crowd that wasn't trying to misinform or terrify me, and which I could identify as my own: it was the only one to call me by my name. It was trustworthy, and it spoke silently, unlike the others. It told me things like: *Donald. Breathe. When the Horror shows up, walk straight into it and don't run away. Let it rise up and break over you like a wave. It can't kill you.* And it said: *This will pass.** Over the next few weeks, things got a little better. Just as the fall had been a wholly embodied metaphor, so was the climb out. I'd find a fingernail crevice and edge up the pit a few inches, but each advance carried with it the risk of a longer drop than ever. It was excruciating, holding each braced pose, waiting for the strength to return to make the next lurch towards the upper air.

Throughout all this, the green-scrubbed auxiliaries, really glorified hospital porters, were scrupulously kind to me. They were working-class men of the sort I'd grown up with, whose survival had been based on the sense of community they now extended to me, unthinkingly: they took care of their own. The nurses were kind too, but distant, and did little but keep a watchful eye; mostly they were too taken up with the running of the ward to spend any time with me. There was one that I'd rather had spent much less, though. Gary, one of the staff nurses, was a horrible boy in his heaven. He looked like a young Owen Wilson, handsome and wiry with a vulpine, expressionless face, a blond New Romantic feathercut halfway to a mullet, and unreadably dead grey eyes. He loved it when

---

* So much Freud is Freudian bollocks, of course, but the superego turns out to be a thing like your feet are a thing.

someone got a little excitable and force could be deployed. When he wasn't restraining them, he enjoyed taking the piss out of the patients, or whupping them at the ping-pong or card table. In my weeks hiding in the corner of the ward, he insisted I either collect my meals myself from the dining hall or not eat. I got there and back by keeping a hand over my head and edging down the wall. We were all afraid of him, especially the women, and we'd all heard rumours of what went on in the laundry room. There were some poor junkie girls in the next ward who could be induced to do anything for some extra pills, or just because they hadn't considered non-compliance as an option. But, as I say, rumours.

There never seemed any way of reporting anyone in those days. Bullies in all professions operated with impunity. In the same year, somewhere in a children's ward in England, a straw-haired scarecrow of a celebrity porter was raping children with the full knowledge of the staff and the protection of the hospital management. The economic historian Carlo Cipolla framed a law of human stupidity; it states that x proportion of *any* cohort – policemen, anglers, artists, Nobel Prize winners, binmen – will be stupid, which is to say they will always operate against both their own interests and those of the group. My not-very-original Law of Narcs states that there is a scalable effect where, within every coherent social group large enough to structure itself around status differentials – extended family, office, military division, political party, university department, knitting circle, brass band, church, mental ward – the person nearest to full-blown narcissistic personality disorder will not just naturally accede to the position of central influence, but be actively facilitated and promoted to it, unless someone consciously intervenes and removes them. This is natural law; much the way that galaxies form themselves around black holes, humans form themselves around gods. A narc is a point of gravitational attraction that structures the social space around them.

One final reflection: as soon as you identify a narc – if you have the resources, if you possibly can – try to let them know you are unafraid of them. Their dead-eyed overconfidence can be quickly distinguished from mere adult self-possession, because its intention and effect is to make you feel all their fear for them. If they feel socially unconfident, they will accuse you of a faux pas; if they feel weak, they will find you insufferably so, and bully you remorselessly to guarantee it; if they fear dying, they will accuse you of malingering; if they feel a failure, all your success will be met with its immediate diminishment; and God help you if they feel they don't exist. But go nose to nose with them and show no fear, and they *all* crumble, because your fear is the cable through which you receive their instructions. Unless, of course, you're their patient, their child, their spouse or their employee, in which case we need the state, the police or the judiciary to intervene and cut the wire for you. They didn't use to do so, because we lived in a morbidly insecure age in which mere self-confidence was seen as strength of character. I wonder what happened to Gary. I suspect he was destined for great things.

Now that I had a centre to hold to, I could concentrate a

little, and had started to read again. As I urgently needed to be elsewhere, and as it was the only available form of escape, my reading needed to be as escapist as possible: so I got stuck into Stephen Donaldson's bloody awful *Chronicles of Thomas Covenant* novels. Iain had lent me *Lord Foul's Bane*. I hadn't read Tolkien yet, and so it struck me as a work of the most splendid originality. Nonetheless, it was, as they say these days, an immersive piece of world-building, and greatly expanded my vocabulary: on every page Donaldson would use a word I'd never heard before, and I had Dad bring me in my Chambers so I could look them up. (Infamously, most pages of *The Chronicles* also saw him use the word 'clench'. It's worth running your literary output through a concordance program to check on your unconscious favourites. Mine is 'discreet'. I don't know what to tell you.) I was therefore fooled into thinking Donaldson was a great intellect, even if it's obvious to me now that he'd only just learned the word too, and had hammered it in with a thesaurus – or, as he'd say, malleated it with a synonymicon – after the first draft, with little regard to tone or context. Still, it inspired me to improve my vocabulary.* Looking at those books now, I honestly don't know

---

* I supercharged it in the mid-eighties, when I read Tony Harrison quoting Arthur Scargill in his epigraph to 'V': 'My father still reads the dictionary every day. He says your life depends on your power to master words.' I was thirty before I realised Arthur and Tony were dead wrong. A large vocabulary has been useless to me. Cultural authority is won not through the mastery of lexis but syntax, pure and simple. The posh lads win by knowing how to speak in full paragraphs,

what you'd have to pay me. The villagefolk came out to stare and wonder; The Unbeliever tried to focus on the elven-fire in Dai Stallforth's hands. Meanwhile, Kevaan's eyes, interred deep within his ancient visage, performed a weary saccade. He had seen it all before. But suddenly Meg the Holborn cleaved the sky with an exsanguineous scream, rending her argent faerymail to bare the twin pups of her silken breasts – and at this signal, all the Rynyhynihyn stood to attention on their warhorses. 'Now fight we must!' she vociferated. 'Aye! Aye!' came the rugged antiphon. I mean, I just made that up, but that's the general vibe. For three thousand pages. But the Land was a huge improvement on the Ward, and it taught me the art of readerly transport.

This was aided by the soundtrack of the early ECM records I fitted to it. I had tapes of Terje Rypdal, Ralph Towner, Eberhard Weber and Keith Jarrett records, but got stuck on John Abercrombie's *Characters*. This is a quiet, watercolour record of solo and multitracked guitar, with which I have been obsessed for forty years – hence my describing it in the present tense – and with which one's lovers have become thoroughly acquainted. (Really; put it on very low and have it fill the room and notice the difference in your attention to the small gesture.) Abercrombie used it as a bridge passage to dissociate himself from his early jazz-rock clone, and it is the sound of

which they have completed while you were rifling through *Roget's* for your elegant variation. They were also reading Wodehouse, Woolf and Walter Pater while you were reading about fucking elves.

someone waking up and realising who they are. It helped me do the same. It's a walled garden of a record, and gave me the keys to a space I could be safe in, and dare to feel something – no small matter, as psychosis makes you quite happy never to feel anything again. Its garden is the one I dreamed myself in as a little boy, the one high above the clouds with its strange tall rocks, trees, ponds and streams, the place which held a distinct flavour of melancholic eternity every time the light changed a little, like a wholly new chord; the place in which you waited, without fear. (The long, lonely single-note solo John plays on the electric mandolin at the start of 'Parable' *is* that little boy.)*

I wasn't what anyone would call 'better' at the end of my sixteen weeks, but I had to be discharged, as some kind of recovery was clearly under way. Liff wouldn't have helped it. Nonetheless, there was a shaky fortnight when I thought they'd transfer me. I was assigned a psychologist, a really fine consultant called, Jungianly, John Martin, a tall, handsome, moustached, curly-haired man who exuded both compassion and authority, and whom I immediately trusted. He was the first shrink I'd seen who had offered anything like actually useful advice, and he drew up a daily plan of gradual exposure to get over my agoraphobia. I could talk to him openly about my lingering fear of God's wrath, and hence of masturbation.

* I wept when John died. I met him only once, in the adjacent urinal at a London rehearsal studio, and decided it was not the moment to grab his hand.

He insisted that I should go home and make a determined effort. So I did, and found I could. Not only was I not struck down where I stood (okay, kneeled; it was hard to balance the thick Grattan's catalogue on the cistern, as the Shower Curtains section was at the back), but it almost had the counterproductive effect of reviving my faith. If your first wank isn't a divine encounter, you're definitely doing it wrong.

I could now see that my hospitalisation had been more of a kill-or-cure quarantine, where something improperly understood had just been allowed to run its course. It was no more sophisticated than the sort of World War I field hospital routine where you'd enclose a wound in plaster with some flesh-eating maggots and some garlic and let the whole thing stew in its own juice, in the hope that, when you cut the cast off later, you'll be left with a healed and gleaming limb, not a putrid black mush. I wasn't quite healed, but the infection was being beaten back by the multiplying antibodies of sanity, for which I now had a working definition: the ability to control one's own thoughts. I had almost no psychotherapy whatsoever, which was probably a good thing, given that back then psychiatry was still indulging the wacko fringes of Freudian doctrine. (I was trying to work out the logic in switching from imipramine to Nardil in the treatment of agoraphobia, and happened on this from a 1975 paper: 'agoraphobic adults experience sudden, unexplained, panic attacks and are unable to travel independently. They are typically women. Freudian theory posits that the symptoms are due to an unconscious, anxiety-provoking, prostitution wish: the women's phobic avoidance of the outside world prevents the activation of an incompletely repressed wish to be a streetwalker.')

About a year later, as part of some kind of ongoing attempt to own the experience, I made a return to the ward. The nurses remembered me, even if they couldn't put a name to the face, but I hadn't made much of an impression. I was unremarkable. The ward was unchanged. The patients were new, bar Davie the Faker, who was lying on his bed with a cup of tea and the paper, and Arnie the panto dame, who was in bed with the covers drawn up to his neck, lying on one side, his head the usual disco ball of sweat; a green-scrubbed auxiliary was seated next to him, talking gently. Gary made an appearance, briefly. He stood with his hands on his hips at the head of the ward, and surveyed the bays to see all was in order. He was wearing the blue uniform of the charge nurse.

It was, however, many years before the experience ceased to define me. I was in my mid-twenties before I stopped thinking about myself as 'one who could go mad'. But it also gifted me something. You knew that the ego was a construct, not because you'd read it in Lacan, but because you'd watched it be dismantled. At the centre of us is not a self, but a clean hole. It can be a pit, or it can be the well from which we raise the clear water of nothingness; this allows us the knowledge without the annihilation. Or we can do instead what nearly all of us do, which is ignore the hole completely, and subscribe fully to the myth of ourselves. The reality will make itself known sooner or later.

35 Adventures in Clubland

It should go without saying that my climb back took much longer than the descent. Descents are a breeze. There *was* a way back up out of the well, but the hand- and footholds all seemed further apart than my hands and feet. There were no ladders, only snakes. Sure and steady does it. I was pursuing a ten-point plan to try to get the better of my crippling agoraphobia. Mum would drive me to the shops, and I'd buy something, and crawl back into the car. That was it for the day. I'd be drowned in sweat, and fit for little but curling up in bed. The distance from the house was slowly increased, and the day I managed to step from the car and nailed a five-minute walk in the city centre, I felt like Neil Armstrong, if Neil Armstrong had gone to the moon for a Scotch pie and a tin of Lilt. But some days I couldn't face it. Alfie declared he wouldn't see me again until I walked down to his house alone. I made it, but the panic attack halfway down Harestane Road meant I almost didn't. But I deployed my new technique, and remembered that the way to break the fear-of-fear-of-fear vortex is, firstly, to accept that panic attacks don't kill you, and secondly, turn and walk *into* them, deliberately, knowing that great wave rising angrily above you will just crash over your head, and leave you quite unharmed.

But how on earth I worked out that the *stage* was the only place my panic could be kept in check is a mystery. I'd worked as my father's occasional sideman since I was fifteen or so. He dragged me along one evening to help set up the PA, just to get me out the house, and tricked me into sitting in. I found, standing on that raised semicircle again, that the psychic palisade I had spent years laboriously nailing together was still intact. I am, like my father, temperamentally unqualified for this kind of work, but this means the overcompensating defences we develop are a long time in fading. Up there, I was someone else. So I felt at my safest where most folk might feel at their least, i.e. at the St Mary's Country and Western Club on a Tuesday night, standing under the Confederate flag playing Elvis's Trilogy (or 'Triology', to give it its local pronunciation: 'Dixie' / 'Hush Little Baby, Don't You Cry' / 'Mine Eyes Have Seen the Glory'), while the cowboys and cowgals stood in a solemn ring below me, their eyes closed and their Stetsons doffed and their hands flat on their hearts until they could contain their emotion no longer, and they fired off their replica Smith & Wessons, joining in with the Hallelujahs as we all reached our collective screaming climax.

On these nights I was technically invalidating my Invalidity Benefit, but I needed my weekly dosed exposure to the isotope of tiny fame; its therapeutic necessity would have taken far too long to explain to the angry DHSS doctor who grudgingly (too light a word: it positively grieved him to do so) renewed my claim every few months. Eventually, about a year later and apoplectic at what he incorrectly saw as my malingering – I was still very ill, by anyone's standards – he sent me to the rehabilitation centre. This involved a week of 'assessment', which consisted of laying a path of paving slabs that went absolutely nowhere. The slabs themselves were removed from another path to a different nowhere, built the week before. If you collapsed, or managed to demonstrate a genuinely terminal incompetence, you'd be sent to receive some training in light clerical work. After one morning in this gloomy Tartarus spent imagining the afternoon, I reclassified myself as unemployed and set about honestly not looking for work. (As, I recall, a shepherd; although sadly employment had long been thin on the scheme for us ancient stewards of the woolly commons.)

Signing on was no humiliation, unless you'd been working the C&W clubs and were recognised by the clerk. However, the chances of them challenging your claim were pretty remote, since it would have entailed a more embarrassing disclosure on their part, i.e. that they had spent Friday night cosplaying Wyatt Earp or Calamity Jane. Once or twice we exchanged a resigned shrug, but that was as much grief as I received. Anyway, my father – inspired by my phaser-drenched machine-gun solo based on an Indian raga in 'Truck Drivin' Man' that almost lost him his next booking at Lochee Gunslingers ('Could we have less of that Hawaiian shite') – soon forced me to answer a small ad in the Dundee *Courier*. The Management were looking for a new lead guitarist.

I went along to the Fairmuir Social Club to meet the band and the outgoing guitarist, Jock: a genial, rough-as-fuck, good-looking moustachioed outlaw-type. Jock played well enough in the Gregg Allman style everyone in Dundee was obsessed with at the time, and was leaving the band, he told me without irony, to concentrate more seriously on his drinking. I did the machine-gun raga solo on 'Three Times a Lady'. Jock – a muso, and thus capable of terrible suspensions of taste – was impressed, and his word carried some authority, despite the rest of the band's reasonable misgivings. Jeff, the spiky-mulleted, Rod Stewart-obsessed singer, bandleader and manager, gave me the thumbs up, and I was in.

Jock stayed on for a couple of weeks to show me the ropes. Not that I'd much to compare him to, having hitherto only really kept the company of children – but Jock was the first person I had ever seen who was *brilliant* with women. His spectacular success, I observed – hell, I was taking notes and abstracting formulae – was down to one thing: he simply preferred their company to ours. By any normal yardstick, the success of the rest of The Management was also spectacular, but anyone in a clubbie band who couldn't get laid three times a week was either a clinical sociopath (like me; technically I probably was) or had some weeping facial elephantiasis (like Shug McCafferty of our near-rivals Jack Black and the Threepenny Tray, who performed in shadow by popular request). The strange cachet conferred merely by randomly hitting an instrument while standing one foot higher than the rest of the audience – dressed in what would be wholly inappropriate for one foot lower – says a lot about both the social function of glamour and its highly relative nature. It got you permanently shagged. In those days nearly all male musicians seemed to regard it less as a perk than as a responsibility. To not shag *all* the time was an abuse of privilege, equivalent in its perversity to a council bus driver paying his fare home, and things like restraint, temperance, particularity and marital fidelity were frowned upon as a betrayal of the whole guild. Some band members seemed in competition only with themselves. I remember Billy the keyboard player set himself the task of having knowledge of three generations of the same family, a feat he achieved in unusual sequence.

Jock's braggadocio was as brash as the rest of the band's – but while their chat-ups were conducted as public performances, whenever Jock talked to a woman everyone else in the room disappeared. I once watched him score from literally thirty yards out. 'Check this. Check this. I'm in.' All he did was catch the eyes of a pretty girl at the bar; the two of them then proceeded to stare each other out, the way those wonderful people do, for almost a full half-minute. She lost her nerve first, though, disguising it as a behind-hand aside to her neighbour. 'Ye bastard – won!' Jock yelled, and punched the air. She laughed. The band laughed. Jock laughed too; with her, not us. After the gig, she was carrying his guitar case, while he wound up his leads.

I think the band knew deep down I was the wrong guy for the job, though, and my ant-infested solos were totally inappropriate for the simpler terrain of 'Stand and Deliver' and 'Karma Chameleon'. But the speed I could deliver the notes at was enough to blind weaker musicians to the order, and I had the sense to keep it from getting too outré. But I considered the popular music of the era beneath contempt, and I would approach the guitar solo from 'Baker Street' less with cynicism than with a sense of doing my bit for interplanetary relations. Christ knows it must have sounded like it. Nonetheless, I diligently learned the set: it was mostly top-twenty hits from the last five years, so this meant covering everything from 'Ebony and Ivory' and 'Maneater' to the guitar solos in Lionel Richie's 'Easy' (it was) and 'Hotel California' (it wasn't), plus the usual classics from the last-bell clubbie songbook, like 'Wild Mountain Thyme' and 'Flower of Scotland'. However, at least my sound had improved. I had a new Gordon Smith, a very plain, elegant guitar with a lovely flat ebony fingerboard and hand-wound pickups, which I was paying up weekly. This purchase was part subsidised through the sale of my Burns Black Bison, a twin-horned satano-bombastic British-made classic with a neck a mile long that was as heavy as a tree. It had a hilarious four pickups, and as many different toggle positions as a set of bike gears. I sold it to some dude off the Charleston estate for a hundred quid. If I'd kept it, I could've paid off the mortgage tomorrow, but I didn't know a soul back then who owned *two* guitars. Jock had sold me his Fender Twin Reverb outrageously cheaply – pitying me, correctly, for my awful 'tranny' HH amp head and the speaker cabs my dad had made from chipboard. The Fender Twin was a giant box full of glowing valves and weighed like the Ark of the Covenant. Compared with the HH, it also *felt* like plugging into the Ark of the Covenant, and was the difference, acoustically, between opening your lungs in the Concertgebouw or a chip shop. And, much like the Ark of the Covenant, I'd imagine, it also had the great advantage of staying hot for two hours after the gig.

clubbie musicians had been vouchsafed something of a basic feminist insight: many women thought about sex just as often as we did.)

In my time, there was only one verified claim on a ten-pointer. The wedding was, inevitably, in Fife. Fife, last bastion of the Picts, whose broad face and beaky nose I bear. The social immobility of certain areas has led to an impoverished gene pool: there are settlements in central Fife, too dangerous for scientific survey, that make the Pitcairn Islands look like the West Village. Hordes of identically terrifying children – who anywhere else would all be singularly terrifying – will eat the legs of any traveller stupid enough to pause to ask directions. Weddings, and hence the presence of visiting gametes from Tayside, therefore represented unmissable opportunities for the locals. It was the drummer's call: in the van, in the car park, between the meal and the evening dance. The bride called it, with questionable timekeeping, her 'last wee fling'. He kept the garter and wore it on his head as a sweatband, after the happy couple had been waved off into the night.

The Management also gave me my first studio experience; we went in to record Jeff's self-penned number 'Motel'. The rest of the band were musos into soul and funk, but our lead singer and bandleader was the only guy who really shared the tastes of our audience. 'Motel' was a shamelessly derivative Rod Stewart-esque, fag-hoarse, she-done-me-wrong anthem. After the third chorus of 'Mo-tel, sheez treatin' me laarg uh mo-tel (*in-an-outta-gen*)' I had an eight-bar guitar break; I went all George Benson and filled it with many notes. The guy on the desk was impressed, if no one else was. The studio was plastered with the promo flyers of previous clients. Jim Jackannelli was an accordionist forever getting accidentally booked as a trio, and then sent home by disappointed promoters. The Threepenny Tray were a kind of poor man's Barron Knights, or would have been had their impersonations borne the slightest relation to the impersonated; you could watch an entire set and remain wholly oblivious to that dimension of their performance. Bonny and Ronny were the pond life of the Dundee club scene. Bonny, God love her, was an Afro'd plane crash of a lassie in specs like two fishbowls, in which one of the fish had died. Ronny was an essay in hair, dandruff, paisley pattern, green corduroy and soup stains. They specialised in a sort of urban Kailyardery, songs in praise of specific council estates – 'Fintry's the Schemie for Me'; 'My Heart Is in West Kirkton'; 'Mid Craigie's the Schemie for Me' and 'When I Get Back to Ardler' – in limited-edition Christmas releases sold in handmade cardboard dump-bins in strategic outlets, as well as covers of songs they didn't know, with a have-a-go attitude wholly commendable in its lunatic bravery. Big Rab swears he heard someone request the Hank Williams classic 'Your Cheatin' Heart' at a wedding Bonny and Ronny had been hired to entertain. 'Your cheatin' heart,' Ronny gamely essayed, 'your cheatin' heart. Your cheatin' heart; your cheatin' heart. Your cheatin' heart . . .', the rest of the song drowned in screamed abuse, hurled glasses and flying lumps of cake. Rab also relates that after their first studio recording, Ronny had asked the engineer for his finished demo. For a laugh, the engineer scraped up a handful of bits of old quarter-inch tape from the floor, and handed them to Ronny. Ronny, child of God that he was, thanked him, cheerfully stuffed the knotted mess in his pocket and walked straight out into the street.

The Wee Orange Light was a particularly dreaded feature of certain clubs, and many bands refused to play in any room fitted with one. The light was the signifying end of a device that the council could forcibly install if enough noise-related complaints were gathered from local residents. It would flicker if a certain decibel threshold was reached, and on the third flicker a power-breaker would be triggered and cut the supply to the stage. This would not only risk surges that could blow the valves on your lovingly reconditioned Vox AC30, but destroy all the synth presets in your DX7 that had taken three months to programme. It was usually accompanied by several bangs, flashes and clouds of coloured smoke from exploding equipment, and was invariably mistaken for an unusually tight ending complete with stage pyrotechnics, thus sending the crowd into delirious ovation. Indeed, if it occurred towards the end of the evening, that's just how you would pass it off, ignoring the cries for an encore while you hunted for the fire extinguishers. Three numbers in, though, the effect was less desirable. The entire band would end up watching the Wee Orange Light throughout the gig, waiting for the second flicker that would place us on our final warning; thereafter we would turn down to an inaudible tinkle, and the drummer would switch to brushes for 'Eye of the Tiger', which was then sung like a barbershop quartet hired to serenade your dying mother. With five pairs of eyes locked on the wee bulb, arguments of the aye-it-did/no-it-didnae type would break out continually – and if it *did* flicker, who had been responsible. In our case it was usually Glen Southwood, the bassist, a nice enough but deeply insecure and bumptious lad with an excess weight, hair gel and aftershave problem and a soul patch he could never quite centre. Glen was given to terribly mistimed boutades of overenthusiasm, particularly in the backing vocals Jeff could not dissuade him from contributing, where things would come out much sooner and louder than he'd intended. Thus, in 'The Theme from *Fame*':

– *Erv-uh-ree dayyyeee is lak sur . . .*

– *SURVAAHVAL!!*

– Fuck's sake.

– Sorry lads.

[. . .]

– *Arm gunna leerve for eh-eh-vurr, am gunna lurn howdda fl . . .*

– *FAME!!*

– Fuck's sake.

– Sorry lads.

– *And* ye've set that fuckin light aff again, ye useless fat prick.

– Huvnae!

– Huv.

– Huv *nutt*.

– Huv *sutt*.

– Huv *nutt*!

– Huv *SUTT*!*

KAABANG!! (followed by mass cheering)

– Aw for fuck's sake . . . *THANK YOU LOCHEE!*

Jeff was correctly afraid of getting caught by the taxman; all clubbie gigs were paid in cash, and no one ever declared a penny of it. We had to take turns to sign off the invoice for the fee at the end of the night ('Mak up some shite and skelly yer handwriting' was Jeff's instruction to me), and this week it was Glen's. We were in the car park while Jeff split the money.

– Forties the night.

– Braw.

– Glen, what name did ye put?

– Oh, somethin' *pretty* clever.

– What?

– Get this. 'Cliff Northtrees'. Get it?

– Eh?

– Glen Southwood. Cliff Northtrees. Get it?

– You're no sposed to leave them fuckin *clues*!

– Dye think this is fuckin *Scooby-Doo*?

– Naw.

– And who the *fuck* is called Northtrees?

– Aye right enough.

– Ye useless fat prick.

– Sorry lads.

* 'Sutt' is the emphatic Dundee form of 'so', mostly confined to the playground.

Glen departed soon after, to popular acclaim. The bass chair was briefly filled by my brother Stevie. Stevie is a sculptor, but also one of those irritating musicians who can pick up an instrument and then sound professionally competent about two weeks later; though, as he would admit, he levels the playing field through his principled refusal to ever practise again. Clubbie bass is not a complex gig, and I think he learned the bass guitar by staring at it hard for ten minutes. He slotted in well, not least in his ribald banter and solid drinking, and all went smoothly until we had a 5 p.m. birthday party slot at a care home, and he didn't have a chance to change before the gig. The band were initially amused by the sight of the heavily bearded man in school uniform, but then suddenly realised that it wasn't some Angus Young shtick, and that their bassist was still only fifteen. Stevie was sadly released, for licensing reasons.

36 You Are a Dundee United

Some humans one falls for, or cultivates an obsession for. Others are your fate, and you love them immediately because you always have. Sometimes you initially *resent* them, for just that reason. It can be frustrating to feel you've been offered no choice. Karen Pettigrew was my first proper girlfriend. I was slowly putting the hospital behind me, and gaining a little confidence again. Karen had been in the year below me at school, and a vague fixture at our half-assed parties; something in me could tell we were an inevitability, and we recognised in the other something we both required to catalyse to the next stage, as the larval was boring us both. She was given to hypocoristic squeaky talk when we were together, but was self-aware enough to know it was defensiveness, though also sexual fear. She was from a blue-collar family who, for years, had lived in a top flat in the Ardler 'multis', a series of monstrous sixteen-storey high-rises that would sway in a gale, and made visitors seasick. They spoke the broad Dundonian known as 'oary'.* I went from fairly well spoken to oary in the course of about eighteen months, and stayed there. I'm now effectively

* This is derived from 'orraman', the odd-job man who worked as farm factotum, an occupation not synonymous with the Queen's English.

bidialectal, and for all that some find me still incomprehensible even when I'm making an effort – I'm a career mumbler – my going Full Oary usually introduces enough noise to scramble the signal completely. But I didn't adopt her accent to be more 'street'; I did it because we often just blend with those we love. (My longer cohabitations have been with New Yorkers; for years I had perfectly unselfconscious at-home shtick that sounded like the disgraced offspring of Joan Rivers had been packed off to Dundee at fourteen.) I also wanted to be accepted by her family. My mum wasn't too pleased with my new accent, since for years I'd been one of the more nicely spoken boys on the estate; once or twice she accused me of affecting it. When one shifts one's accent in the direction of *less* prestige, it's often called out as much more of an affectation than when we upgrade it – see 'mockney' – but this is because it makes the aspirational in one's circle especially insecure. But I also heard the active delight that Karen took in her own speech – a pride, not a shame, in the people and place she was from – which I didn't particularly take in mine. I was envious. Karen taught me to speak like the native I am.

(I gave a class on Robert Burns to two hundred undergraduates a few years back, using what I optimistically think of as my 'lecture voice'. Afterwards, an impressively self-possessed first-year student from the Home Counties approached me and suggested that, while he was grateful for the effort I was plainly making, I should perhaps do a little work on my accent if I actually cared to make myself understood to him and his kind. I should have saved time and failed him pre-exam, given the talk he'd just attended was on how the cultural authority of any language is a construct, and how Burns, driven by social and artistic ambition and hamstrung by the low status of his own native speech, had sought a more prestigious register that had, for a while, ruined his poetry. But then I remembered that we don't cover irony until Semester 2, so I cut him some slack. I reminded the young man that, while St Andrews may seem to him at times like an English fort, I was nonetheless born ten miles away; therefore it was technically *his* accent he was struggling with, not mine, for all that he remained a very welcome guest in my beautiful country. I believe he understood this lecture a little better, but then again by this point I was yelling.)

The transformation was nonetheless slow enough to be unconscious, although one or two words were entirely new to me and had to be learned. Her family's speech was peppered with the older, weirder Dundee words derived from French through the Auld Alliance: 'cundy' and 'stank' for 'culvert' and 'drain' (from *conduite* and *estanc*), 'cassie' for paving stone (as in *chaussée*), 'ashet' for large plate (from *assiette*), 'fash' for 'to fret pointlessly' (as in *fâcher*); but I'd never heard of 'goosie' for a segment of an orange (which I'm pretty sure must be from *gousse*, as in *gousse d'ail*, a clove of garlic).

Karen was tall, curly-haired and large of tooth, with a slightly boyish, babyish face that was also incredibly pretty. (I have no 'type' whatsoever, and somehow manage to find myself attracted to all women on principle, but am a total sucker for smiles that seem to trick the sun out of hiding.) She had decent

323

taste in music and tolerated my Keith Jarrett obsession with some forbearance. The family had an awful shadow over them: one member was in prison, forever, on account of an act few of us would have managed once in several lifetimes, but which he'd pulled off twice. They still proclaimed his innocence in the face of what seemed to me some farcically conclusive evidence, and were all in principled and collective denial. This false sense of injustice was also fuelled by some genuine injustice, not least the way Karen's grandmother had been hounded by the Scottish press. They protected each other from the reality, and projected any familial shame onto their tribal enemies, mainly Dundee FC supporters.

But while her voice was like a sweary Tinky Winky, she had a brain like Gottlob Frege. She was a mathematician of prodigious ability, and later took a first at Dundee and did her postgraduate work in Glasgow. She introduced me to the idea of dedicated study, which I had never even remotely contemplated. Her desk had ring binder upon ring binder of notes and formulae, each three inches thick, filled with handwriting small enough to count as microfiche. It was the first time I'd actually seen someone get their shit together, close up. I realised I'd best start actually studying, as opposed to just frantically woodshedding scales against a runaway metronome whose weight had already sunk to *presto* and was still falling fast, and made a start on some actual book-learning.

Besides linear algebra, matrix decomposition and the stout defence of her purity, Karen's other obsession was football. She was a Dundee United season-ticket holder, and taught me about the game, patiently, and from scratch. Hitherto I'd only ever been to one football match: Dad had taken me to a traditional Dundee charity fixture, The Butchers vs The Ministers, when I was about seven. It was awful. Not only was the play clearly not of a professional standard, the novelty wasn't even exploited: the butchers did not pelt the goalie with offal or attack the ministers with cleavers, and the ministers did not kneel and pray for their lives, or to be not shite. But going to a real game with Karen was a total thrill. Even more impressive than her extensive tactical knowledge – 'Can you fuckin *believe* he's pushing Kirkwood into defensive midfield against a four–four–two?' 'No' – was her genuine and heartfelt wish for all Dundee FC supporters to be dead. Dundee FC and Dundee United enjoy the most incomprehensible rivalry in UK football, and therefore, in a sense, the purest. It had to be conjured from nothing: the grounds were eighty yards apart; the fans were drawn from no particular side of the city, and often from the same family; there was no sectarian basis on which one could divide the support. Yet 'Shed or Derry?' – the stands at either stadium where the home support would throng – was one of the most dreaded challenges of my childhood. United fans are known as 'Arabs', a name that dates back either to the time the perennially waterlogged pitch used to be treated with sand, or to a cheerleader in the Shed end who used to scream 'I am Nasser and you are my Arabs', back in the days when such an ejaculation would have been widely understood. Some enterprising morons who'd forgotten all this briefly tried to upgrade the Shed/Derry rivalry to a

Standard Liège. We cuffed Barcelona home and away. (Yes, *that* Barcelona. The most absurd stat in world football is Dundee United's record against Barcelona in competitive matchplay: 4–0.) We supplied around half the Scotland international team. We cuffed Roma 2–0 at home in the European Cup semi-final. We were openly cheated of a final place by an Italian referee who provided Roma with as many free kicks and penalties as were required to keep his family alive, and he punched the air at his own final whistle. This provided one of my earliest and most searing contacts with the reality that life isn't fair; I would neither forget nor forgive. (That we had been openly defrauded to maintain the status quo was later acknowledged by UEFA, but not to the extent of reversing the result.) Having known only success, like a child I assumed it would go on forever.

But then the reality treadmill caught up with us. The horrible pace of our rise and fall was incarnated in the figure of Ralph Milne, now only remembered beyond the city walls as the worst signing in Manchester United's history. Alex Ferguson recalled Milne's lubricious talent from his years managing Aberdeen, and reasonably thought that Milne, being still a young man, might have something to contribute. Karen and I had watched Ralphie reduce the defences of the best teams in Europe to skittles. He had that Messi-like ability to bounce the ball off the toe of his foot like the elastic on a paddleball, while running full pelt through the defence – running so fluidly that it looked like they were all politely getting out the way so as not to impede his perfectly straight line, when he was actually feinting and dancing between them.

town we were, and slowly, but inevitably, we returned to being one. I stuck it out for a couple of seasons while the open chequebooks of Rangers and Celtic restored the natural order; I don't mind losing, but I hate its perfect guarantee, so I gave up on them.

Scottish football is a godawful waste of time, and our children are born into a lifetime of support for teams for whom a best-placed third or fourth is the inevitable outcome of natural law, not anything resembling actual competition. (I am of that unpopular number who would relocate Celtic and Rangers to Dublin and Belfast – or indeed two adjacent villages in Sakhalin – tomorrow, for all that one retains a strong admiration for Celtic fans' longstanding support of the just cause. But there is simply no immediate territorial, cultural or political dispute between Catholics and Protestants in Scotland that justifies the Old Firm's idiocy, and I for one am tired of hearing that it's 'Scotland's shame'. Nah: it's Glasgow's.) True story: 'Dundee United' is still employed as a noun in parts of Nigeria, meaning 'idiot', even if the origins are forgotten; they lie in a disaster of a pre-season friendly tour in the early seventies, when we were beaten by every pub team and scratch eleven in the country. It is now often simply shortened to 'Dundee', as in: 'My friend, you are behaving like a total Dundee.'

Away from football, my virginity seemed eternal, and weighed on me like a curse. It was a bit of a zero-sum game: Karen losing hers made her the Fallen Woman; me keeping mine made me something less than a man. She kept me waiting a long, long time. For some reason we had to wait until after her sister's wedding, on the grounds that it would upset the natural order, which struck me at the time as a quirky but not illogical compunction, though it sounds completely insane now. For a while I was still on Nardil anyway, which by now had rendered me almost incapable of bringing anything to a conclusion, by my hand or anyone else's; I suspect it wasn't much of an inconvenience to her. When it finally happened, I fully expected me to do all the bleeding just from the sheer relief, and frankly I would have been happy to fly the stained sheets from Edinburgh Castle just to make sure everyone got the news. Anyway, it's none of your goddamn business. We lasted around two and a half years, I think. Towards the end she got bored of the relationship, and to my deep chagrin started mooning after an angelic boy with a stubble beard and golden ringlets who was the double of John Martyn, circa 1972, and who with any luck has aged along much the same timeline. There was real love, but not enough to derail the sensible plan that the relationship would end when one of us left town to make our way. She had reasonably assumed that would be her, and given I hadn't left town for about ten years, so did I.*

* I started writing because I had a long poem of self-expiation and apology to write to Karen – and because I didn't know any other poets yet, I did what she would have done: I read right through an etymological dictionary, a thesaurus and some books about versification and prosody, highlighter in hand – assuming, with an immaculate naïveté, that this was surely what trainee poets did.

37 Kammakammakammakammakamma

The Management might have been a little under-rehearsed at times, but compared with the geriatric Bob Dooley Combo we were drilled like the SAS. Having first okayed it with Jeff, who viewed all other bands as the enemy, I accepted a few gigs while their hundred-a-day guitarist recovered from the subtraction of his remaining leg. Bob was an accordionist turned Cordovox player. (The Cordovox is an 'electronic accordion', two words which sit together about as happily as 'adult diaper'. Most of the human ingenuity directed towards the Scottish accordion, that out-of-tune tartan fairground nightmare, has involved ways of getting it to be quieter or indeed prevented altogether, but the Cordovox boldly amplified the offence.) They said they'd send charts before the gig, which was a promising sign. They arrived in the post. Big Rab later told me he'd had the same experience: by 'Can you read?', Bob had meant the alphabet. The 'charts' were bits of paper ripped from a school jotter, each tune consisting of a row of large letters to indicate the order in which the chords should occur – but, with the absence of bar lines, no indication as to when. (The 'when', it transpired on the gig, I was to take from the bassist's cues, which he gave in a series of violently mimed headbutts. The fast ska chord changes of Madness's 'Baggy Trousers' induced a near-blackout, though, and he had to complete the song sitting down.)

Their regular gig was the old Dundee FC Supporters' Club. I arrived an hour early, as agreed, for a run-through of the material. I couldn't get in as there was a fight in the foyer; two drunks had pulled knives on each other and were frozen in a stand-off. Someone called upstairs, and a five-foot MC in a Zapata 'tache, frilly shirt and plum velvet suit with matching bow tie came down to sort things out. He said nothing, but merely opened the left side of his jacket: in the inside pocket was a small axe. The two men muttered their apologies and shook hands. Then the MC let them both *in*.

I headed for the dressing room and got changed into the band uniform, or as near as I could get to it – my old way-too-tight school trousers and a black nylon shirt of my dad's. The band had conceived the idea, which I have encountered several times subsequently, that black shirts are a charm against BO, on the principle that they don't appear to need washing. Five minutes after we were due to go on the rest of the band showed up. Although initially annoyed, I soon saw the pointlessness of the run-through. The Bob Dooley Combo were an education in what could pass for music amongst the tone-deaf. I once had a conversation with the late traditional music scholar Mícheál Ó Súilleabháin on this subject: his theory was that, as long as there was something resembling a tune and a regular rhythm, you could harmonise a song like Boulez or Cecil Taylor, and a rustic audience would have no strong objections, being less indifferent to harmony than oblivious to its existence. (Towards the end of the evening, he claimed that the tune itself could be abandoned, and a random series of notes substituted; as long as you could still dance to it, all would be well.) This was pretty much Bob's approach. Bob, like Cecil Taylor, had driven a cab to subsidise his art; but the harmonic freedom Cecil had won through years of intense study and cautious experiment Bob had achieved instantly, through the brilliant expedient of not giving a fuck. His left hand was like the upper body of an Irish dancer, present but terminally infarcted; it was simply dragged along for the ride. It crashed and bumped around on the bottom half of his keyboard like a trailer on a loose tow bar, and aspired to no greater accuracy nor accomplishment than finding his balls if they got itchy.

The drummer was also something of an innovator, and had a specially constructed kit, with a ring-holder for his pint and an ashtray welded to the tom stand; in place of the second tom, he had welded the top half of a music stand, on which he'd place a copy of *Hustler* or an *Edge* Western. The difficult procedure of turning the pages while playing was brilliantly solved by just stopping playing and then turning the page. I could always tell when he was on prose, as the drop-outs grew further apart. His brother had three fingers on either hand – the result, he told me, of an accident at Tayport sawmill. I swear to *God* this is true, having heard it subsequently repeated as an urban myth: the first finger was lost when a plank slipped under a bandsaw. The second finger was lost demonstrating how he'd cut off the first.

I have heard covers bands in South-East Asia who produce immaculate live versions of songs the original artists took months in the studio to perfect, and would themselves be incapable of delivering. Bob was the precise antithesis, and given to the most spectacular approximation. There was nonetheless a kind of genius of economy here: knowing the two or three bits of the tune by which his cloth-eared audience – by whatever somnambulant verification procedure – might identify it, he would present these as semi-random prompts, while the rest of the song fell into an atonal mish-mash. The most important bit was the intro, when everyone feels the sugar rush of recognition, security and reassurance; this was often accompanied by cheers of relief, as the working classes are raised with a well-founded terror of the unknown.* Then there was the middle bit: so as long as 'Karma Chameleon' went *kammakammakamma-kammakamma* at some point you were home and dry. But if you really wanted to ingratiate yourself, you would end abruptly together, anywhere, and on any note. This was taken as a sign of thorough professionalism, of the kind the audience would dimly pride themselves on being able to recognise, and the jolt administered would always provoke spontaneous and wild applause. In this anti-aesthetic there was only one possible criticism: *for fuck's sake play somethin' wih ken*; and one possible compliment: *yous lads werenae too loud nor nothin.* Between the whirlpool of alienation and the rock of annoyance, the Bob Dooley Combo steered an unerring and masterly course.

* Next time you're wondering why the English working class didn't vote for Jeremy Corbyn, interrogate the phrase 'programme for radical change'. The lower orders know intuitively that 'radical change' is code for 'You lot are first against the wall when it all goes tits-up again.'

They were also responsible for some of the most bestial sex I have ever witnessed on a gig. I had been warned to expect it: Big Rab told me he once stumbled in on the drummer and a lass getting it together on a radiator in the dressing room. She was, considerately, holding the drummer's pint for him, and had told her mum that she'd just gone for a pish. But one scene etched itself into my soul, and to this day I am trying to parse what I think I saw, and still hope it was something else. In the endless second between my opening the dressing-room door and swiftly pulling it closed, I'm pretty sure it involved three band members and far fewer women, possibly one. Technically, I suppose they may have been enacting, in live tableau, one of those later chapters in *The Perfumed Garden*, where the woman allegedly demonstrates the simultaneous pleasuring of many men; though given the advanced years of all four participants it looked more like a game of Twister gone horribly wrong at a hospice Christmas party. Usually such liaisons involve three contortionists and one uncomfortable woman, but in my memory the woman looked like the only relaxed party, de-corseted and at ease in her open gussets while three scarlet-faced arthritic wrecks wheezed away in their shirt-tails and socks. I think Davie the bassist raised his hand in a pained gesture of greeting, and possibly even invitation – to do what, and where, and to whom, I shudder to think. But as I say, I may have misinterpreted the whole thing, and perhaps they were merely getting changed. I dearly hope so.

I only ever visited one club in Dundee lower down the food chain. It was a surreal evening anyway: I had turned up at the wrong gig on the wrong night with what turned out to be an empty guitar case, like a novice in some Zen fable, the point of which was lost on me, but perhaps that was the lesson. I saw a neighbour I knew, and he bought me a half. The place was a long, low-ceilinged, windowless bunker between the two worst schemes in the city. The dim orange uplighters gave it the look of a torchlit crypt, and concealed its filthy plush and scorched carpet. It was obviously a condition of membership that you had to be able to walk upright under a parked artic and emerge with your bonnet still straight; at five foot eight I was a titan. Everyone was either silent or comatose with drink, though some would rouse themselves to a brief incoherent rage every ten minutes or so. The club was Men Only: a superfluous edict if ever there was one, though the woman-ban was in place not because of the club's chauvinism – which would have required the energy to sustain a prejudice in the first place – but because it retroactively accommodated the fact that no woman would have set foot in this place. And you could tell sex or its distraction wasn't even a *thought* for them. Sex is at least a sign of being alive, in some recognisable way. A student of tantra might have said that their kundalini had now retracted to lie coiled at the base of the spine, at the muladhara chakra, where man becomes a kind of mobile plant life. These guys seem to have found another chakra six feet below their arsehole, and couldn't move at all. They all died there in the club, on the floor or in the toilet or slumped at the table, and their friends took three hours to notice.

Throughout all this, I was studying jazz fairly intensively.

Bar the local virtuoso, Kevin Murray – a genuinely accomplished player by whom I was wholly intimidated – there was no one in Dundee worth taking a lesson from, but I'd got hold of copies of some jazz theory books that helped a lot, and a few guitar methods that didn't, most memorably Mickey Baker's *Jazz Guitar* – inexplicably still in print and indeed highly regarded by many, for all it strikes me as a niche situationist gag. Baker's book was the first time I experienced the stylistic offence: Mickey had apparently pulled up a barstool to yell the whole book into a Dictaphone in fifteen minutes flat. 'Now we are up to what we call Rhythm changes.' (At no point does Baker say what they are: a set of chord changes based on Gershwin's 'I Got Rhythm'.) 'Rhythm changes are pretty much the same as Vamps.' (They aren't really.) 'I can go so far as to say that every Jazz musician, ever to have a Name, has recorded these changes over and over, again.' (They haven't.) 'So you can see just how important rhythm changes are.' Not really, Mickey, because you didn't say what the hell they were, or where they came from, or what was the point of them. And a critic, alas, was born.

I also pored over Ted Greene's notorious harmonic studies. Greene, like Mickey Baker, was the last person who should have written a guitar method, but for very different reasons. At the time I assumed that my failure to get my knuckles round his études was my own uselessness; but an encounter thirty years later with the handful of extant recordings by Greene on YouTube revealed him to be a double-jointed, one-off, completely inimitable minor genius, dead in middle age, possibly by chordal injury. (His one album, *Solo Guitar* – in Ted's case, this title takes on a certain omen – is one long ripple of cluster-chords and angelic counterpoint and Lenny Breau celesta-like waterfalls of harmonics, all delivered in a sine-wave country-church organ tone, with some natural vibrato and a little phaser. It is nothing, really, and everything, and sounds like the elevator music in heaven.)

I was also working with a wee band I kept secret from Jeff, called Ghosts, after the Albert Ayler tune which sounds like a cross between a Sousa march and a demonic invocation. We had about four and a half numbers I'd written, which I could nonetheless barely play (this turned out to be something of a life-game). Among them, I recall, were 'Elephant Rut', 'Titular Absence' (a title stolen, wittily I thought, from Derek Bailey, the doyen of avant-garde free jazz guitar, from whom I later took a couple of lessons in London) and 'My Italics'. We were a trio, with Iain on the bass. (In his natural affinity for the low end, he took after his uncle, the bassist in a popular UK rock combo called . . . Milk, with Derek Clacton and . . . Sometimes this anonymity rule gets a bit strained.) Our drummer Doug had, as they say, 'a lot of shit worked out in 7/8', but actually much less in 4/4. He would play 4/4 by playing 7/8 four times, i.e. in multiples of twenty-eight, and every seven bars we would coincide, like those trains on the London Underground you suddenly find yourself riding parallel with for a few cheery seconds before plunging back into the lonely dark. We had a cool wee poster drawn by an art school friend of Karen's, strange, scribbly figures drawn from the inside out. (I never thanked her for doing it, and do so now. Just seven thousand, three hundred and nineteen apologies to go now.) We played a couple of gigs in the Dundee stoner quarter to much nodding of heads. These took place in the Tayside Bar, a terrible auld gadgies' pub the hipsters had taken over and kitted out with UV lighting to disguise the pish and beer stains, and where Billy MacKenzie occasionally held court. Dundee has always prided itself on a kind of deranged eclecticism, and we once found ourselves sandwiched between a mad classical guitarist called Bob Flynn – who berated the stoned audience for applauding between movements, like it was the Wigmore Hall – and a band called The Scrotum Poles.

When Jeff found out about the existence of Ghosts he went berserk at my perfidy, and threatened to sack me. I should not be forming or working for the competition. To reassure him that we were unlikely to challenge The Management for their spot at the Battle of the Bands Night at the Mains of Claverhouse, I sat him down and put on a tape of our last gig. His face initially assumed an attitude of horror; then it contorted in pity. He raised his palm to signal he'd had enough (frankly so had I; it was halfway through the free-improv arco bass solo in 'Titular Absence', and it sounded like a six-foot bee trapped in an art supply cupboard) and then spoke to his in-turned fingernails.

– Don.

– Aye?

– Look, man. I ken ye've had a hard time. Like . . .

– What?

– Like when ye were in the hospital and aa that.

– Oh aye.

– We'll no' say anything to the other lads aboot this.

– Cheers, man.

Ghosts was never mentioned again. However, now my dark jazz secret was out in the open, the fun was gone. Even if no one else gave a hoot over my lack of note-for-note sincerity, I found, implausibly, that I did. The Management had started to kill my playing, and I quit practising. (Ghosts evaporated in a cloud of bong smoke; I think Doug discovered 4/4 and joined another clubbie band.) The end came with astonishing swiftness one night in the St Joseph's Club. I was, from the vantage of the high stage, watching a lad in a dark corner manually bringing his girl to climax while he affected to read the back of the *Courier* (actually, now that I think of it, he was also genuinely reading the back of the *Courier*); a particularly ugly fight had broken out over the pool table, and a guy was being forced to admit the black ball into his mouth. We were halfway through Barry Manilow's 'Bermuda Triangle'. I could hear Jeff singing somewhere far above me, as from the bottom of a well. 'Burmoo-da Trah-yangle / It makes pee pill dizza-peer . . . Burmoo-da Trah-yangle . . . Dung go doo near . . . She dunt see mah-yangle . . .' One bar into my guitar solo, I suffered what can only be described as an acute failure of the will, and found myself unable to play a note. It was identical to a panic attack, with the usual choking sensation and drone's-eye view of myself, except there was no panic. It was a relief to be out of it, my body, this club, this life, this particular godawful song. Jeff turned his head slowly towards me to meet my lifeless stare, and all was instantly understood. I fired myself on the spot.

38 The One Note

In the 1980s BBC Scotland produced a jazz series, hosted by Oscar Peterson. (Yes, you read that right. One's licence fee was well invested back then.) Oscar would play a short and torrid set with Niels-Henning Ørsted Pedersen, then probably the greatest living double bass virtuoso, and the English drummer Martin Drew. Then Oscar would introduce, in a scripted and mildly bewildered fashion, an act drawn from the cream of European jazz. One week it was a Norwegian singer called Radka Toneff. (Her name remains little known except to aficionados, but *Fairytales* – a duet album with the pianist Steve Dobrogosz – is Norway's best-selling jazz record of all time, which may sound like a 'fastest snail' kind of boast, unless you're familiar with the superiority of Scando jazz to all international variants outside the US.) Her musicians were unknown to me then, but included the bassist Arild Andersen and pianist Jon Balke. I fell in love with Radka on the spot. All women are beautiful when they sing beautifully, and she was beautiful anyway. She was maybe the last of those archetypal beloved faces from my childhood, one I'd somehow always known, one I'd foolishly search for later.*

---

* My entirely subjective impression is that singing and orgasm render the faces of women astonishingly beautiful. Both activities turn them

The Note occurred during Radka's performance of her own setting of an insufficiently known Fran Landesman poem, 'Wasted'. Radka had already recorded a fine version of 'Spring Can Really Hang You Up the Most', probably Landesman's best-known lyric, set in the fifties by a genius called Tommy Wolf. (Wolf's use of the first bar *after* his gorgeous middle eight to pull off a smoke-and-mirrors modulation back into the original key is one of the most what-the, goosefleshy moments in the standard repertoire. When you play it, it feels like stumbling on a secret door back into the walled garden you thought you'd accidentally locked yourself out of.) 'Wasted', though, was arranged by Radka herself, and with almost equal sensitivity. In the middle eight is the line 'Sequins, stars and silver moon'. She sings the first syllable of the word 'silver' in the upper end of her range. The note starts off straight and pure, and is then sustained on a very trained, Oslo Conservatory high-note vibrato. But then it suddenly yields to some hidden ache it finds in itself: now there are two entirely different vibratos going on simultaneously, the faster and lighter somehow being subject to a rolling sob below it. The note lasted for the fatal length of the 'phonological loop', the three-second tape recorder in your brain which degrades

wholly interior and self-absorbed; this is always a privileged sight, as ten thousand years of patriarchy sees many women rest naturally in presentation mode, for their own safety. Singing and orgasm, by contrast, tend to contort the male face, often hideously. I suspect many men request to finish from behind for purely charitable reasons.

after a few repeated playbacks, but which is enough time to commit a sound to memory as *itself*, in a non-encoded, eternally present way. I had never heard a note remotely like it in my life. (Nor have I since.) It was inhuman. It seemed to induce a shaking sob in me too, less by sympathetic resonance than by straightforward command: *This is almost more than you can bear.* I'd videoed the programme, and replayed the note a thousand times, never properly able to believe my ears, wondering if it was just a fluctuation on the VHS tape. No, it was there, and it had happened. Then an odd thought occurred to me. That it was hard to imagine anyone singing that note without consequence. I wasn't sure how you could get away with it. The myths are full of those victims of jealous gods who either claimed to possess a divine talent, or hit some note to which their merely human talent didn't entitle them; at least this was the explanation I offered myself when Radka died later that same year. Information was hard to come by, but the official word was that she'd been in a car accident. She was barely thirty.*

Perversely, I realised, when I chased down her short back catalogue, one of the reasons Toneff was such a great performer was that she made herself a more human singer than she need

---

* 'Car accident' was the form of words her record company used, the actual circumstances of her death being too depressing to relate. Yes, there was a car, and yes, there was an accident. It seems to have been that most pointless death, the botched cry for help. Radka drove into the Bygdøy woods and swallowed some sleeping pills. She may have choked on them, or miscalculated the dose.

have been. Despite being gifted with a huge, powerful voice courtesy of her Bulgarian heritage – an early record includes a solo Magyar folk song (her father was Hungarian) impossible to recognise as the same singer, two minutes of bloody, full-throated ululation, all whoops and growls and yodels, and her first album, *Winter Poem*, sees her soaring stridently over a full orchestra – at some point she made an odd pact with the void. Her credo was, as she put it, to 'sing piano, master the sounds that are closest to silence'. Half the time she sang just the right side of a whisper, as if she were imparting a confidence. (Perfect whispers impart only secrets.) This creates intimacy; but at a practical level it also means you simply have more difficulty controlling the note. Classical singing technique, with its fat vibrato and emphasis on projection and diaphragm control – whether you love it or consider it a painful distortion of the voice – is at least a guarantee of the consistency of vocal production. Toneff abandoned that for something riskier, and things *did* go awry – her records aren't for Diana Krall fans, and there are tiny fluffs and mispitchings. But what's down there on the shoreline of silence is audible breath, the point at which the voice shades into the sea of nothing. Jesus. What was it with nothing? Why did you have to play it so close to annihilation to have anyone *feel* anything?

Much of this was, of course, romantic projection on my part, which her early death fuelled considerably. A few months later, I went to play the tape – marked 'DO NOT RECORD OVER' in red marker – to be greeted with Les Dawson and Roy Kinnear in drag, having a conversation over a garden fence

39 Let's Get Horsin'

The truth is that there were entire years when nothing much happened. Open *Speak, Memory* anywhere, and – well, let's do it. Oh look: Volodya is being shown a cool trick with matches by General Kuropatkin on the sofa, on the same day he assumed command of the Russian army in the Far East. Let's throw a dart at my wall calendar between, say, 1981 and '82. Nothing; try again. Nothing; once more. This day just reads 'Battenberg cake'. No idea. Long months would pass between things one could call actual events; between, say, the primary teacher known as Snorkel getting fired for assisting a wee lad in the boys' toilets who'd got his toby trapped in his spaver* (less for the act than for the full hour it took him to free it), and the time Eleanor over the road tried to stain her wallpaper with tea just before her anniversary party, and Dad had to repaper the entire room in two hours flat. ('I meant *cold* tea.' 'Who makes *cold* tea?' '. . . Disnae matter.')

Then again, incident was something I studiously avoided. In the years between leaving hospital and leaving Dundee, I went out of my way to minimise all drama; as a born queen, this should tell you how sick of it I was. I also went in fear of all intoxicants. I couldn't trust my mind to report the world

---

* Correct: junior penis; flies.

347

back accurately, and had a horror of losing what might prove only a temporary control over my own thoughts. Instead, I sunk myself completely into music, books and homosocial bonding. My tight gang of Baldragon stoners, musicians and maths wonks usually assembled at my place, since I had the most laxly indulgent parents; after my breakdown, they were so pleased to have me home I could've kept bees in the kitchen. Not that we were any trouble. Mostly we just sat around drinking unbelievable amounts of tea. Though God knows how Mum and Dad slept through the constant flushing of the toilet at the top of the landing, six feet from their bedroom; I hope all their dreams were set in Malibu.

Stevie and I decided to paint our little bedroom black to hide the dirt. We swapped our beds for a couple of shapeless foam fold-outs to make space. It was decorated with posters by Dalí (*The Persistence of Memory*, with the melty watches), Magritte (*Time Transfixed*, with the train coming out the fireplace) and de Chirico (*Arse with Bananas*, I forget the actual title), and my pencil drawings of various musicians; some of them – Maggie Nicols, odd members of Henry Cow – were folk I'd be playing with in London five years later. We'd also hung up a few knackered old guitars rescued from the cowp,* some of

---

* The municipal dump; 'cowp', to tip, to tip over. It'll be from the French, the way 'coup' also becomes 'overthrow'. A 'cowpie' was a sheep or cow which had fallen on its back and couldn't right itself, or one deliberately tipped. A 'cow pie' was something my dad coloured in when he was on Desperate Dan.

which had been sawn in half and positioned so they appeared to emerge from the walls, *Time Transfixed*-style. The black room was essentially just a listening-chamber-cum-salon. Tea was drunk; shite was talked; records were spun; that was it. The listening was both utterly snobbish and madly eclectic, on snobbish principle. (Because you just have to know, an average evening might see you blasted with Tim Buckley and Loudon Wainwright, Scritti Politti and Jon Hassell, Weather Report and Steely Dan, Coltrane and Miles, Julian Bream and John Ogdon, Bartók and Shostakovich, Bach and Dufay, Meredith Monk and Carla Bley, Townes Van Zandt and Willie Nelson, Van der Graaf and Holger Czukay, Talking Heads and Laurie Anderson, Nick Drake and Joni Mitchell, Gong and Henry Cow, Dick Gaughan and The Bothy Band. We hated only opera, prog, reggae and 'rock'. Especially 'rock'. I mean, honestly. 'Rock'.) In between records, we sat around discussing big things about which we knew little. Soon we all had girlfriends (mercifully, all around the same time; young men can find themselves suddenly and dangerously isolated if they're late to the party here), which meant we stopped talking about sex, at least in any sexual way. Nonetheless, there was much agony-aunting of practical matters.

– Sandra makes me wear three johnnies and I can't feel a thing.

– Maybe try nearly wanking yourself to the edge just before?

– Aye, I'll try that.

– What do yous lot think about to stop yourself?

– Middle-game strategy. 'Agadoo'. Thatcher.

– Nah, that'll just bring him off.

– Michael Foot.

– *Shagging* Michael Foot?

– If I have to.

– Do you ever get that stabby pain in the back of your head just before you go off?

– Nope.

– Nah, that's literally just you.

– Aye, I'd get that looked at.

– I'd avoid coming again. Ever.

– Fuck off.

– Aye. Time to start faking it.

– Fuck knows Morag is.

– Fuck off.

– Aye, that'll kill ye that.

– Fuck off.

I was in love with my girlfriend. I was also in love with George's, inconveniently, and seriously. (Later, in our adult incarnations, it became a fairly defining relationship for both of us, albeit one of those on–off, colossally messy ones whose purpose seemed to be to demonstrate, in an exhausting and final way, that love most definitely does not conquer all. Apologies to her for speaking for us both.) I was confused by this, and had to accept another miserable truth about myself, and possibly men. Since I was five, I'd understood that sex and love could get along quite independently. I later came to accept, when gay guys explained it to me, that this is normal. Only then did I feel partly absolved of the guilt of not being able to live up to the ideal of their interdependence – an ideal straight men will often insincerely host, because we love women. (For all that women often experience *exactly* the same separation of heart and loin, the traditional risks of pregnancy and financial abandonment tend to make it a far less uncomplicated proposition.) When we were taught about sex at school, it was always in the context of 'a loving relationship'; this is sweet, but ludicrous, since the only really important thing to teach about sex is respect. Sex without love, and sex experienced as distinct from love, is perfectly fine for men and women, provided your contraception's dependable. What I wasn't prepared for was discovering I had the capacity to love more than one person, in a way that was unconflicted, or conflicted only by the atrocious hurt I knew it would have caused others. And the only thing I learned subsequently was to keep this knowledge to myself.

I can see now that we were also furiously encouraging of one another's talents, however small, mostly using the Dundee pedagogical method of public humiliation. The averagely talented were shamed into excelling, and even no-hopers were embarrassed into a passable standard: how the hell are we meant to get a shot in at your head if you can't even make it to the parapet? Even George, the least musical of us, could play some classical guitar; his younger brother was a virtuoso who ended up Guitar Prof at the Royal Conservatoire. Sandy was also a decent player, and for a while we tried to put together some kind of half-assed jazz–rock thing; we briefly recruited

Tommy, a gifted fifteen-year-old drummer. (Tom Doyle, the music journalist, as it turned out, though he won't have been introduced to himself yet. His riveting account of the rise, fall and fall of Billy MacKenzie, *The Glamour Chase*, explains more about the weirdness of Dundee than I ever could.) Sandy often had to be levered apart from his girlfriend, the beautiful and brilliant Gwen, just to get him plugged into his Fender Champ; it felt like taking an axe to Baucis and Philemon, and in the end it proved easier to leave them be. My mate Steve was the sole rocker, and had a metal band called Stonehenge – he really did, pre-'Tap – in which Alfie briefly took lead vocals, to his own astonishment and dismay, before someone heard Doad Clancy singing in the shower after his binman shift and pointed out that he was a preposterously great David Coverdale clone. He literally hadn't noticed, and thereafter did it for a living.

The competitive culture also occasionally afforded you the time-saving luxury of hitting your talent-ceiling almost immediately. In the case of chess, I sat upright and bopped my head on the coffin lid. George and I played a lot. I was terrible. This was despite my having hit the books pretty hard, and the fact that we were being tutored by Paul Motwani, who lived round the corner. Paul, a fabulously sheltered and sweet guy with a remarkably runny nose, was already threatening his first international master norm (he became the first Scottish grandmaster a few years later, just before Colin McNab, another Dundee guy). Despite the fact that every game had the same guaranteed outcome, I spent it practically fainting from the adrenaline and hypertension; while my clock ticked down and I mulled my next stupid move, my heart clicked in my throat, the veins clicked in my temple and my stomach ached like it was tensed for a punch. This high excitement was totally incommensurate with any chance I had of actually winning. George was becoming increasingly expert, and the handicaps he offered me more and more humiliating. He would start a whole piece down, then agree to play a deliberately terrible opening like the moronic Grob's Attack, and then put twenty minutes on my clock and five on his. And then win. I less planned my moves than told myself the tale of my step-by-step march to glory; this relied on George not seeing the clever traps I had set along the way. From his perspective, they made Wile E. Coyote look like Alexander the Great: I dug holes and invited him to fall in; I tempted him with exposed pawns booby-trapped to explode. These cunning plans would unfold just as I'd intended, right up to the point that George actually moved, invariably in a part of the board to which I had been paying no attention and left fatally undefended. One always learned something, though. Sure, chess players look at a board and see lots of branching paths, but they also have a sense of the chess position as a gestalt, and can decide what constitutes a true and beautiful move as much by instinct as by analysis. And you could also hear, by the way he talked about it, how Motwani was thinking in whole sequences of moves, strung together by a grammar of inevitable logic, just as we think in whole phrases, not individual words. I had no feel for the language of it. I was good at mate-in-two chess puzzles, which have nothing to do with real chess, as any two half-decent players would never find the board in that position; someone would have resigned by then. Me, I realised. I tipped my king for good.

After I left The Management, most paid work I did was with Iain. We got a gig playing with a large French singer who had a nice line in Hot Club rhythm guitar and spoke broad Dundonian with a heavy French accent through a thick black beard. He had some bizarre but contagious turns of phrase: 'Let's get horsin'' meant we had to leave, apparently. His name was Jean-Louis Vandeberg, and his name was Alan Breitenbach, as I now realise even the most carefully economic description of Alan still leaves him instantly recognisable and is like trying to conceal a space hopper behind a pencil. Alan forced me to start learning standards, which is of course the work of a lifetime; the simpler numbers favoured by the Django/Grappelli school are a great place to start. It was not our kind of thing, but we learned the set, and then inevitably found it was our kind of thing. We played the gypsy jazz defaults of 'St Louis Blues', 'Sweet Georgia Brown' and Django's lovely tune 'Nuages', written in 1940 to take everyone's mind off the Nazis and suggest that they might stare up into the summer sky for five minutes. And, of course, bloody 'Summertime'.*

---

* I hate Gershwin's fake spiritual with a passion. It's awful. No, it really is. The cotton is high, eh? Whose cotton? Your rich daddy's? Dude, this is a lullaby, which has a long tradition of false reassurance. This song is about your abject poverty. And since *he's* not rich, ergo

But no sooner had we nailed it than Alan promptly horsed off to an oil rig for four months, and we were left with a bunch of gigs and no bandleader.

Fortuitously, Iain had woken up with a lady at the weekend – who, upon enquiring, in his chivalrous way, of her name and occupation, turned out to be a fine young fiddler and singer called Deirdre. We promptly renamed ourselves Deirdre and The Clot Hub. That left us just having to find a drummer. The same eight drummers were pooled between every band in Dundee, and so had to be hired on a one-off basis and could not be permanently retained. Every gig involved a desperate dive down the food chain. The lowest we got was Eddie Iddendon. Any lower would have involved placing a landed turbot in an empty biscuit tin, sticking a mic on it and hoping for the best. It was literally Eddie or nothing. O that we had booked nothing. Eddie was, we discovered, a drummer only in the loosest sense of 'one who possessed some drums'; but we had interviewed him on the phone, where his confidence seemed reassuringly boundless. Then we rehearsed. A sort of ancient, eclamptic Andy Serkis in fisheye specs, less a man than a handy place to keep tics from escaping, Eddie gave the impression of having just been given the drums for his

---

your mama is probably no oil painting either. Oh, I could go on, but suffice to say that this is the kind of sentimental, fake-aspirational, poverty-celebrating muddle that results when middle-class white folks write black songs. O I know you love it; I *know* but your friend Lizzie sang it wonderfully at Sarah and Geoff's house-warming. Tell her to sing something else.

birthday, and played with both the joyous innocence and the sense of discovery that phrase implies. As for his technique: Zeno himself could not have contrived a moment so fleeting that Eddie could not speed up in it; no bar was so short that Eddie couldn't lose the count. In 2/4, he'd have started on 3. His enthusiasm was tremendous, but almost miraculously uninfectious, like leprosy. He was clearly skint, though, so we felt it was too late to drop him.

Our first engagement was an open-air concert in Baxter Park. Access was via a wide and steep flight of ornamental steps which ran from the Victorian pavilion down to the lower level, where the stage had been built. We parked the van at the pavilion and staggered down with the gear. We had warned Eddie that the get-in would be tricky, and that an early arrival would be sensible; Eddie gave his breezy assent. Five minutes before we were due to go on, there was still no Eddie. With much cursing, we made plans to do the set as a trio. Then we heard a frantic honking from above, and left the stage to help Eddie down with his gear – only to be met with Eddie's Ford Escort edging over the ornamental stairs like Fitzcarraldo over the rapids. Then it all went Ealing Comedy getaway as he rattled down the steps, crashed to a halt, fought his way out of the airbag with much accidental honking, and immediately started to unload. 'Bang on time!' he offered, cheerily and without humour. We had to kick off, but Eddie insisted he could set up and play at the same time. Since he couldn't play at all, this seemed unlikely, but he gamely started hitting things with one hand while assembling the rest of the kit with the other. By the start of 'St Louis Blues', the mid-point in the set, his kit was complete. By the end of the song he had started to dismantle it again, and was loosening wingnuts and dropping his cymbals in a pile while still playing one-handed. 'The *fuck* are you doing?' Iain asked. 'I've got another gig in the Ferry,' Eddie explained. By the end of the set he was twatting away on a single ride cymbal, with the rest of the kit in pieces. Thank heavens there was no encore, but then again there was never going to be an encore. The Clot Hub disbanded, having fulfilled their engagements; Deirdre went off to teach music, and Iain changed his name, confusingly, to Nico, and joined The Proclaimers for about thirty years.

I was in a post-Management doldrums then, and God knows how I was passing the time. I certainly wasn't practising. Then Big Rab called: Ken Hyder, the jazz drummer, was up from London to visit his mother, and wanted a gig. Ken Hyder's Talisker were then a kind of groundbreaking Celtic free jazz ensemble – perhaps still the only kind of Celtic free jazz ensemble – who may not have been the last word in technical finesse but made up for it with a terrifying brass neck, or more precisely a steroidal version of the Scottish quality of 'gallusness' ('gallus' being somewhere between reckless, bold and shameless; literally 'fit for the gallows'). They had albums out on the Virgin label, and even I'd heard of them. I had no idea Hyder was from Dundee. Back then Rab still played double bass a bit, and suggested we form a trio. I hadn't really worked with an actual professional musician before, and almost turned down the gig in fear.

Rab and I met up with the somewhat lupine and man-spreadingly over-centred Ken. I found him brash, loud, disturbingly volatile and full of the rather performative Scottishness of the expatriate. (I have met too many Lowland Scots who actively regret not having had a famine to justify their exile.) But Ken was also magnetic, hyper-awake, a coiled spring of a man, and his confidence as a musician had an active and generous energy that asked you to draw on it, not cave in to it. The Restless Natives (we were early to the joke) then played an hour of loud improvised mush at Dundee Student Union, with Rab spontaneously titling the tunes as we went along. 'Thank you. That was "Forfar's Ache". This next is a nostalgic piece by Ken that he calls "I Used to 'Bide' There".' The gigs went as well as they could have. Rab kept it simple and solid; I did my thing, which was then a completely deranged mash-up of mutually incompatible styles: John Martyn open-chord folksy picking, Mahavishnu Sten-gun pentatonic bursts, Bill Frisell drifty dissonance, and a whole bunch of bluegrass licks copped off my dad and Tony Rice. Ken did his signature *bish* (ominous pause) *bash* (ominous pause) *bosh* Paul Motian cymbal thing, and some pretty thrilling rat-a-tat rolls and ratamacues that drove us along at a ferocious tempo; if you ever forgot that Max Roach had been taught by a Scottish pipe band drummer, Ken wasn't likely to let you forget for long. Not least because he was always telling you. Ken was still some years away from discovering Tuvan throat singing, which drew even more attention to himself, but he was nothing if not a commanding performer; he was also deadly serious in a way that made me realise the extent to which I'd been merely playing at art. The music was a godawful mess, but terribly exciting. Afterwards Ken asked me, in his direct way, what I was planning to do with my life. I had absolutely no idea, but I didn't want to say that. For the first time it hit me that I hadn't a clue. So I did my usual, and blagged it. 'Uh, I dunno . . . I was maybe going to move to London and see how the music worked out.' Was I hell. London? My single foray over the English border had been our terrible holiday in Whitley Bay ten years before, and I could still barely manage Dundee city centre on a Saturday.

Two weeks later, Ken called the house and my bluff. He said flattering things about my playing, and that if I was serious about moving south, there was a job in Talisker going. Only three gigs in the book, couple of festivals, no money, but y'know. Could I let him know by next week. He hung up, and I stood there for a long while, holding the dead receiver and staring out the window, past the bus stop and off into the clouds, suddenly open to the wonder and horror of an actual future. It afforded me a simple clarity I only ever really get on planes, in turbulence. Death is a breeze. It's life that's terrifying.

40 Near by Dundee and the Bonnie Magdalen Green

If the end of this tale is a little abrupt, so was my departure. There was very little time – perhaps just three or four weeks – between my declaring I would leave and my leaving. Any longer, and I'd have found a reason not to. Karen met the news with shock but understanding. Although we'd time-limited the relationship, it was supposed to have concluded with her heading off to postgrad study. It was a wretchedly hard and tearful way to finish things, but kids can be far more sensible in these matters than adults ever can. Age makes us weak, frightened and change-resistant; perversely, only the young really appreciate that our time is short.

Back then, it still held true that London was to working-class Scots what America was to the Irish, the ancestral proving ground where we could rise or we could fall; neither were really possible at home, where there was blessedly little risk of either success or failure. But my mother didn't want me to go, and could see no reason why I couldn't make my jazz name in Glasgow or Edinburgh. The answer was that there was no jazz scene to speak of. The Scottish Musicians' Union was at the time raising the money to get the sixteen-year-old saxophonist Tommy Smith the hell out of the junkies' wonderland of the Wester Hailes estate (then known as 'Waster's Hell') and packed off to study at Berklee, as they knew Scotland had no way of providing the competition and mentorship his talent needed.

Mum wanted me to know that if I decided to come back after a year, or even the weekend, she wouldn't be disappointed in me. Indeed, she'd be undisappointed to the point of delirium. By contrast, Dad was nothing but an iron pillar of support. His excitement was partly vicarious; he'd have loved to have had such an opportunity as a young man. But mainly he wanted this for me. He knew these chances were rare and random, and only a fool quibbled over the details of their timing: I must go. I loved him then. Now I was about to place a border between us, I could finally accept what I felt for him, like a man, for all that I still needed the distance from him, like a boy.

My family scraped together the cash for the one-way Dundee–King's Cross train fare, and I sold my beloved but non-portable Fender Twin; I'd use the money to buy an amp in London. I had too much stuff to travel down on the bus, which is to say I had everything. I couldn't really afford to come home (I didn't, for a year), and so the commitment had to be absolute. I had two old-fashioned cardboard suitcases with spring locks, a guitar, and a few books. Having weaned myself off his influence a couple of years previously, I had seen less and less of Alex Thom. He too was heading south to make his mark, and we agreed to travel down together.

I had no job, nor any intention of seeking employment beyond playing music. Signing on back then worked like a kind of inadvertent universal basic income for young artists.

The system was lax, and God knows there were plenty of benefit lifers. But I was anything but lazy, and couldn't have studied for either of my own professions without the time the Bru bought me.*

I don't think the state should provide young self-declared artists a comfortable living; but I'd propose that it might afford them an uncomfortable one. You are free to place faith in yourself, but that doesn't oblige anyone to place any faith in you without some evidence. There's nothing wrong with young folk finding it tough going in their garret and basement years, and I have some sharply unfashionable things to say about grant culture, which disburses the same pot in a colossally unfair and inefficient way. But an indifferent Bru inadvertently offered me some subsistence when I needed to spend my days doing nothing but writing and practising, while not more than occasionally distracted by hunger or cold. (Universal Basic Income would achieve the same thing more honestly. Apart from, obviously, its more important role of supplying a wage for those traditionally unremunerated but intense forms of labour still predominantly carried out by women, UBI would fuel a huge artistic revival. Unless you'd prefer the arts to go the way they're going, and be populated entirely by the family-subsidised middle classes, UBI would provide

---

* 'Bru', contraction of 'buroo' or 'bureau', short for 'Labour Bureau', so metonymically 'unemployment benefit'.

anyone sufficiently driven with the opportunity to put in their ten thousand hours without wondering where their next Twix, Pickled Onion Monster Munch, packet of custard creams and tin of Heinz Beans with Pork Sausages on four slices of toasted white bread* was coming from.)

Beyond that minimal income, little awaited me in the capital. A few gigs with Talisker, fewer than I'd realised. A tiny room in a terraced house in Risley Avenue off Bruce Grove in Tottenham, where Stevie's school pal Andy already had a bedsit. A deaf, porn-addicted Greek Cypriot landlady who would address me as 'Toe' and did a heroin run to Karachi every second weekend. A little second-hand Polytone amp in Finsbury Park. (I hated it. Because it's meant to make you sound like Joe Pass, the Polytone has exactly one tone, 'muffled', or two if you count 'off', which I soon decided was an improvement.) And no friends, bar Ken, who according to the Tube map lived just outside London in a village called Balham, and (thank God) Big Rab, who had moved down the year before to work at a music agency, and was in Battersea. I hoped the dogs weren't keeping him awake at night.

There was also the red Sony Walkman I'd buy from Andy on my arrival. This would be my principal company through my initial year of almost total isolation. (Andy moved out two weeks later; at least I then inherited a slightly bigger room

---

* My entire daily nutritional intake, 1984–6.

with a toilet and an electric cooking ring.) One song that got me through some bad days in the eighties was 'Davy', from the first Danny Wilson album, the tale of a brother who'd left the Dundee schemie for the Smoke. 'Remember, if you want to come home / I won't throw the first stone, Davy . . .' Few songs have ever felt so directly addressed: the flight from your own low expectations of yourself, the raw fear of the clueless provincial in the big city, the fear and hope and the love of the community that follows you there, and reminds you – dangerously – that you only have so far to fall.

We got to the station around 9 p.m., with Mum miserable and weeping, and Dad smiling and weeping. I was light and blank and stomachless with fear, and astonished that I wasn't doing what I'd imagined doing a thousand times, and bottling it on the platform. The decision to stay or go, at that moment, seemed to hang on a whim. But it didn't, really. No, as one must learn to do on all thresholds – because they are notorious places to trip and stumble – you trust not to your head, not to your heart, but to your feet. I watched them walk me to the train; I watched them climb me aboard; I watched them find my carriage, where Alex had already taken his seat opposite mine. I felt his equal now; I could see he was as afraid as I was. I also knew this would be the last time I saw him.

I left Dundee for London in late September of 1984, in the window seat of an old-fashioned compartment on the sleeper train. I was twenty years old and I had been to Whitley Bay once. *Breathe*, said the voice. Alex tried to get a conversation going. So: was the future what you made it, or did it make you? Discuss. The sun was going down on the Tay, and had turned it to a vast, glorious, ten-mile slick of rose and jade and orange and vermilion and blue that seemed somehow far brighter than the sky it mirrored. Which was the truer? It was all light. Same thing, I said.

Acknowledgements

I lied; it was not T. S. Eliot who originally commissioned this book, but Hannah Griffiths. I'd like to thank Han for her initial faith in the project, when for so long it must have seemed grievously misplaced. Very early versions of some of this material appeared in *Granta*; thanks to John Freeman and to the late and much-missed Ciaran Carson for their early encouragement. Thanks to my dear friends Rob Adams, Jane Feaver, Lisa Gee, Rebecca Stott and Gail Wylie for being supportive early readers of the text. I am greatly indebted to Alexa von Hirschberg for her editorial guidance and wise counsel, and to the copy-editing genius that is Silvia Crompton; thanks to my long-suffering agent, Peter Straus, the almost-as-long-suffering Kate Burton, and to the newly suffering Alex Bowler at Faber. I'd like to thank that beloved circle of humans to whom I am variously known as Don, Donald, Dad, Uncle Don or fannybaws. What's that? You've forgiven me everything in advance? Braw. Lastly, I'm afraid I can't thank my wife, Lisa Brockwell, and not just because I wouldn't know where to stop. My reasons are mainly superstitious: I am not sure what cosmic filing error left me householded with the best person I know, but I do know that I do not want to draw the gods' attention to it.

I'm surprised at the number of song lyrics I've casually

quoted throughout, so allow me to non-casually supply their provenance:

page 128: *'What did I know'* From 'Those Winter Sundays', Robert Hayden, *Collected Poems of Robert Hayden*, Liveright Publishing Corporation, 1966.

page 159: *'I'll play anything you ask'* Sparky's Magic Piano (Alan Livingstone), Capitol Records, 1948.

page 162: *'Up, down, flying around'* 'Those Magnificent Men in Their Flying Machines' (Lorraine Williams/Ron Goodwin), Stateside, 1965.

page 166: *'Wir fahren, fahren, fahren'* 'Autobahn' (Schult/ Schneider-Esleben/Hütter), Kraftwerk; from *Autobahn*, Philips, 1974.

page 167: *'The young man stepped'* 'The Hall of Mirrors' (Schult/Hütter), Kraftwerk; from *Trans-Europe Express*, Kling Klang Records, 1977.

page 186: *'We're so pretty'* 'Pretty Vacant' (Paul Cook, Steve Jones, John Lydon, Glen Matlock), The Sex Pistols; from *Never Mind the Bollocks, Here's the Sex Pistols*, Virgin, 1977.

page 188: *'With me roo-run-rority'* 'The Royal Forester' (trad.), Steeleye Span; from *Below the Salt*, Chrysalis, 1972.

page 191: *'There's no excuse for torture'* 'Let It Go' (Swarbrick/ Pegg/Denny), Fairport Convention; from *Rising for the Moon*, Island, 1975.

page 210: *'too boiled and shy'* 'Man and Wife', Robert Lowell; from *Life Studies*, Farrar Straus & Giroux, 1959.

page 235: *'Tea and biscuits secretary's legs'* 'Mr. 9 'till 5' (Mauro Pagani, Mussida, Permoli, Sinfield), Premiata Forneria Marconi; from *Photos of Ghosts*, Manticore, 1973.

page 236: *'Citadel reverberates to a thousand'* 'Still Life' (Peter Hammill), Van der Graaf Generator; from *Still Life*, Charisma, 1976.

page 238: *'Partly fish, partly porpoise'* / *'Joking apart'* 'Sea Song' (Robert Wyatt), Robert Wyatt; from *Rock Bottom*, Virgin, 1974.

page 239: *'In the gardens of England'* 'Little Red Riding Hood Hit the Road' (Robert Wyatt), Robert Wyatt; from *Rock Bottom*, Virgin, 1974.

page 337: *'Now we are up to'* Mickey Baker, *Complete Course in Jazz Guitar*, Lewis Music Publishing Co. Inc., 1955.

page 364: *'Remember, if you want'* 'Davy' (Gary Clark), Danny Wilson; from *Meet Danny Wilson*, Virgin, 1987.